POSER

POSER

My Life in Twenty-Three Yoga Poses

CLAIRE DEDERER

BLOOMSBURY

LONDON · BERLIN · NEW YORK · SYDNEY

First published in Great Britain 2011

A portion of *Poser* first appeared, in slightly different form, in *Vogue*.

Grateful acknowledgment is made for permission to reprint the following: 'A Ritual to Read
Each Other' by William Stafford, from *The Way It Is: New and Selected Poems*. Copyright ©
1960, 1988 by the Estate of William Stafford. Reprinted by permission of Graywolf Press,
Saint Paul, Minnesota. 'Comin' Down' by Cris Kirkwood. Copyright © 1994 by Meat
Puppets Music BMI / Administered by Bug, All Rights Reserved. Used by permission.
'Letter to Wagoner from Port Townsend' by Richard Hugo, from *Making Certain It Goes
On: The Collected Poems of Richard Hugo*. Copyright © 1984 by the Estate of Richard Hugo.
Reprinted with permission of W. W. Norton & Company, Inc.

Bloomsbury Publishing, London, Berlin, New York and Sydney

36 Soho Square, London W1D 3QY

A CIP catalogue record for this book is available from the British Library

ISBN 978 1 4088 0250 2
10 9 8 7 6 5 4 3 2 1

Printed in Great Britain by Clays Limited, St Ives plc

www.bloomsbury.com/clairedederer

FOR

MOM

DAD

AND

LARRY

Even in favorable conditions, a person encounters struggle.

—SWAMI KRIPALVANANDA

AUTHOR'S NOTE

Some of the events and people in this story have been "run through the scrambler," to use Clive James's phrase. I've tinkered with the chronology of a few events for the sake of narrative flow or discretion. I've changed the names and identifying characteristics of some, but not all, of the people.

Those changes aside, this is a true story, constructed from memory.

CONTENTS

POSER

PROLOGUE: CAMEL

Taking up yoga in the middle of your life is like having someone hand you a dossier about yourself. A dossier full of information you're not really sure you want.

I hadn't been doing yoga long when the information began to come in. One cloudy January afternoon, twenty of us were lowering ourselves backward into camel pose, as slowly and tentatively as swimmers entering cold water.

We knelt on our mats, our feet sticking straight out behind us. The idea was this: You reached back with both hands and grabbed your heels. You thrust your hips forward. Meanwhile, your chest rose up into the air. It seemed a little porny, but I was willing to give it an honest try.

I did it once. My hands reached. My hips thrust. My chest, I hoped, rose. My lower back crimped. I came out of the pose, which was at least as scary as going into the pose.

I sat for a moment and watched the other students, reaching, thrusting, rising. Not crimping, at least visibly. God, they really had the hang of it. I sank back in child's pose for a rest and caught a whiff of onions from my hands. I had stuffed a chicken and put it in the oven for Bruce and our one-year-old, Lucy, before I raced off to yoga. The chicken was my passport out of the house. I left them food as though it were a piece of me. Synecdoche: a part representing the whole. A sail representing a fleet. A crown representing a king. A chicken representing a mother.

There was really no need. Bruce was a fine cook, of the manly, spaghetti-with-sauce-from-a-jar school. Yet I cooked. A chicken roasting in the oven was virtue discernible. There it was: love, concern, nurturing, all rolled in a four-pound organic fryer. Camel. All right. Time to try again. I lowered gently backward into the pose, at the same time reaching, reaching upward with my chest.

"Release into the pose," said my teacher, Fran. "Breathe into the tightness. Let the mind empty of the day's concerns." I wondered if Bruce had found the good bread I had left on the counter. Guilt bread. They could chew on it while I hung out in this room, pretending to be in India. I should've bought them roti.

Suddenly I got a fluttery, scary feeling across my breastbone. It felt like something might tear.

I carefully lifted out of the pose and spoke up: "Uh, Fran? When I'm doing the pose, I have this feeling in my chest, kind of a scary, tight feeling."

Fran was adjusting someone across the room. She had a way of looking like a thoughtful seamstress when she made adjustments: an inch let out here, a seam straightened there, and everything would be just right. She might as well have had pins tucked between her lips and a tape measure around her neck. Without missing a beat or looking up, she said, "Oh, that's fear. Try the pose again."

Fear. I hadn't even known it was there.

1. TRIANGLE

Creamy and flushed and covered with fuzz, our baby daughter was like a delicious peach. Only much heavier. Even though I fed her on a diet of breast milk and nothing else, she grew fatter and fatter. She was dense with good health.

The story of how I nursed my daughter has a catch-22 ending. The child was thriving on this milky, unending flow of a food designed perfectly for her. When she was ten months old, I began to feel like we might weigh about the same amount. I would haul her onto my lap, and she would gaze up at me with delight, and, in the parlance of the day, latch on. I would gaze back at her, amazed that I could so easily satisfy another creature. She was intent and happy as she suckled away.

The only problem with the baby was that when I held her in my lap for these marathon feedings, she was crushing something crucial inside me. Maybe my spleen, or possibly something larger. I tried lying on my side to nurse her, but she required so much food, provided in such lengthy sessions, that this wasn't really tenable. The milk was making her so, ah, healthy that it was getting harder and harder to actually deliver the milk to her. (That's the catch-22 part.)

Cast your mind back to the late 1990s for just a moment. Nursing, at least where we lived in Seattle, was a strange combination of enthusiast's hobby and moral mandate. Drive thirty miles to the north, where my husband's cousins lived in suburbia, and you'd find mothers happily plugging a bottle of formula into their babies' squalling mouths. In Seattle, only full-time working mothers gave their babies bottles, or rather their nannies did, and those bottles were filled with the mother's very own milk, expressed through a breast pump.

Weaning wasn't allowed until at least one year. This was by the consensus of who, exactly? Us. We were mothers with books. We looked things up. We knew stuff, like, for example, that the American Academy of Pediatrics said that at least one year of nursing was optimal for the baby's immune system and brain development. For the kind of mothers we were, optimal meant mandatory, and one year meant a few. Seattle at that time was a town where little dudes strolled up to their moms at the playground for a quick top-off, said "Thanks, babe," and rejoined the soccer match.

Lucy wasn't yet ten months, and I wasn't supposed to quit nursing until at least a year. If you think this sounds like a frivolous dilemma, or not worth losing sleep over, then that just goes to show you were not a new mother in a liberal enclave at the end of the last century.

While I debated whether or not to wean her (and Bruce, my husband, feigned interest), the inevitable occurred. My back went out. The middle of my back pinched me all the time, like a salacious old man. I couldn't sit in a straight chair. I couldn't lie flat on the couch. I couldn't lift the groceries. So I weaned her.

Now that I've been doing yoga for ten years, I'm tempted to say something wise, such as: I was ready to wean and my body made the decision for me. But back then I didn't believe in that kind of crap. Instead, I paddled around in a complicated gumbo of guilt and relief. I claimed to feel cheated of my full, god-given, federally mandated year of nursing. I apologized to my husband for my subpar performance. I told my friends: Oh, no! I can't nurse the baby! Inside, I secretly exulted. I had my spleen to myself again.

We lived in Phinney Ridge, a North Seattle neighborhood filled with educated, white, liberal, well-intentioned people. Which pretty much describes all North Seattle neighborhoods. Phinney Ridge is notable for being even more liberal and even better intentioned than most. In Phinney Ridge, people don't have BEWARE OF DOG signs. They have PLEASE BE MINDFUL OF DOG signs.

When I complained about my back, which I did often and with gusto, the people of Phinney Ridge all had the same answer: Do yoga. My doctor said, "There are poses that will strengthen your back." The checker at Ken's Market told me I could buy a good yoga video at a nearby New Age bookstore. The homeless guy selling the homeless-guy newspaper outside Ken's Market said, "Be sure to get a mat! It's really hard to do yoga without a mat."

I had a number of preconceptions about yoga. I thought yoga was done by self-indulgent middle-aged ladies with a lot of time on their hands, or by skinny fanatical twenty-two-year-old vegetarian former gymnasts. I was also unsettled by the notion of white people seeking transformation through the customs of brown-skinned people—basically, to my mind, a suspect dynamic.

Despite these sloppily thought-out but strongly held reservations (my specialty), I had suspected for years that I probably ought to do yoga. I was a nervous kind of person. A self-conscious, hair-adjusting kind of person. A person who practically burned with worried energy. I had a constant tremor in my hands, so that the whole world knew how anxious I was. Just a couple of weeks earlier, I had been hanging out at a coffee shop, feeding Lucy bits of cracker and navigating the coffee cup from the saucer to my mouth with trembling hand. A gentleman approached and introduced himself to me as an "energy shaman." Before I could think of a way to get rid of him, he took my shaking hand in his and pronounced gravely, "You could use a lot of work."

"Oh!" I said, grinning nervously. "I'm sorry! I just, I have this tremor that I've had since I was a little kid, and I'm not getting a lot of sleep because of the baby. And I guess I've had a lot of coffee," I concluded lamely.

"Do you eat a lot of chicken?" he asked. "That can cause energy problems."

I stood up, spilling my coffee, and swiftly loaded Lucy into her stroller.

"Well, goodbye!" I waved cheerfully, and left the café, fairly thrumming with energy problems.

Yoga seemed like just exactly what I wanted: something to calm me down. It also seemed like just exactly what I didn't want: a place where everyone could see what a mess I was, could see my tremor and my anxiety and my worry. There was something about holding still, about inhabiting a pose, that was scary. What was under all that anxious chatter?

But now things were different. I had a baby. It was imperative that I be able to lift her. I would do anything to be able to lift her. Yoga class, however, was beyond me. Like everyone else, I was terrified of a roomful of people who were good at it. Little did I know then that only very occasionally in yoga do you stumble into an entire roomful of people who are good at it. And when you do, they often turn out to be assholes.

I figured a video would be the best approach; maybe I could get the benefits without all the pesky humiliation. On an Indian summer afternoon I decided to head over to the New Age bookstore. Amid much pinching, I wrangled the baby into her stroller. This engendered another form of mother guilt: recently strollers had come under the North Seattle mother's list of banned substances. Apparently the baby felt alienated so far away from its mother, and preferred to be snuggled up against the mother's back or—there was no escaping its Perón-like hegemony—her breast. You were supposed to strap your baby into a sling or a Snugli (known around our house as a Smugli). There was some theory about the baby wanting to see the world from the same perspective as its mother. Which looks crazy as I type it, but that was the argument. At any rate, putting your child in a stroller was fast becoming yet another way of letting the world know that a) you didn't really love your kid and b) you were an uneducated dumbshit.

That was all well and good for people with those lightweight babies made from balsa wood, but my pleasingly substantial daughter and I were devoted to strolling. And so we made our way through the fall afternoon to the bookshop, the baby graciously tolerating her dumbshit, unloving mother.

I had walked by the New Age bookshop many times but had never gone in. Wrestling the stroller through the door, I was hit with the ecclesiastically grubby smell of incense. Everything in the store was dusty and slightly off plumb. The magazine racks tilted; the books were piled haphazardly; the posters of chakras and mushrooms and stars were at various subtle angles.

I found a teetering wire rack of yoga videos. Some of the people on the covers were orange. Some wore headbands. Some were peeking out from behind swirling, vaguely medieval purple writing. I chose a beginning yoga tape. It looked safe. The woman on the cover was not orange and she wore no headgear. The graphics did not look as if they'd been drawn up in an asylum.

I located a yoga mat, and paid, and then the baby and I got the hell out of there.

That night, Bruce gave her a bottle (to which she had adapted nicely, thanks) and I went into the room with the TV, which, like everyone on Phinney Ridge, we refused to call the TV room. I put on my tape. The blond woman gazed into the camera from her serene world, a place where potted orchids thrived. There was some discussion about not overdoing it and going at your own speed, and then the yoga session was under way. The woman sat there with her eyes shut. I sat there looking at her. Apparently we were warming up.

This pleasant state of affairs continued for a while. Unfortunately, soon it was time to do asana. This had a forbidding sound.

"Jump your feet about three feet apart on the mat," said the blond lady. This I did. "Turn your left foot in about forty-five degrees, and your right foot out." Done and done. Check me out! "Extend the right hand over the right foot, and gently rest the hand on the shin, the ankle, or the foot, wherever is most comfortable." Tippy, but I was on it. "Slowly rotate your torso upward, and extend your left arm toward the ceiling." Aaand I'm out. I sat down with a thud and watched the woman with her strangely unshifting expression. She was a puddle on a windless day. In a calm voice, the way you talk to old people when you're convincing them to take a few steps across the hospital room to use the bathroom, she said, "Tri-ko-na-sa-na." She lingered on the word, obviously enjoying the sound of the . . . what was it? Sanskrit? "Triangle pose," she translated.

I rewound the tape. I tried again. Right leg out. Feet turned at an angle. Extend right arm. Drop right hand to right shin. I started to worry. How was I going to get that left arm up? How was I going to turn my torso? Oh, shit, now or never. I flung my left arm into the air and twisted my torso maybe a millimeter up. Pinch.

I caught a glimpse of myself reflected in the darkened window. I was hunched up like "It's Pat!" from *Saturday Night Live*. I rewound the tape again, and followed the directions again, and ended up, again, bunched in an odd shape. I could feel parts of my body bumping together that had never bumped before. Something hurt. I had a feeling it wasn't supposed to hurt.

Looking back, I can see that I had just learned a paramount yoga lesson: Get a good teacher. Or at least a live one. My back still hurt, and though muscle relaxants exerted a powerful allure, the muscle-relaxant lifestyle was not really doable for me. I made my living as a book reviewer. (A terrible idea, by the way.) When I took muscle relaxants, the novels I read for review tended to improve dramatically. Since my critical faculties were really all I had going for me, I reluctantly went drug free.

There was this notion in my mind that somehow yoga was going to make me better. Better than I'd been, better than everyone else. More virtuous. I liked the idea of myself as a yoga person. (I could not bring myself to say yogi, or yogini.) Lithe, probably thin, with some kind of ineffable glow. And my back wouldn't hurt. Clearly it was time to try an actual yoga class. The following week, on a rainy October day, I left the baby with my mother and drove across town to the yoga studio my friend Katrina went to. Katrina was sort of nutty, but she had a gorgeous ass, so I thought, What the hell.

Inside the front door of the studio was an entry vestibule, decorated in the style of "Don't Be Afraid, We're Not a Cult." The walls were painted white and screened with tasteful shoji panels; the blond-wood floor was uncarpeted and spotless; neat cubbies awaited shoes. All was white and clean, as though the room had been designed for surgery, or Swedish people. The only spot of color came from the Tibetan prayer flags strung over the doorway into the studio.

In flagrant defiance of my longtime policy of never entering a structure adorned with Tibetan prayer flags, I removed my shoes, paid my ten bucks to the wan girl at the desk, and walked into the studio, where eight or ten young women were sitting on their mats. Even though we were there for a beginner class, they all looked incredibly fit and somewhat stern. Their ponytails were glossy and neat. Those ponytails were ready for business. The women sat cross-legged, with straight backs. They all gazed straight ahead into the middle distance, as if they were about to break out into a collective fit of landscape painting.

I smiled apologetically. This is my worst habit, and I hope to break it by the time I'm eighty. When I'm an old lady I'll finally be able to swagger into a room with a fuck-you attitude. I laid out my mat and sat on it. I felt the onset of the deep sorrow that, maybe peculiarly to me, precedes any new physical undertaking. I have never been good at sports; I always feel like a spectator, even when I'm in the middle of a game.

The shoji screens filtered the light from the vestibule, spreading it on the floor in a grid. My sense of futility grew larger. I looked at the serene ladies and wondered if they really believed that enlightenment would find us here, in a drafty room in a strip mall in North Seattle.

As I looked around at the fair-skinned women and the prayer flags over the door and the little altar in the corner, my preconceptions about yoga seemed immediately and all too amply confirmed. The scene was the very picture of white female self-indulgence. There were no Indian people in this room, that was certain.

A woman in her late twenties entered and rolled out her mat in front of us. Her thick blond hair was cut in an expensive bob. Her eyebrows were fancily mowed. Her outfit was black and tight. She looked as though she had been a step-aerobics teacher until about five minutes ago. She looked like her name was Jennifer.

"I am Atosa," she said. Like hell you are, sister.

"Come to a comfortable sitting position," she said. "Please bring your fingers into the gyana mudra. Mudra is the yoga of the hands." She made a circle with the thumb and forefinger of each hand, and I followed suit. It felt corny but sort of wonderful at the same time. My hands looked enlightened.

"We will begin the class with one long om," Asha intoned. "Breathe in, and om on the exhalation." I sneaked peeks around the room. The other women looked peaceful and relaxed, as if they were in an ad for bubble bath. I breathed in and let out my om, which came in a wheezing gasp. Atosa's om boomed and wavered beautifully.

"The om travels up from the seat, through the heart, and out the top of the head. It passes through all the chakras." Atosa listed all the chakras by name, location, and color. Yoga seemed to involve a lot of talking.

We did a series of wildly uncomfortable movements that I now recognize to be sun salutation A. We reached for the sky, we touched our toes, we lunged one leg back. Then we pulled back into downward dog: both hands on the floor, both feet on the floor, bottom jutting up toward the ceiling. We lunged again, touched our toes again, and there we were, where we started, reaching for the sky. I was red and breathing hard and trembling. As we sank into a deep runner's lunge, Atosa looked at me with worry. It wasn't "I'm worried about you" worry. It was "I don't need anyone collapsing in my class" worry.

"You need blocks," she said abruptly. She got some foam blocks from a shelf and had me prop my hands on them. She kept an eagle eye on me.

"We're going to work on trikonasana today," she said. My nemesis. "Please turn your mats so they're perpendicular to mine. Jump your feet apart about three feet," she said, and then we were off to the races.

We did trikonasana over and over: at the wall, in the center of the room, with a partner pulling on our front arm. Each time I bunched up like a cluster of grapes. I shook; I sweated; I clenched. It was exactly as I had always suspected: yoga was a kind of magnifier for my limitations.

Triangle was especially baffling because it was, in essence, so simple. You stood with your feet apart and rested a hand on your shin. Easy as pie. Except it wasn't. (Even pie itself is not that easy, if you make your own crust.) There seemed to be an infinite number of ways to get it wrong.

Atosa began to lecture us. Well, actually, she began to lecture me. "Think extension. The pose is about creating space." I thought extension. I tried to create space. I bunched.

At the end of class, we all lay flat on our backs in savasana, or corpse pose, sprawled loosely with our arms at our sides. Even this seemed painfully beyond my reach. My eyes were shut tight, but I could sense Atosa looking at me, noticing my tensed shoulders, my knit brow, my clenched jaw.

Finally we sat up. Atosa led the class in a final om, and said that if anyone had questions to feel free to approach her after class. I took her at her word, more fool I.

"Yes?" she said, raising a perfectly shaped eyebrow.

"Uh, I was wondering if you could help me with triangle."

"Oh, you mean trikonasana?" she asked.

"Yes, trikonasana."

"Well, you just need more extension. Here, look at this." She stepped into a beautiful shape, legs angling apart, torso twisting gracefully, eyes gazing upward as if she could see infinity beyond the acoustic tiles. She jumped back to standing. "See?" she said brightly. I was reminded of Julie Peterson showing off her cartwheel in first grade.

I gave it a go. "No," she said. "Try extending your trunk more. You're too hunched."

I smiled apologetically at her and said, "I'll work on it." And I left.

I never wanted to see Atosa again. In a just world, she would've been deported, maybe to an island populated by fully extended human beings.

Even so, for some reason I still wanted to try yoga. The next week I noticed a little storefront yoga place near my house. It didn't look like much. It had a stylized brushstroke drawing of a yogi—or was it a Buddha?—as its logo. I didn't want to do yoga in a place that looked like a half-assed noodle joint. Nonetheless, it was only five minutes away and offered a beginner class at 7 p.m., which is the time of day when I customarily begin to be alert and look around and notice things. I thought I'd give it a try.

It was dark by the time I got there, and the foyer to the studio was a pool of cheerful yellow light.

I approached the desk, which was manned by a serious-looking fellow with a dork knob. My heart sank. After Atosa, I couldn't take any more coldhearted grooviness. I introduced myself and gave him my ten bucks. "Welcome," he said ominously, Vincent Price in a tank top.

I went into the studio. The room was filled with not-girls! Which is to say, there were all kinds of people there. A few young men in workout gear and two older women in stretchy purple Lycra and a couple of slightly lumpy women my own age, clearly moms, all but lactating through their leotards, and one old fellow who was wearing jeans and a leather belt. A leather belt! Even I knew better than that. I enjoyed a nanosecond of feeling superior, but was thrown off guard when the students turned and smiled and said hello. In all my days—well, day—of yoga-going, I had never seen anything like it.

Dork knob came in. He sat down silently and I got myself ready for some more vague sanctimonies. Instead, he looked around the room and smiled. Something in him lit up, like there was a big switch on his back that had just been flipped on. He started laughing before he started speaking. "Hi, I'm Jonathan," he said. "Beginning is hard. But it's also lucky. Because you have the chance to build something beautiful from the ground up, with no old mistakes, no bad habits." I know now that this was basic yoga boilerplate, but the thing was, Jonathan really believed it. He finished the speech and laughed again, like: Can you believe we're all doing this crazy thing in this room together? I looked around. Everyone was smiling.

We sat and breathed for a while. Then Jonathan popped up and said, "Tonight we're going to work on triangle!"

I got ready for the bossing: First we would jump our feet apart, then we would try to extend, whatever that meant, and then I would look like "It's Pat," and then the teacher would frown at me. Alrighty.

Jonathan did have us spread our feet apart, but we didn't jump. We just lazily separated them. Once our feet were positioned, he said, "We're going to work on angulating our hips. That's all triangle really is. It's a hip position."

His right foot was in the leading position. He cocked his left hip to the left and said, with excitement, "Look! See how the simple action of pulling my left hip back creates a crease between the top of the right thigh and the hip? That crease is what we want. That's where triangle comes from."

We all cocked our left hips. As one, we gazed down at our right thighs. And, lo! There were creases. We beamed.

"Look at those hip creases. That is triangle," said Jonathan. He looked genuinely happy for us. "You are doing it. You can add more. You can extend the right arm out over the right leg, and drop the hand, and turn the body, and raise the left arm to the ceiling. But those are all additions. You are doing triangle right now."

I cocked my hip over and over again, and watched that crease appear. I had been living inside of my body more than thirty years, and it was showing me a shape I had never witnessed before.

After a while, we tried gesturing forward with our right arm. It felt great, like the movement was growing from that creased hip. Then we dropped our right hands. "Just anywhere," said Jonathan. "Anywhere that feels good." Mine landed on my knee. We turned our bodies gently. And then we raised our left arms as best we could. Mine was not exactly straight up. It was in the general direction of up. It was the beginning of up.

Jonathan walked around the room looking at us. He stopped by me and said, "Try pressing the little toe of your back foot." I tried it, and all of sudden the pose made more sense to me. I was able—or abler—to understand what I was doing, and didn't feel quite so much like I was at war with my own body. I was amazed by the change. It was like having someone show you that you could fix a car's crankshaft by adjusting the side mirror.

Here was a place where someone would tell me what to do, and there were identifiable results. Unlike motherhood, where the rules seemed to shift all the time and the standards seemed as high as the moon.

Of course, this was no different from what happened at any exercise class—at step aerobics, for instance, they were only too happy to tell you what to do, and had the headsets to prove it. But I intuited, or guessed, or, let's be honest, devoutly hoped that in yoga there was another outcome. You would do what they said and you would be better. Yoga would allay my anxiety by teaching me to breathe and relax. But it would also allay my anxiety by elevating me to a more superior, evolved state of being, where I would no longer have to worry about whether or not I was doing everything right.

Jonathan continued. "Imagine your body is being pressed between two huge planes of glass. Gently pressed, of course."

I tried to imagine this. It seemed sort of silly.

Jonathan went on. "This plane, this space between the two imaginary panes of glass, is called the coronal plane. You want to keep your body within this plane while you do the pose. Don't lean your torso forward or let your behind stick out. Keep it within this coronal plane."

This seemed like the most pointless piece of information I had ever heard. In fact, triangle itself was an exercise in pointlessness. Who could imagine herself into being a triangle? It brought to mind that old They Might Be Giants song about "triangle man," who goes around beating people up. Maybe that song was secretly about yoga.

These thoughts ran through my mind as I tried to fit myself into a triangle. At the same time, Jonathan spoke with such confidence, as though the coronal plane and fitting oneself into it were crucial information. Maybe he was right. Anyway, I couldn't quit now. I just stood there and held the pose. This small submission would yield huge and strange returns that would reverberate across the next few years. Yoga had come into my life, with its strange, unknowable, even funny logic. For good or for ill, it had arrived. What the hell, I thought, as I extended my hand toward the sky, and creased my hip, and tried to fit myself into the coronal plane.

At the end of class, we lay in savasana. I felt tired and content. The immobility had a pastoral quality to it, as if trees swayed overhead.

Jonathan's voice was quiet now. "Thank you for sharing this evening with me. In yoga, we say 'Namaste,' which means 'I bow to the divine in you.'" He bowed his dork-knobbed head and said, "Namaste." We bowed back and mumbled, "Namaste." On my tongue, the new word felt as though it contained its own foreign spice.

2. EAGLE

We were a generation of hollow-eyed women, chasing virtue. We, the mothers of North Seattle, were consumed with trying to do everything right. Breast-feeding was simply the first item in a long, abstruse to-do list: cook organic food, buy expensive wooden toys, create an enriching home environment, attend parenting lectures, sleep with your child in your bed, ensure that your house was toxin free, use cloth diapers, carry your child in a sling, make your own baby food, dress your child in organic fibers, join a baby group so your child could develop peer attachments. And don't quit your job. But be sure to agonize about it. And enjoy an active sex life. But only with your spouse! Also, don't forget to recycle.

Bruce and I were doing our best with the baby. In fact, we were always doing our best. These were the rules: Get your thousand words written, cook your organic dinner, call your parents, good, good, good all the time. We tried to do everything right, along with all our friends. Plastic toys were avoided because they might off-gas, a terrifying—yet strangely fun to say—word. Mother and baby consumed only organic milk: We had heard the rumors about hormones in dairy causing nine-year-olds to menstruate. Meat had become a problem. You couldn't just run to the corner store and pick up a cut of whatever. You had to schlep over to Whole Foods and buy one of those ruinously expensive grass-fed roasts.

Goodness ruled me. I was thirty-one. All the moms I knew, at least the ones who were my age and lived in my zip code, lived by this set of rules. It was a variant form of that oldie, perfectionism, but without the hang-ups about appearances. We didn't want to look good. We wanted to be good. We wanted a kind of moral cleanliness to touch our lives. This was symbolized by the cleanliness we sought in the world: We wanted the oceans denuded of mercury and the soil divested of arsenic; we even wanted the coal-plant smokestacks scrubbed. We eschewed Formula 409 and discovered the wonders of vinegar. We avoided preservatives and bought organic soda pop. We wanted to be clean inside and out so we could be worthy of our children. We could see they were pure. We didn't want to be the ones to screw up that purity.

Our goodness was driven by an underlying terror: What if we stopped? We didn't want to know the answer to that question. So we never stopped.

Or maybe I was the only one with the terror. Maybe I was the only one who, grinding steamed organic carrots in the baby-food mill, felt as if turning the mill's little handle was keeping something awful from happening. There was trouble lurking at the edge of my effort; all I could do was everything, and do it right. Having recently become a mother, I was surprised by the level of dread that filled me at almost all times. There was occasional pleasure, but it often consisted of the cessation of dread. It was as if by turning into a mother, I had also turned into Camus.

Certainly I made fun of the ridiculous dictates of motherhood; but I also succumbed, utterly. Yoga was part of my project of becoming a new person. Maybe if I appeared to be serene, I would stop with the existentialist dread, the likes of which I had not felt since my overcoat-wearin' teenage days.

I ate and slept and dreamed yoga that fall. I was like a thirteen-year-old girl with a new pony. I practiced at home, forward-bending while I did the housework. I taught Bruce how to do downward dog. I extolled Jonathan's virtues and quoted him constantly. I fantasized about traveling to India to study with his guru. At night I lulled myself to sleep by re-creating in my mind the exact sequence of the poses that had been taught that day. I could usually remember the first twenty minutes or so of class pretty accurately, then it all merged together in a sort of indeterminate yoga stew and I would drift off to sleep. The days cooled down and the wind moved coldly through the trees; the trees went red and orange and then too quickly turned brown; and I thought about yoga all the time—yoga and Lucy were my twin polestars. Bruce wasn't really in there at all. At the time, I didn't know this situation was dangerous.

My life organized itself around Tuesday and Thursday evenings; they were camel humps on the workaday back of the week. In between I worked on my poses, my breathing, myself.

I wasn't sure exactly what I was doing. I mean, literally. Was this exercising? Or meditating? Or what? Jonathan explained that hatha yoga simply meant any asana practice. There were lots of types of hatha yoga: Iyengar, which was concerned with alignment; ashtanga, which was vigorous; restorative yoga; and, it seemed, countless others. "In this class, we don't do a particular style. We take from all traditions. So we simply call it hatha yoga. 'Ha' refers to the right side of your body, to the sun's energy, to vigor. 'Tha' refers to the left side, the moon, to passivity. 'Yoga' literally means yoke. We yoke these two kinds of energy together. We also yoke ourselves to the infinite."

This seemed unlikely. I was distrustful of these definitions. At the same time, I had a strange feeling that what I was doing was something a little more than exercise. When we finished up in savasana, I didn't feel like I'd worked out. I felt more like I'd churched. I didn't believe in the infinite or in the energy of the sun and the moon. I didn't believe that saying "om" connected me to anything outside myself. More than that: I didn't care. I didn't have an atheist's fervor about this nonbelief; I had an agnostic's indifference.

But. There was this idea that yoga was going to make me better. Maybe it already was, just a bit. Calmer. More grounded. Less afraid. So I chanted and posed and sat. I carried on as I had begun: What the hell. Maybe some of it would take.

On Halloween afternoon, Lucy was napping in her crib. The house was decorated with homemade pumpkin and ghost cutouts. I was boiling potatoes for potato salad. It would be dark soon. The end of daylight savings time was serious business in Seattle, a curtain dropping.

I felt a surge of an under-documented emotion: domestic happiness. It seemed a static, permanent thing, domestic happiness. It involved so many objects: folded, red-checked dishrags in a pile; a bowl of lemons; narcissus in a flowerpot on a windowsill.

But domestic happiness was in fact as fleeting as any dream. It was predicated on labor, and money, and good fortune, all things that exist in a state of flux. Most of all, it depended upon doing what you were supposed to do.

In the movie *Wings of Desire*, there's a mysterious line. In fact the whole movie is willfully, ridiculously mysterious, but this one line is really great: "The dream of the house in the house." There was the house we lived in, and there was also a kind of domestic dream, a dream of order and contentment and beauty. The domestic dream is a dream for grown-ups, full of pride and ambition and effort. It's a dream of a world transformed through labor, and taste, and some love. It's a dream that's tinged with dread: What if I can't keep up with it?

Over the course of this evening, others would join me there in my kitchen: Bruce, my baby, my mother, her boyfriend, my father, my friends, their parents. But no matter how many people joined me there, it would remain my kitchen. It was a great machine that produced domestic happiness, and I was the engine that ran it.

We were throwing a Halloween party. Our parents would come and look at Lucy in her bear suit, with her tiny nose painted black and whiskers eyebrow-penciled on her cheeks. Our friends would bring their kids and hang around and eat candy. It would be great.

I drained the potatoes into a colander amid a great whoosh of starchy steam: a potato facial.

Bruce came in from the office, looking for more coffee. We had converted a little garage in our backyard into an office. When we were talking to editors in New York, we tried to make it sound romantically rustic. We called it a garden shed or a writing shack. Since we didn't have the benefit of being able to schmooze our editors at the cocktail parties that we were sure occurred every evening in New York, we tried to make lemonade out of our provincial status by cultivating a raw Western allure.

Bruce kissed me and said there was an e-mail for me; someone wanted a rewrite by the end of the week. It was our way to share an account and browse through each other's e-mails. It made the writing life a little less lonesome, a little more like a cheerful cottage industry and a little less like being trapped alone with your weak brain.

"Rewrite! Who invented that, anyway?" I asked.

"Tell me about it." Bruce, also a writer, worked for a magazine that set editors upon his stories like snarling dogs who liked to tear stuff up just for the sport of it.

He poured some coffee into his cup and leaned against the counter, looking at me. He was a tall, thin person with a beautifully craggy face and a single black eyebrow. He looked like an Egon Schiele drawing come to life and occasionally consumed by teen passion. He was a person in whom ethnicity was palpable. Like me, his family went way back, or at least what passed for way back in Washington State. Some of his people were Norwegian farmers from the Snohomish valley; some of his people were Croat fishermen from Everett. He was mostly Norwegian farmer, shy and austere, but the Croat in him grew voluble when he was alone with me.

"Halloween!" he said. "The best holiday of the year. The holiday of candy and fright. What could be better? So, when are people coming?" He plucked a piece of potato from the colander and dropped it; too hot.

"Shh!" I said. "Lucy's still asleep." The line was delivered with a certain amount of bitchiness. I was fanatical about the baby's sleep. In fact, I was always shocked when I heard about other mothers who napped when their babies were napping. How could they fall asleep? I needed to stay awake to worry about when the baby would wake up.

Bruce made that little apology rictus people make when they've unthinkingly spoken too loud. It was easy to wake up the baby in our house, a small bungalow on a hillside street, a street in fact just right for Halloween: houses tightly packed together and filled with kind, liberal folk who would have plenty of treats on hand (though they did not eat sugar, usually).

"OK, I gotta go back out there." He was working on a big feature about decommissioning dams.

As he headed out the back door, my mom came in the front, as though we were in an episode of *The Benny Hill Show*. But without the French maid's costumes.

"Hi, honey! Is Lucy up from her nap yet?"

"Let's go check, she's been asleep for a while."

We crept up the stairs and peeked into Lucy's room under the eaves. Eyes still shut. Some waggling of the rump, but it could've been dream related. We crept back down and my mom took charge of the ham.

"Ooh, you got a honey-baked! Good!" She pulled it from the fridge. "What platter are you using?"

I was still thinking about that rewrite but pulled myself together. I gave her the big plain white platter and watched as she transformed the ham from a glistening hunk of fatty flesh into a Main Course, simply by placing it on the dish. How'd she do that?

The baby snuffled faintly and my mom was upstairs like a shot. "Oh, my darling girl!" My mother caught the baby up in her arms, right from the crib, no easy feat.

My mom was a slender thing, long-haired and artistic-looking and deceptively frail, like a shrinky-dink Vanessa Redgrave. But there was might in her. Her small body possessed a secret toughness. She could hold the baby for hours, it seemed; she ran a perfectly clean house; her garden, which she took care of herself, always looked as though Vita Sackville-West had just spent the day there, attended by a team of burly men. And she had a will like a root; it was sometimes hidden underground, but it was there, tough and fibrous and sustaining every single thing she did.

The enormous, peachy baby tucked onto her slender hip, my mom moved around the house in her efficient way.

"Do you think the dining table really works like this?" she asked. "Maybe we should move it against the wall."

My mother had a kind of mania for shifting tables. No table was ever in the right place. It was part of getting ready for a party. And of course, maddeningly, she was always right. These tables, moved from their old locations into their new locations, made people know what they were supposed to do and where they were supposed to go at my mother's parties. Released from anxiety by my mother's table place-ment, partygoers moved more freely, chatted more easily. It was typi-cal of my mother. Finally you just had to lay yourself down and let her roll over you, pushing a table as she went.

I sighed. "Let's move it. Just put Lucy in the playroom for a moment."

Mom set the baby on the floor and placed a few toys around her.

"Where's Larry?" I asked as we lugged my huge dining-room table across the room.

"Oh, he had to work this afternoon. He'll be in here in a bit."

Larry was my mother's boyfriend. He had been for twenty-five years. Even though my mom was still married to my dad. Let me just lay it out:

Mom and Dad married in the early 1960s. Broke up when my mom met Larry, who was at the time a young hippie. Mom and Larry have been together ever since. Mom and Dad decided to stay married, thinking it would be easier on me and my brother, Dave.

And that's how it had been ever since. My parents were still functionally married. Dad still got his mail at Mom's house. Dad and Mom still talked on the phone practically every day. Dad and Mom still had their financial lives intertwined. I told a friend once about this arrangement, and she said, "Well, there are all different kinds of marriage." I said, "But they're not really married!" And my friend said, "Oh, yes, they are."

It read like a false syllogism: Mom and Larry were a couple; Mom and Dad were married. Therefore . . . what, exactly? I would be tempted to say, "You do the math," but there was no math. Hmm, you might be thinking. This woman appears to have two husbands. All I can say is this: Maybe that's how many husbands my mother needed. Did I mention her will of iron? On the other hand, maybe my dad needed only a fraction of a wife.

"There!" said my mother. All we had done was move the table, and the room no longer looked like my dining room. It looked like party central. "A tablecloth and we'll be set!"

We looked into the playroom and found Lucy sitting on the floor in front of the towering fiction bookcase. A pile of M's (our library was still alphabetized, a relic of pre-children days) faced her: Maupin and Mitford and Munro. She was gnawing on a corner of *Tales of the City* when my mom swooped down on her.

Parties were complicated. This complication was usual for me and my family, as it was for lots of people of my generation. Mom and Dad and Larry clustered in the kitchen, exclaiming over the baby, while Bruce's nice parents milled around a bit. Their incomprehension of my family's background was palpable, but they Norwegianly kept it to themselves and we all rubbed along just fine.

My dad, with his flyaway hair and his observant eyes and his lanky frame, toggled between the majestic and the laid-back. At the public relations firm he had helped run, he was known as "The Great One," but now that he had retired, he favored the laid-back. He leaned against the kitchen wall, his arms crossed against his chest, chatting animatedly with Larry about some early snow in the Cascades. My dad was made for skiing.

Larry, sixteen years younger than my dad, was a tugboat captain. Really. And he looked it. Imagine a handsome Italian tugboat captain, with a beard and an elegant nose. Now imagine him cracking up, quietly. There's Larry. He was wearing flip-flops—he usually didn't give them up until December—and jeans and a plaid shirt.

My dad and Larry were civil; my mother was charm itself. The whole thing ran like clockwork. Except it didn't. Lately I had been impatient, even crabby, with my parents. They were bugging me in some obscure way. Now that I was a parent, they got under my skin almost all the time. I ordered them about and sighed when I spoke.

To wit: As I got the white wine out of the fridge to put out on the table, my dad loped in. "Can I get a glass of water?" he asked.

"Sure. Go for it," I answered tersely, gesturing at the cupboard where we kept the glasses.

My dad got this look I'd been seeing on his face more and more often lately, the look of a person who is a little offended but is suppressing it.

My brother, meanwhile, had bailed. He didn't come to family parties anymore. This had begun years ago, when he had been in a band—the Presidents of the United States of America—that toured incessantly. We thought he would come back to the fold. But he never did, even after he left the band and became a PR guy like my dad, and then a new-media exec. He stayed away. He sent middle-of-the-night e-mail pleas to my parents, on which he CC'ed me. (He was kind of officious, for a former rock star.) "It's time for a divorce," he would write. Or, "My birthday is coming. For my gift I would like a divorce!"

His disappearance was a function of his total immersion in his wife and daughters. He folded himself into his family tightly, as though he was tucking himself into bed. There didn't seem to be room for anybody else. He and I communicated by means of e-mail, little semaphore signals, mostly about music and our parents, that we sent back and forth across Lake Washington. I was happy to take what I could get.

When we were all together like this, I missed him.

Larry was holding Lucy in his arms, and she was giggling and burying her hands in his full, ex-hippie beard.

"Give me that baby!" I said.

Larry laughed and handed her over.

Larry laughed at everything; it was his great charm. Larry and I had become more related since I had Lucy. She was certainly his grandchild, therefore he and I must be related by blood. Another faulty syllogism, but it had an undeniable emotional truth.

We sat down on the sofa with Bruce's parents near the fire. I loved a shoulder-season fire. A winter fire was pedestrian, but there was something wonderfully profligate about an autumn fire, when you didn't quite need it. I began to maneuver Lucy's legs into her bear suit. She glanced up at me, adoringly, as though I was a rock star.

As I drew a tiny black bear nose onto her tiny face with an eyeliner, friends and neighbors began to arrive. Bruce got busy leading kids on short candy-extorting tours of the neighborhood, with Lucy in his arms.

People brought food. The ham glistened fatly. The waxy, sweet smell of Halloween candy filled the air, and for the next three hours people bustled in and out, spilling wine on the rug, taking handfuls of fun-size Milky Way bars.

I overheard my mom talking to my old friend Isabel.

"Did you know that the house out back is for sale?" asked my mom.

"Which one?"

"The one just past the backyard."

Isabel started laughing. "Are you going to buy it?"

"I think I should!" said my mom. Her hungry eyes looked at Lucy as she said it.

"Not funny," I said.

"It's not meant to be funny, Claire. Wouldn't it be nice? We could make a little path between the two houses."

"It's not funny, Mom. Knock it off."

"Well, I'm not joking. I might just call a Realtor."

"Are you moving?" asked my dad as he walked by. He had a vested interest. After all, he was married to my mom. They still co-owned her house, even though he lived across town in a wooden houseboat on Lake Union.

"Well, did you see that the house behind this one is for sale?"

"Huh!" said my dad, and sloped off lankily to graze on a ham sandwich. Their relationship was friendly and a bit incurious, like the slight emotional distance maintained by, say, longtime next-door neighbors.

"I'm going to buy it!" said Isabel. "I'm calling a Realtor."

"No way," said my mom. "It's mine."

Nobody would buy the house, I knew. It was just a way to show that they were enjoying my domesticity. Claire, with a house! And a husband and a baby. There was something absurd about it. Except my mom. My mom might buy the house. You never knew. My mom and Bruce's mom, all the moms, were like barbarians at the gates. Their need for the baby's proximity was huge; it was the most important thing in my mother's life.

Larry came in and opened another bottle of wine. My ex-boyfriend, there with his wife and beautiful sloe-eyed baby daughter, demanded another glass. The web of relationships surrounded me, tightly.

I slipped upstairs with Lucy and lay down with her on the bed while she lulled into sleep. The sounds of the party, of complications, of life roared softly below.

The next day Lucy and I were slated to go to baby co-op. This was a highly desirable baby class run at the neighborhood center. I had applied right after Lucy was born. At this cooperative preschool, babies socialized with one another while volunteer moms helped run the school. It was impossible not to imagine the babies lounging in armchairs, holding martinis and cigarettes, and lifting their feet from the carpet to let their work-worn mothers run the vacuum.

Even so, it was part of the law of North Seattle that your baby "did" co-op. It was always put like this—"doing" co-op—as though you were doing lunch, or heroin.

At the urging of other moms, soon after Lucy was born I had called the co-op contact line and spoken to a harried-sounding mom, the kind of person whose small efficiencies barely concealed the fact that her life, with its children and part-time job and not quite helpful spouse, was always about to go haywire. Just by talking to her, you could tell she was a person using Scotch tape to hold together a writhing ball of snakes. There was a lot of screaming in the background. She put us on a wait list but warned that it could be months, "or years."

Now, after nine months, Lucy and I had discovered that we were in. On the day after Halloween, we strollered up to the giant gray building that housed Phinney Neighborhood Association. Outside, the vinyl sign reading JOIN PHINNEY KIDS CO-OP! lifted and dropped heavily against the chain-link fence.

I had dressed carefully, in my one really expensive striped T-shirt, my most flattering jeans, and a pair of Dansko clogs, the official footgear of overeducated liberal moms. Lucy sported a tie-dyed T-shirt (because "co-op" sounded a lot like "commune," and we wanted to get this thing right), a pair of overalls, and a hand-knitted beret, a form of headgear which I felt sent the right message. I didn't plan to tell anyone that I had not knitted it myself, that it was a hand-me-down from a friend who actually did knit for her child. But its obvious handmadeness would imply that I was a craftsy type. It was quite a house of cards I was building with that knitted pink cap.

I was supposed to go to the Dragon Room. Given the long wait list and the lectures from my fellow moms, I entered the room expecting a kind of nurturing, wooden-toy-filled Shangri-la. What I found was a basement full of women wearing Dansko clogs.

I looked around nervously: The women were moving randomly and ceaselessly around the room like electrons around an atom; I half expected them to do that thing modern dancers are forever doing where they fiercely thump their breastbones. Some of the women were carrying babies on their hips. Some were tailing crawlers. Some were holding the arms of beginning walkers, which made the babies, arms joyfully shooting straight up in the air, look like they were about to testify at a gospel meeting.

It was a strange scene, hidden from the unsuspecting eyes of the people whizzing by up on Phinney Avenue. I set Lucy down at a basket of wooden fruit and said hello to the teacher.

The image of those women, sitting on the floor in the yoga studio in North Seattle, flashed in my mind. I had wondered whether enlightenment would find them in a strip mall. Here I had that same feeling. There was the same earnestness in this room, the same intensity of purpose, and, I discovered over the next weeks, the same difficulty of knowing what, exactly, that purpose was. Maybe the other ladies knew. They certainly looked like they knew what they were about, with their nifty slings and their well-packaged baby food and always, always their clogs. The ubiquity of clogs was like a commentary on our lack of ability to care for ourselves: We could run elaborate food mills and operate breast pumps and launder cloth diapers and juggle complex part-time work arrangements, but we could not, would not tie our own shoes. That first day I was quickly absorbed into the group and became one of the women following my crawler around the room. No one really talked to each other. There was an almost meditative quality to the scene.

After a while, we sat down and sang "The Wheels on the Bus." This shocked me deeply. No one told me there would be singing. I had occasionally sung to Lucy when she was tiny and colicky and clearly inconsolable. Singing was a last resort, after negotiations and sanctions had failed. The last song I had sung in public was the Sex Pistols' "God Save the Queen" to a group of very startled Japanese people in a karaoke parlor in Kyoto sometime during the early 1990s. I was to find that singing was a big part of the social life of the North Seattle good mother. We were a flock of very large out-of-tune birds, warbling away, communicating . . . what, exactly? Love, concern, devotion.

After "The Wheels on the Bus," it was time to go home. The other moms were making plans to meet for coffee. I felt shy, and so we slipped away and walked home through scattered raindrops.

When we got home, Bruce was sitting at our big scarred wooden dining-room table. He had moved it back to its usual non-party spot in the center of the room. Papers were spread across it.

Bruce seemed to be working all the time. It was hard to know how much we were supposed to work. We were freelance writers; we had no office and no boss and no dependable means of support—and a mortgage. How'd that mortgage get in there? It didn't belong.

He looked up at us with the gaze of the astigmatized. He did not, in fact, have anything wrong with his eyes, except pure immersion in what he was doing.

He visibly wrenched his attention away from his work on his article about dams. "Hi, guys!" he said. "How was it?"

"It was . . . weird," I said, inarticulate as a preteen. "I don't quite get it."

"Well, what did you do? What was it like?"

"It was like what we do at home. Lucy played and crawled around. She liked the cooking table, but I think it was just because it was the right height for pulling herself up. Oh, and we sang."

"You sang? Like, you yourself?"

"You don't need to sound so horrified. We sang 'The Wheels on the Bus,' if you must know."

"How does that one go again?" he asked with a grin.

He glanced over at his laptop. I set Lucy on the table to help retain his attention. She wore stout little brown leather boots that she kicked on top of a photocopied article from the *Journal of the American Water Resources Association*. Her eyes shone. I'd never known someone with such shiny eyes.

"So," he asked, making an effort at conversation, "did you pow-wow with the other moms? Does the teacher watch the kids while you hang out?"

"No, no, it's not like that at all. I played with Lucy and sort of followed her around, and then we had a little class meeting to plan the snack schedule, and then I came home. Oh, and I had to sign up for a job—everyone has a co-op job. Mine is babysitting for the board when they have their monthly meeting."

"What? How many kids do you have to watch?"

"I think there are eight board members, so at least eight kids. One of them has twins, I know."

He started cracking up. "OK, so let's go over this again. You had to get on a wait list for this thing. Now you have to pay them . . . what? Seventy-five bucks a month? And there's no child care? And you have to do a job? Are you really sure you want to do this?"

I was really sure. This was what you did. You got your baby into co-op, and then they developed stable relationships and didn't suffer separation anxiety when baby co-op turned into toddler co-op and then preschool. This was best. Everyone said so.

Bruce's attention drifted in a way that I knew was irrevocable. He had a new focus on his work since Lucy came; it was as though the urges that governed me and told me to fold napkins and fuss over baby food and nurse until I could nurse no more were giving him another message altogether: earn, earn, earn. (A funny message for an environmental journalist, but there you go.) He worked now with an almost maniacal gleam in his eye, like Squirrel Nutkin putting away nuts for the winter.

Our anxieties were driving us to become other people—he was Earner; I was Mother, like characters in some phenomenally boring Ionesco play. We both worried all the time and often didn't remember to laugh. I could find relief in the baby's smile, or with my friends, or, now, in yoga. I didn't see that Bruce was headed someplace where there was no relief.

That night I went to yoga. I always went at night. The day was work time, time to get stuff done. We tried some balances. Balances seemed somehow the heart of the thing. We started with tree. I shifted my weight onto my left foot, as the teacher said, and set my right foot on the inside of my thigh, just above the knee. Solid jackson. It was my first real moment of yoga competence. This was truly no problem. I could stand around on one leg all day, probably. I could probably just hop to the store from now on. I caught sight of myself in the mirror.

I was shredding the rad, to use the parlance of snowboarders. And of course as I thought all this, I fell out. I pulled my foot back onto my thigh, and gazed at the ground and thought about nothing at all. Solid once again.

"Nice!" said Jonathan. "There's good balance in this group." We beamed at him.

"OK," he said. "I wouldn't normally do this, but I think we should try eagle. It's a little advanced for you guys." My eyes immediately started roaming nervously around the room. What in tarnation was eagle? What if everyone could do it but me?

Eagle: We shifted our weight onto our right legs. We bent our right knees just a bit. We hooked our left legs over the right, as though we were about to sit cross-legged in a chair. This seemed like enough; this seemed like plenty. But there was more: We hooked our left feet around the back of our right calves. My foot slipped back there easily, as if it had been waiting its whole life to find this cozy location.

When I was in high school I had a best friend who was a boy. We never had a sexual relationship, never even kissed. He liked girls who dressed mod and had straight, shiny hair; I liked boys who were mean. We had a thing we used to do while we lay on the couch watching TV or listening to *Special Beat Service*; we found what we called "perfect fits." His chin inside my elbow; my shoulder in his armpit; his one foot resting between my two. That we never pursued the ultimate male-female perfect fit only made these couplings sweeter and more relaxing.

Left leg hooked over right knee; left foot hooked behind right calf. It felt perfect. It was a perfect fit, but I was alone. Good lord, there was more. We were supposed to do arms. Right elbow fitted on top of the crevice of left elbow; then we twisted them together so the hands caught each other. Another perfect fit; my arms and hands seemed made to slip into this strange arrangement. My legs wavered, but I snugged them tighter.

"Lift your elbows," said Jonathan. "Bend your knees a little more deeply."

Staring at the floor fixedly, I accomplished these motions. I felt like some advanced, 2.0 version of myself. I glanced up. The rest of the class had come out of the pose. Jonathan was standing there, openly laughing at me. "Claire has found her pose," he said. As he spoke, I caught sight of myself in the mirror. I felt completely at ease in the pose, and yet I looked utterly unlike myself.

I had discovered something; there was a pleasure in becoming something new. You could will yourself into a fresh shape. Now all I had to do was figure out how to do it out there, in my life.

3. LOTUS

I took beginning lessons from Jonathan for another month, but the higher-level classes were calling to me. I wanted to improve! With some trepidation I bumped up to the all-levels teacher, Fran, a beautiful dark-haired woman with a somewhat bodacious figure. Fran's classes were always packed with regulars: Ryan, who'd injured his back skydiving; Elizabeth, who ran marathons; Greg, whose wife was pregnant; Lindsey, who'd been a serious gymnast as a child; the other Claire, a Scottish masseuse, and her sardonic husband, Ralph, whose back hurt a lot.

Fran's classes met in the early evenings, and we'd come rushing in from the wet, dusky streets, where rain was the sky's lingua franca. Night descended during our time with Fran, and the room where she taught felt like the most perfect, secret, happiest room in the city.

Fran set us tasks and then she would walk among us, tapping her long fingers together. She walked in a continuous loop, like a shorebird. Or a drill sergeant. Often she would see something that would stop her dead in her perambulations. "Look!" she would cry. "Philip, when you came to us, you couldn't lie flat on your back. Now you're doing a full backbend. Everyone, stop! Look at Philip." And we would flump pinkly down from our own backbends and gaze admiringly at Philip, who was beginning to tremble from staying up so long.

Like any great teacher, Fran never ran quite the same game twice. Sometimes she came in with an elaborate plan, where she eased us through preparatory poses without telling us where she was headed, and the next thing we knew we'd be attempting something truly tough: full splits or an arm balance. Sometimes she was inspired by the weather and only did poses that felt autumnal or wintry to her— she seemed to favor lingering seated forward bends as it grew cooler. Sometimes she simply asked what we wanted and stitched our random desires into a seamless class.

I always asked for the same thing, but, being me, I led up to it gingerly, like a kid buying condoms. "I was thinking we could, uh, maybe try lotus?"

In fact, I had become obsessed with lotus. Lotus was my new boyfriend. I thought about it all the time. Since then, I've become used to this phenomenon: A yoga pose will take hold of my imagination, and I will dream of it like I'm a lover in some terrible Victorian poem—as I fall asleep at night, as I wake in the morning. It's often a pose that I've just mastered. Once I get hold of the edge of it, I want to pull the whole of it toward me.

Lotus was like a puzzle: You got the bottom foot wedged up against the hip, and then began the process of pulling the other foot on top of it. The bottom foot would begin to hurt; the ankle would torque. At this point, the whole thing started to seem like a bad idea. And then. You flexed your feet, and did that magical thing yoga teachers call softening the hips, and breathed in a determined, thoughtful way, and you got into the pose another inch, or another millimeter. Or you'd just get the idea of the pose; you'd feel the upward movement of the feet and the downward movement of the hips. The elusiveness of that feeling was part of the pose's irresistible lure.

My fascination with lotus had something to do with its formal perfection: symmetrical, compact, elegant. The Buddha did lotus; you did lotus. I'm not saying I believed that the syllogism concluded with you turning into the Buddha, but still. At least you were working inside the same set of propositions.

I worked and worked on lotus. Well, actually, I cheated at it. If you think it is impossible to cheat at a yoga pose, you are wrong. It is all too easy. Fran walked, and tapped her fingers, and repeated over and over: "Do not continue if your ankles or knees hurt. If your ankles or knees hurt, take half lotus." My knees and my ankles both hurt quite a bit, but I did continue. I just loved the way my feet looked, folded into lotus. It looked like virtue. Never mind that it hurt.

The baby was growing into something more than a baby and less than a toddler. She was pleasant to spend time with, and certainly ornamental. Nonetheless, I was experiencing a severe case of anhedonia. I was just too tired all the time. I read once about a big, manmade surfing wave at an indoor water park in Yokohama, Japan. The wave was engineered to never stop. It just kept crashing onto the beach. Exhaustion was this: a great powerful wave, cresting eternally and ceaselessly, ready at any time to pull you under.

I looked around and saw eye bags everywhere. When I got together with my girlfriends, fun seemed not to come into the picture. Forget about going out drinking or dancing; we seldom even met for coffee anymore—nothing for the baby to do. Also, not very improving. Instead, day in and day out, we met at the flat, weed-choked lake that lay in the center of northwest Seattle. Green Lake had no color at all; it was the most ill-named lake ever. But, a little shy of three miles around, its paved path made a just-right walk. You'd meet your friend there, and after a while, you got so sleepy and worn out, it hardly made a difference which friend. We were all merging into one woman, and sometimes I felt I couldn't tell my friends apart. They were all new moms. They were all part-time workers with interesting, creative, exhausting jobs. They all wore cute corduroy pants and hipsterish hoodies covered with spit-up. They all had haircuts that were once really good but were now growing unpruned and wayward. They were all, all, all married, and they would complain about their husbands in slightly ironic voices, voices that said they knew how good they had it; after all he loaded the dishwasher every night, after all he still played in a band, after all he was just plain someone else, someone not a baby, in the house.

I would go for a walk with anyone, anytime. I just wanted to get out of the house. But I had three best friends, and they were my favorite walking companions.

Ruthie was petite and fierce and wildly in love with her baby boy. She had huge eyes and an elegant nose. When she put on a dress and mascara we called her "The Contessa," but this no longer happened very often.

Lisa, the first of our group of friends to have children, was slender and blond and Valkyrie-beautiful. While the rest of us drank and did somewhat random career development, Lisa got married and started producing children at the tender age of twenty-three. We felt this was criminal. There was an unspoken rule that we would not be wed until at least our late twenties, and not have children until we were thirty. Lisa now had four gorgeous green-eyed, towheaded children, and if she seemed scattered and exhausted, who could blame her?

Isabel, our childless friend, was a tall, goofily elegant artist who made minimalist drawings and sculptures. Her pieces were all line; that was all there was to see. She still went to rock shows and she still had friends who were men. She and her glamorous punk-rock design-builder husband went places like Portugal and Marfa, Texas, and hung around with people like John Doe from the band X. (You'd forgotten all about John Doe, right? Well, guess what? Still really cool.) She was the only one of our friends who still ate lunch with all the people we knew from the Sub Pop record label, which had unleashed Mudhoney and Nirvana upon the world. She had always been cooler than the rest of us, but now that we had kids, she was hopelessly out of our league.

Ruthie, Lisa, Isabel, and I, along with our boyfriends, had wended our way through our lost youths together. I made college last almost a full decade. Classes and travel were interspersed with rock shows, crappy jobs, brunches we couldn't afford, rabid poker nights, more rock shows, more crappy jobs, inner tubing at the beach. We stuck with it. We were very consistent for at least a decade. We were dedicated to our leisurely, exploratory life.

Not an unusual story for a woman of my generation. Hardly worth focusing on the details, except to say that for almost a decade I was elevated and illuminated by love. Not love of any boyfriend in particular but love of my friends, one of those couple groups that clump together in your twenties. Our group was made up of artists and musicians and carpenters. En masse, we were possessed of a mean sense of humor and reflexive, total forgiveness of one another. A perfect combination of qualities, I felt: We made fun of one another incessantly and then let one another off the hook.

REI, the local outdoor emporium, had a sale of ridiculous turquoise-striped polypropylene skullcaps and I bought one for each of us. We took to wearing them out at night, so we could spot one another across crowded rooms. This was love.

This story—the story of fucking around through your twenties, of devoting yourself to your friends, of drawing out adolescence right up to the breaking point of thirty—is not the only story of my American generation. But it's one of them. This phenomenon has begun to be noted by the kind of people who note such things. It's been called extended adolescence. The psychologist Jeffrey Arnett called it emerging adulthood. I like that one; it sounds like something the NEA might give you a grant for. The *New York Times* columnist David Brooks dubbed it the Odyssey Years.

Here's the thing of it: We did exactly what we wanted in our twenties. I wasn't always happy, and it wasn't always easy, making it up as you go along. But I was running the show. All my trouble was of my own making, and so was my fun. So was my job and so was my series of underfurnished apartments. I was a free agent moving through the landscape I chose: bars and classrooms and cafés and poker tables. My friends and I had lived by the slippery dictates of coolness for decades (or tried to). We, as the Cat Power song says, lived in bars. For years and years, we worked casual jobs so we could make art or write or just go to rock shows.

Then, with the advent of children, we had done a massive about-face. We stopped going out, stopped drinking, stopped going to shows and openings. We just didn't have the poop to care anymore.

I watched my former hipsterdom sail away from me. I had thought it was my home, but it turned out to be a ship and I a temporary passenger. Goodbye, I waved from the shore. See you in fifteen years, when you come back to pick up my child. Goodbye!

Goodness was new to me and my friends, and we took to it with the fervor of the newly converted. We switched our allegiance entirely and unswervingly. We were like a marching band, all swinging our trumpets away from the sun at the exact same moment.

Today I was meeting Ruthie. I pulled into the parking lot and hauled the enormous baby out of her car seat, making it through that potentially disastrous twist and pull without injury to my back. Lucy was starting to grow soft blond curls that sausaged around her face. The effect was almost ridiculous in its cuteness, and I stopped to admire her for a moment before heading across the street to meet Ruthie.

I had known Ruthie for well over a decade and every year she surprised me: She worked in wildlife rehabilitation, and she would show up for a night out with a bear cub in the back of her Jeep—"I just have to drop it off at the shelter, it won't take long." She once was the lead singer of a punk-rock band named Charm School. She could pick up a Canada goose in a city park and carry it around in her arms like a writhing feathered bagpipe. A lifelong vegetarian, she started eating meat because her vegetarian underlings at work began to annoy her with their righteousness; she thought she ought to "set an example." It's like Versailles in her brain, room upon room upon room of unexpected stuff.

Ruthie and I were figuring out the motherhood thing together. Ruthie seemed to have a knack for it. Her son, who was now a toddler, still slept in the same bed with Ruthie and her nice husband,

Henry. (In North Seattle, co-sleeping, as it was called, was the very definition of good parenting. Even your dreams would be sacrificed!) She nursed on demand. She followed James as he waddled around the house, offering him organic snacks. These behaviors—sleeping in the same bed as your child, nursing ad infinitum, making sure needs were met in the instant they were expressed—were the very essence of Seattle parenting. Ruthie was, by the lights of our community, an excellent mother. And she was happy.

Her son was a year and a half older than Lucy, and I watched Ruthie closely, trying to figure out how to be as good as she was. So far I was failing.

Everything was gray: sky, water, tree branches. The wind blew the gray around a bit. Ruthie fit right in, with a gray cap pulled down over her dark hair. James was in a backpack on her back, waving merrily.

Ruthie and I hugged; she always said "Hi, Claire" in this special tone, as if I was the best thing that had happened to her all day. We set off like penitent anchorites: once around the gray lake for our sins. James pulled her hair, but her "Ouch!" was good-natured. She still seemed dazzled by this creature she had made.

"So James is really into Jimmie Dale Gilmore."

I started laughing. "What?"

"I've been playing it for him and he smiles and dances. The kid has good taste."

Our group of friends had fallen collectively in love with the freaky Austin country singer Jimmie Dale Gilmore one night at the old Backstage in Ballard. We bought him beers and sat rapt, even the guys, listening to him drawl to us about how much he luuuved Seattle and what guuud beer we had here. Now James was listening to him. James, with his bald head and nonsensical chatter. It seemed this was how things would go from now on. Anything good, even our music, even our Texan crushes, would be taken over by our children. It seemed unfair.

We walked a while, and then stopped as Lucy's blanket caught the breeze and tried to blow away.

"Henry and I are thinking about having another."

"Another what?" I asked, tucking the blanket in tightly.

"Uh, another baby? Hello?"

"Oh, one of those. You know my position on that. I have a baby. Why would I need another? OK, let's walk again. Just ignore her crying, maybe she'll go to sleep."

"James needs a sibling. I don't want him to turn into one of those asshole only children." We cracked up. My ex-boyfriend was an only child. To be fair, this was a joke he often made about himself.

"They've all got good self-esteem, though," I said, thinking of my ex's monumental self-confidence.

Anyway, that was clearly the end of the discussion. If James needed something he would get it. Probably Lucy needed a sibling, too, if James needed one. The thought was unwelcome. I felt like I was extended to my very limit with just the one.

"Um, don't you have to stop nursing to get pregnant?" Ruthie, sleepy as she was, planned to nurse for as long as James needed to nurse.

"I've heard you don't. I'm gonna try." Ruthie had this hilariously rueful way of speaking, as if each sentence came prepackaged with its own regrets.

My mind was working over something. "Where's the baby going to sleep?"

"Henry says we'll have to get a king-size bed and we'll all four sleep in there."

"What? Are you serious?"

"Yes," she said definitively. "We can't just kick James out."

This was wild to me. I knew people co-slept, but I could barely stand to have my husband in my bed, let alone my kid.

"What if you roll over on one of them?"

"You don't. You just kind of know where they are."

I thought about this for a while and we walked a few strides in silence. Ruthie knew I was mulling it over. And I was. Would Lucy turn out to be a hoodlum if she didn't sleep with us? Was I making a big mistake?

This was the pattern of every walk: We made a circle around Green Lake, and so our talk traveled. We started with our babies and tried to decipher all the new rules we had to follow. The talk opened out to work, maybe briefly touched the real world, and then, like a tight, magic circle, closed back in on babies again. It was a dark enchantment.

We came to the work segment of the walk. Ruthie ran a division of PAWS, which rescued animals who found themselves in the weird interstices of suburbia, where developments stole land from bears and coyotes and raccoons. The animals wandered confused through this new landscape, snacking on trash cans full of delicious food, until Ruthie found them. Ruthie would swoop them up and take them back to her facility, where they were rehabilitated and released. Now she was thinking of quitting; they could get by on Henry's salary. They were offering her a raise if she would stay. I, meanwhile, had gotten my first assignment from *The New York Times*—a short book review of an obscure novel. I had been working my way up to this, reviewing for bigger and bigger newspapers, getting the right clips to secure an assignment from the *Times*. And it had worked. These developments were beyond both of our wildest work dreams, but somehow they didn't seem as interesting or pressing as Lucy's feeding schedule or James's lack thereof, and our talk telescoped back to sleep and milk.

As we got back to the parking lot, it started to rain, sideways spit that made me realize that *pluie*, the French word for rain, was onomatopoeic.

"D'you think this is the kind of weather Axl Rose was thinking of when he wrote 'November Rain'?" I asked.

"Damn, I was going to wear my wedding dress to meet you, just like Stephanie Seymour. But I forgot."

We kissed goodbye.

Ruthie drove away in her little Jeep, a whirlwind of surety. Ruthie was doing it; she was going all out; she was a real mom.

————

Every once in a while I'd meet Isabel or some other childless friend for a walk, and it was like taking a peacock out on a leash. Look at her! I'd think. The childless friend would talk about her trip to Vietnam or Zihuatanejo and who said what to whom at which barbecue and her new interest in xeriscaping or Roller Derby, and as she talked I would just gaze, secretly envious and secretly superior. I no longer had interests. I had a baby.

If I was unsure about my performance as a mother, Bruce had concerns about his performance as an earner.

These concerns came to the fore whenever he went out to work at a café. And he went completely haywire whenever he took the laptop to a specific café: the Caffe Ladro in Fremont. Fremont was the neighborhood just to the south of Phinney Ridge. It had been truly weird in my teenage years. My friends and I went to Fremont to eat Chinese humbow, drink espresso (then still rare), buy vintage overcoats, and gape at real live bike gangs. Now it was home to tech corporations like Aldus and Getty. The funkiness had been commodified into condos with creative metalwork and a plethora of brightly painted, overpriced restaurants frequented by young white men clad in expensive bicycling gear.

The Ladro was always filled with consultants, the leisurely underemployed, and freelancers like us. It was a crucible for Bruce. It had big tables and lots of outlets to plug in your computer, and there were other humans, but he always ended up rankled by the place.

He felt that as a freelance print journalist he was surrounded by new-technology assholes who didn't understand the value of what he did. He felt he was in a pitched battle with these guys, and he was doubly pissed because they didn't even know it.

The day after my walk with Ruthie, Bruce hit Ladro while I worked at home. (Our budget stretched to one laptop.) The baby was being minded by Joelle, our nanny. Or babysitter. Whatever. She didn't care either way. We adored Joelle. She sang in a band. I mean, she belted it. The first time we saw her band, they covered "Son of a Preacher Man," and she imbued the song with a deeply burlesque, almost vaudevillian sexiness. Bruce put his fingers over his eyes and watched from behind them, like he was at a scary movie.

Joelle had a wicked sense of humor married to a wholesome farm-girl persona. She was beloved by everyone except our mothers. They looked askance at her. How come she got to be with Lucy when they wanted to? (The answer was that she, being dependent on our money, was more reliable.) She was a basically depressive character who liked jokes. She fit right in at our house.

I had left her and Lucy on the couch, reading a book, and was working away at a story when an e-mail came in from Bruce:

Who are these assholes? Where did they come from?
B

I was still composing a response when the next e-mail appeared:

These are the phrases I've heard in the last ten minutes: Getting eyeballs. Metrics. Driving traffic. Aargh!

I tried to think of something calming to say and another came in:

Now one of them is talking about the three-month Buddhist retreat he just went on. Took a little time for himself after leaving Microsoft. These fuckers sit there in their two hundred dollar jeans and get to feel all morally superior!
Love you.
B

Oh, dear. This was getting distracting and I had to finish this piece before Joelle left. I closed my browser window and resolved not to read any e-mail for at least an hour.

Twelve minutes later, I checked my in-box:

All this cash seems to flow to them, and yet they don't seem to DO anything. It used to be that you could either work for money, or be a creative type. Somehow these guys get credit for being bohemian and also get to make all the money.

I shut down my browser again. I finished the article, finally, and went in to get some lunch. Joelle and Lucy had gone for a walk.

I was flipping a quesadilla when Bruce came in.

He dropped his backpack on the kitchen floor. "Look at my fore-head!" He pointed his long, knobby, beautiful forefinger at his head. "Do I have a big L stamped on it? Am I just the town loser?"

"Want a quesadilla?"

"Yes, please. Just let me bitch for like ten minutes. Ducatis are lit-tered in front of that place. And everyone has a brand-new laptop. You know these people are all from the East. They went to, like, Williams. They think Seattle is cute but too small and too far from everything. They deign to live here. They used to like microbrews and now they're into small-batch bourbon."

"You're ranting."

"Damn right I'm ranting! I'm making a living as a writer. Which is a feat! But I'm judged by the standards of the people around me, who are all making a mint. It's ridiculous! Every time I go out for coffee I feel like a chump."

"Don't feel like a chump! Feel lucky. You're making a living. Here's your quesadilla, it has avocado."

When Bruce and I met, we worked at a newspaper. The week we quit, Bruce was ecstatic. He had a contract in hand from a national magazine and an office in his backyard. What more could any man want?

Maybe the isolation was wearing him down; maybe it was the pres-sure of providing for his family. But his mood appeared to tank frequently. I tried my best to jolly him out of it, with cheerful encour-agement, with quesadillas.

We bent to our lunches and read the paper. It was Tuesday, the Science Times. So boring. I handed it to Bruce and read a review, of a show by a band I'd never heard of.

That night, during lotus (requested by me), Fran stopped in her tracks in front of Elizabeth, who was folded neatly into the pose, her blond hair curling around her eyes-shut face. She looked great: serene, softly lit, folded up, Buddha-ish, if the Buddha were a competitive marathoner/corporate lawyer. You're not supposed to look around at the other people in class. Yoga and my granny agree on at least one principle: Comparisons are odious. But I always found myself peeking, and my gaze often landed on Elizabeth, who appeared as slender and strong as Artemis with her crossbow.

Fran closed her eyes, as she always did when she was really thinking. "Lotus is a dangerous pose," she said slowly. "Because it's the perfect yoga pose. It's the pose that people who don't do yoga imagine when they think of yoga. If you follow me." She smiled, white teeth gleaming, dark lashes still laid low on her cheeks. Fran had the most devouring smile, like she was eating air. "When we try to fit our bodies into an idea, it's dangerous. We stop feeling from the inside and take cues from the outside about what we should be doing. This can lead to injury and, even worse, to dissatisfaction."

Sitting there in lotus, with my ankle twisted and torqued, and my hip knotted, and my brow furrowed, I tried to listen to what Fran was saying, even though it made no sense to me. I also checked myself in the mirror. I wanted to see if I looked anything like Elizabeth. I looked pretty good, quite yoga-ish, in fact.

"Close your eyes," said Fran. "Stop looking in the mirror. Just feel the pose." Damn! How did she know I was looking in the mirror? "One of the eight limbs of yoga is pratyahara," she said. "It's a quality of inwardness, of contemplation. Fall is a great time to practice pratyahara, as the year is dying." Have I mentioned that Fran was really into the seasons? "As you do the rest of your poses today, and as you go back into the world, practice pratyahara. Try to feel from within, rather than judging and looking at what's on the outside. Just try it."

My basic attitude toward Fran was: If you say so. She was my teacher, and she was funny, and smart, and beautiful, and could do full splits. So I trusted her. Her words about inwardness were as incomprehensible to me as a foreign currency. The coin Fran was handing me might have been Etruscan or Finnish; I had no idea how to spend it. But I guessed there was some value, some currency in there somewhere.

Until then, I would fake it.

4. CROW

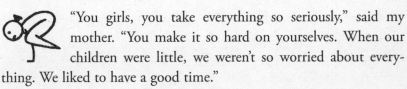"You girls, you take everything so seriously," said my mother. "You make it so hard on yourselves. When our children were little, we weren't so worried about everything. We liked to have a good time."

I was baking a banana cake for Lucy, whose first birthday was the next day. Homemade cake, I felt, was more wholesome than store-bought, and bananas more wholesome than chocolate. My mother sat at the kitchen table sipping a glass of wine.

"Of course you liked to have a good time," I said, mashing banana in the bottom of a large bowl. Its strangely pleasing dirty-lunch-box smell filled the room. "You were, like, twelve when you had us. You had parties and got drunk and stuff because that's what you do when you're young. I'm old."

My mom had given birth to my brother when she was twenty-four and to me when she was twenty-six. I, on the other hand, had cruised past thirty the year before. I felt it.

I had begun to notice that I disagreed with every single thing my mother said, as if I were an adolescent again.

She pressed on. "I'm not saying we had fun all the time. I'm saying we didn't take everything so seriously."

"I don't take everything seriously," I said, crossly. In fact, seriously.

Lucy pulled herself up on a chair and looked at us expectantly.

"Want to help?" I asked. "This is your cake. For your birthday tomorrow!"

I set her on a chair and she slapped at the batter with the wooden spoon.

"Good stirring, Lucy," said my mother in her beseeching-grandma voice. "Go for it!" She gazed at Lucy, her eyes bright and soft. She looked like a witch who was just about to eat the delicious, pudgy child.

"Mom, don't praise her all the time. You'll spoil her."

"Oh," said my mother. "But you praise her all the time, too, honey."

"Oh, well." I started to laugh. "She's pretty great."

"The greatest," said my mom.

We watched Lucy stir the cake awhile, and then my natural impatience overcame me, and I took the spoon from the baby and finished making the cake. My mom sat down on the floor with Lucy and chatted with her while they shifted some blocks around.

I looked nervously at the door. I hoped Bruce wouldn't come in. Lately I had been experiencing cognitive dissonance whenever I was with my mom and my husband at the same time. It was as though I had a split allegiance. I didn't know which family I belonged to.

These days Bruce seemed less tolerant of my family, shorter tempered with my mom. In fact, less tolerant and shorter tempered in general. Every person who came in the door seemed like an encroachment on his work time.

I sank onto the floor with the newspaper—Wednesday, Dining Out—and read while I desultorily watched my mom play with my daughter. She seemed showy with Lucy, as though she knew how it was done and I'd better watch. This was possibly entirely my own imagination.

A thought crept unbidden into my head as the two of them made a tower out of brightly painted wooden blocks: You weren't so perfect.

There is a picture of my mother in the living room of our house in Laurelhurst. Her dark hair is tied into Laura Petrie ponytails. A few years later, she would start to bleach it. Her eyeglasses are black and heavy, perched on the end of her nose. The year is 1969. She is in the foreground of the photo, doing crow.

Crow is a gawkily beautiful pose. The body becomes an angling weight resting upon a shifting balance point. It takes a little doing to set up. My mom, we can presume, has done these things to get into the pose: Squatted. Spread her hands before her on the floor. Bent her elbows deeply and wedged her knees atop her upper arms. Shifted her weight from her feet to her arms. Lifted her feet into the air. And now, she is doing it! She is flying. Her face is triumphant, maybe even a bit smug. If you saw only her face, you might think she was a successful cardsharp. She has pulled off a trick.

In the background of the photo, my lanky father leans against a table, arms crossed, legs extended. He looks pretty good-natured, but he's not impressed. And he's certainly not going to try it himself.

This picture says everything anyone needs to know about my 1970s. My mother, taking flight. My father, not coming along.

When I was a kid, all the mothers started to leave. Gretchen's mother got a business suit and then a job to go with it. Jennie's mother started drinking a lot of white wine, and then began to leave Jennie and Pete with a silky-haired, clog-shod babysitter for long weekends. Natalie's mother, despite what we perceived to be her ancient age, took up with a graduate student.

My mother, poised for flight in crow, began to take off in earnest at a pig roast. Of all places. Pig roasts were big in the 1970s. We went to this one because everyone else was going. We lived in a kind of teeming mass in those days, filled with the people my mother had grown up with in her North Seattle parish. It was a group that kept expanding, having children, acquiring new friends, dragging home colleagues for marathon bouts of jug-wine drinking. The Catholics were spreading out, encompassing more and more humanity in a jolly, disregarding manner that I guess had something to do with being Irish.

My mother's friend's husband ran a company that made water skis, and his shop manager was throwing the pig roast. So my brother, my mother, and I went. My dad, now, says he remembers he went to this party as well. I don't remember his being there; but maybe I choose not to. Maybe it's too difficult a notion to countenance.

My brother and I had been told we were going to a hippie party. We were interested in hippies. They congregated along Fifteenth Avenue on a mangy lawn that edged the University of Washington. We called this lawn Hippie Hill and begged to be driven past it. The hippies were fun to look at, with their long hair and their often-purple clothes. "Hippie!" we would call when we spotted one, as if we were successful birders. Now we were going to a party with the hippies. We would walk among them at last!

This hippie party would take place at a beach, way out in the country. We took a ferry across Puget Sound, our noses filled with the scent of salt and creosote. We drove over snaking highways and then down a dirt track through a forest. Giant ferns brushed the car. We didn't know that we were driving into a new life. I suppose no one ever does.

We parked the car and headed through the throng to the roasting pit.

"Hey there," said a young man with long chestnut hair and a full beard that didn't quite cover his rosy, round cheeks. In fact, everyone present looked a bit . . . not fat, exactly, but well fed. Solid. It was one thing to see hippies sprinkled around town, but it was another thing to see them massed in one place. A hairier thing. Three bare-chested men and a tough-looking girl with long braids stood at the end of the spit, slowly turning it and drinking Lucky beer from bottles.

My mom, always one to mind her manners, asked after the host, and was told he was sick in bed. She went off to say hello to him, and Dave and I spotted some of our pals from the Catholic diaspora. We headed down to the beach to do what we did: walk on logs, get our pants wet, bat at rocks with pieces of wood, pick on Freddy O'Brien. None of us liked the looks of the pig, glistening and naked. It was like a monster, rotating at the center of the day.

There was no sign of my mother. This was optimal. We spent the day in the woods and on the beach, like little savages. Our main objective was to avoid having to eat the pig. Finally, exhausted and hungry, I went to look for her. I saw the other mothers, Rita and Margaret and Patty, near the fire pit, busily absorbing their new friends, the hippies. Long tables had been set up nearby, covered with old flowered bedsheets. Half-empty bowls, made from lumpy pottery and utilitarian shiny metal, were constellated there. The food inside them did not interest me. Five kinds of potato salad, green salad, and some kind of salad made from rice. Salad, the nonevent of the food world, as far as children are concerned.

"Where's my mom?" I asked.

They peered at me over mugs of wine. "Has anyone seen Donna?" asked Margaret in her vague way. She pulled me onto her lap. I leaned against her and absentmindedly patted her frizz of hair.

I stayed there awhile. Margaret's husband, Don, was playing Bob Dylan songs on his guitar and people were mumble-singing. The sun was dropping through the trees over the bay. Finally Rita went into the house to look for more wine and poked her head back out the door. "Claire! Your mom's in here."

I went in. The last of the sun streamed into the large, wood-paneled room. A platform bed was set up in the corner. My mother perched on the edge of it, chatting animatedly. The bed was a wild tangle of sheets. At home our sheets were white and ironed and neat. These were a mess of bright colors: orange, aqua, and green.

There was a person in the sheets, sunburned behind a bushy mustache. My mother's attention was bent away from me, toward him, like a plant that was photosynthesizing like crazy.

"Honey, this is Larry. He's our host," my mother said, in the voice that meant I was supposed to do something.

I said hello. He said hello back. His mustache was frightening and his eyes were green. I went back outside, to the other mothers. It seemed like hours before my mom came out.

I put Lucy into her birthday dress of black-and-white gingham-checked taffeta. Her creamy limbs bulged. Yellow curls lay against her neck. She greeted her public at the front door.

Lisa was there with her four children and her handsome, too-cool-for-school husband, Steve; Isabel and her husband were there; Ruthie and her husband, Henry, and James. Bruce's parents. And of course my mom and Larry and my dad and my brother and his wife and baby were there. Everyone has their "everyone" they mean when they say "Everyone was there." This was my "everyone."

I watched my parents rotate around the room. They were all genuinely lovely people. They sat next to the lame and the halt, or at least the boring and the difficult, and listened and chatted. Larry poured wine and laughed at people's jokes. My mother talked people's ears off, but in a good way. My dad mooched around, laconic and lovable, utterly himself, seemingly unconcerned what anyone thought of him. (Of course all my friends worshipped him.)

My brother sat on a leather ottoman, elbows resting on his knees, and talked with Isabel about her art. He wore a beautiful cashmere sweater. He had become a natty man somewhere along the way. He had an elegant, bony face and close-cropped blond curls. He was as familiar to me as my hand.

My brother and I had been through the biggest events of our childhood with each other. We had traveled back and forth between our parents, always together. He was a couple of years older than me and, even as a little kid, had a personality that was a combination of gravitas and jokiness. He took himself seriously, but not too seriously. I found his attention essential. He was as necessary to me as the other stuff I had to remember traveling from point A to point B. Underwear, library books, homework, brother.

Lately I had started to wonder: What happened? Not just my mom and dad breaking up. It seemed that during that period in the early 1970s when my folks split, everyone's mom and dad had broken up.

It was the women who left. Looking back, I picture a rondo of departures: women fleeing in cutoff jeans, in business suits, in dashikis and Mexican wedding gowns and halter tops. They're like dogs in P. D. Eastman's *Go, Dog. Go!*: They're going in cars, they're going by foot, they're going by bike and boat and airplane. Where are they going? Some of them are going, like those jolly, argumentative dogs, to a party. Some are going to work. Some are going to live on communes. Some are moving into another house not unlike the one they just left, with a qualitative difference: a new man.

Why did they leave? Why did they all go at once? Between 1967 and 1977, the divorce rate in America doubled. Obviously some of the people who were leaving were men, but men had always left. The difference now was that the women were leaving, too.

Some people are just born into an ill-fitting moment. They're born too late for one thing and too early for another. To be a young mother at the end of the 1960s and the beginning of the '70s was to have missed it. The young mothers had washed up on the sandbar of marriage, while all around them the tide shifted into some unfamiliar current. The feminists, the hippies, the protestors, the cultural elite all said, It's OK to drop out. Just go. You know you want to. It's OK to go. And, oh, the mothers wanted to go. They, like everyone else, wanted fun and freedom and meaning.

Liberation was now a story of movement. The idea was to go somewhere. The problem was the children. How was it supposed to work, exactly? If you went, say, to San Francisco, or Marrakech, or one of those other places always cropping up in popular tunes, did the children go, too? Or did you leave them behind? Bring along a babysitter? Or what?

It's a question that sounds small, even petty: What to do with the children? But it turns out to be paramount. The young mothers answered it as best they could. They left their husbands and took the kids; they ran off with bearded, smelly boyfriends; they stayed at home and cooked dinner and drank too much wine and imagined the parties they were missing. These solutions made them crabby sometimes.

To grow up as one of their children was to grow up with compromise, and disappointment, and experimentation, and strange men hanging around. It was also to grow up in an atmosphere of weird, even sketchy optimism. The young mothers had heard a song of liberation, and they were trying to dance.

The generational construct can be silly, but sometimes it holds. We speak of a Depression mentality, a boomer sense of entitlement. We wonder about our children, growing up awash in digital culture. And I can't help but wonder: What happens when a generation of children grows up with all these comings and goings; when a generation of children grows up with parents who want to be free, and who think that freedom is movement? The voluntary nature of our parents' upheavals and displacements makes the whole situation more loaded, more confusing, from a child's point of view. Our moms and dads chose this radical shift. It did not, like war or the Depression, come upon them. And yet, almost paradoxically, for their children that element of volition was missing. We were thrust into this life, not at all by our own choice. Children are famously conservative; given the choice, they would go nowhere at all. They would choose to change nothing, ever.

So: What happened to us, to the kids of the first generation who divorced in huge numbers?

Of course I'm not the first to be fascinated by this question. In the early 2000s, two long-term studies of the children of the first generation of divorce were released. First came Judith Wallerstein's book *The Unexpected Legacy of Divorce*. Wallerstein's sample was comprised of 131 children and their families from Marin County, California. Marin is a county better known for its departure from societal norms than for its adherence to them. Even so, Wallerstein's small sample from an atypical population caused a sensation. Guess what the unexpected legacy of divorce was? Fucked-up kids, that's what!

At least that was the way the story got told in the media. Wallerstein found that kids from divorced families experienced more difficulty in intimate relationships, more drug and alcohol problems, and as adults, a higher rate of divorce than their counterparts from intact families. Her subtle exploration of children's experience of divorce got reduced to a four-word headline: DIVORCE BAD FOR KIDS. The book became a best seller. Right-wing groups rallied behind Wallerstein's findings, and the book's message was taken up as a cri de coeur by conservatives. Lefties were more dismissive. Katha Pollitt made a convincing argument that Wallerstein's study was "pseudoscience."

Three years later came *For Better or For Worse* by E. Mavis Hetherington, a professor of psychology at the University of Virginia. Her book took a slightly larger population, from a larger geographic area, over a slightly longer period of time, and came up with findings that basically said: DIVORCE NOT SO BAD.

My own observations were less quantitative and more qualitative—more narrative, maybe. Here is what I saw: Our thoughts and feelings about divorce by and large centered around our mothers. Our fathers somehow stood to the side, not part of the emotional picture. Some of us were furious with our mothers, and some of us were bemused by them. I myself vacillated between these two approaches. Our mothers did just as they pleased! We could hardly believe it when we thought about it. It made us dizzy. Our mothers broke up our families and left our fathers and thought only of themselves. That was the story we told ourselves.

And so, when we became parents, my brother and I shrunk our possibilities and lived our lives within the walls of our respective homes. Our mother had broken up our family, which was something neither of us would ever do to our own children.

My brother grew up to become a one-woman man. His wife was a girl he'd known since high school. They began dating in their early twenties and were married a few years later. They were devoted to each other from the start, the kind of couple who would leave a party early to go home and hang out, just the two of them. Dave was what you might call a partisan husband. He was entirely on board with his wife's platform; he loved the art she made and he loved her parenting philosophy and he loved her shoes. He was the kind of husband who repeated his wife's jokes. And he was the kind of father who made sure he did everything just right. That meant he followed the same rules I did, only more so. Organic cotton diapers and stylish wooden toys from Europe. He had eye bags for years on end from letting his daughters sleep in the same bed with him and his wife. He was a proud wearer of a baby sling. Of course, being Dave, he made all this look cool.

We made up our minds, my brother and I and so many of the grown children of the runaway moms, that we would put our families first and ourselves second. We would be good, all the time. We would stay married, no matter what, and drink organic milk. That was how it was going to be. My brother and I became the worker bees of family life.

He was serious in his request that my parents divorce. Since he had started his own family, he seemed to rankle more than ever at the odd shape, the strange story of our family. He and his wife had created a beautiful nuclear family; now it seemed that in retrospect he saw just how nuts our own family had been. Two dads! And our parents were still married! It was bananas! Sometimes he called me up with exhortations to join forces in order to browbeat our parents. I was noodly. I just wanted everyone to get along. This need was even stronger than the need to do what my brother wanted, which was very strong indeed.

The eccentricity of my family, the strange grouping that my mother had made and that Larry and my father had agreed to, was unquestioned by me. I tried to think about it when my brother called to bully me about it in his calm, rational way. But somehow my brain shut down when I thought about my childhood. I experienced that mysterious state called "brain fog." I didn't want to think about our childhood one single bit.

I looked at my brother now. He had a coiled, latent power. He was angry, I knew. Not at me. So why did his anger make me nervous?

It was time to sing "Happy Birthday." I lifted Lucy's delicious weight into her high chair and went to get the cake. I lit the candle. Bruce began the singing, and I walked into the dining room. The candle light spangled my eyes a bit.

How did my family look when I came into the room with the cake in my hands? I don't know. All I could see was my daughter, her dear eyes shining, her tiny hands clapping.

In yoga class, my hard work was not paying off. I liked poses that held still, as implied by the word "pose." I liked to get into the thing and inhabit it as perfectly as possible, for as long as possible. Fran told us that poses were not about perfection but process. The yoga, she said, was in the trying. This sounded great and all, but I was addicted to the feeling of finishing a pose. Triangle. Warrior. Lotus. Half moon. I wished I could hold them in stasis for longer, for hours, filling their shapes like they were molds and I was cake batter.

There was no way to do crow right, as far as I could tell. When Fran called out for crow, I'd pad across the studio to the stack of blankets and put a couple on my mat, in case I fell. I was quite frightened of falling. In fact, there was zero chance of my ever, ever falling, since I never actually was brave enough to lift into the pose.

"Crow is not a pose about stasis," Fran reminded us. "Crow is a pose that's about a fine point of balance. It's about maintaining a state of play."

Play. Right. I looked around. People were popping into the pose, and falling out, and laughing, and growing red in the face. Me, I made everything pretty: I straightened my blankets. I squatted on my mat, back like a ramrod. I spread my hands on the mat, widening my fingers and pressing down on each pad. This was the right way to spread your hands for an inversion or a balance, even for downward dog: equal pressure over every part of the hand. Surprisingly difficult to do, so I concentrated and did it right. I leaned my weight forward, my knees pressing into my elbows. And . . . that was it.

This was the point where my feet were supposed to lift off the mat, but they stayed put. I couldn't lift them even an inch. The fact was, I didn't want to. The ground was the place for me.

My mother had flown, though. As a kid, I think I was a little afraid that she might fly away altogether.

5. PIGEON

 I looked like something you'd find at the scene of a car accident. With my left leg sticking out behind me and my right leg pinned under my hips, I leaned forward onto my belly. Legs were not meant to be held in such a position. Legs were meant to stride or cross elegantly at the ankles or wear fancy tights or dance an Irish jig. They were meant to do anything, really, but this.

Really? I thought of asking Fran, the first time we did pigeon. Are you sure?

But now I had been doing pigeon for a month or two, and my attitude had changed. I realized it was not so much a pose as a mining expedition. I was digging in and finding stuff. Each time I did the pose, I got a little farther into my hip muscles. I seemed to pick up each day where I had left off before, and then go a little farther in my expedition, a little deeper in my probing.

My conception of my body changed. My hips came to seem a great dark unexplored area, like Conrad's Congo. Of course, as in the Congo, there had been plenty going on there all along. I just hadn't been paying attention. I had always been dissociated from my hips. A friend, dancing with me in college, exclaimed with real excitement, "Hey! Your hips just moved." Since I became a mom and started carrying the baby around all day, my hips had become intensely impacted.

Today Fran had warned us that she expected us to hold the pose for quite a long time. As we lay there in attitudes of traffic-accident chic, she talked, quite mysteriously, about something called the koshas.

"Our selves are layered in what the yogis call koshas," said Fran. "We can think of them as sheaths. I'm going to describe them, and as I talk, I want you to move through them with me. Think about whether or not you can locate these different parts of yourself. Think about whether or not they can help you do this pose, or if this pose can help you to find them.

"The first sheath, or layer, is the annamayakosha. This literally means 'food sheath.' This is the part of us that is visible. Next is the pranamayakosha, the breath sheath. Or if you think of prana as energy, this is the energy sheath."

The pigeon haters (whose number is legion) in the group were beginning to shift and frown. Fran kept talking.

"The next layer is manomayakosha. This is the sheath of the self, of identity. It is also the sheath of our emotional life. Next is vijnamayakosha. This sheath has to do with intellect, judgment, and wisdom. We often mistake these two sheaths for the deepest self, especially in the West. But there's one more layer: the anandamayakosha. The bliss sheath."

Bliss sheath. I stored it away, as a nut in a squirrel's cheek, for later punning. Fran went on. "The bliss sheath is the truest self, the self most connected to the divine. It is always present in us, and most active when we are asleep. Practicing all the limbs of yoga can bring us closer to it. Release pigeon."

As I swung my leg out of pigeon, I thought about what Fran had said. It seemed entirely true and entirely false. There was something about this idea of the bliss sheath, a layer of divinity inside a person, that made sense. I believed that it might exist, if only as a beautiful and dumb metaphor. But just as entirely I dismissed the idea that such a thing might exist inside of me. It was clearly something that would only ever be a reality for other people, like Vuitton bags or a tidy spice drawer.

"Look at the sutras," she said, not for the first time. "They're not, like, an easy read. But you might find something of interest there."

One of the problems with yoga was that there was no bible. No urtext. No word of god. Really, this is because yoga is a technique for knowing god, or even becoming god. A technique cannot have a bible. It has, instead, a manual. Or many manuals.

I began my exploration of the sutras with high hopes. I looked them up on the Internet, leaning heavily on Wikipedia, I'm sorry to say. Wikipedia is like the *People* magazine of research; everyone looks at it and no one will admit it. Anyway, I learned the sutras were compiled by someone called Patanjali in the second century. They are a compendium of the knowledge developed by yogis up until that point, written in aphorisms. Excellent, I thought. Aphorisms. Maybe they would have an Oscar Wilde–like pithiness. I set out with Lucy to buy a copy.

There was a street corner in the University District, or really, an alley corner, where Forty-second Street met the alley that ran between University Way and Fifteenth. Café Allegro, the oldest coffeehouse in Seattle, fronted onto the alley. Magus Books fronted onto the street.

I once heard a screenwriter refer to "the brown muffin." She said certain films, for instance those made by Merchant Ivory, look as though they've been shot through a brown muffin. That was what life felt like at this intersection. Everything was old, and worn, and amber-colored.

I stopped in at the Allegro first. Years ago, the Chinese restaurant a few doors up had spilled a vat of chicken fat out into the alley. The smell had somehow set in the sun, and now the Allegro always smelled a little animal and rancid. This was just right, because the Allegro was a mean place. The servers could barely tolerate the sight of the patrons. My husband referred to the girls who worked there as "the bitches in their sweaters." My mother said that the disappointment was palpable every single time she walked in the door. My friend Scott said it was the most ill-named coffee shop ever—it should, he said, be called Café Triste. I loved it. It was a relief from the constant niceness of our life.

I ordered. The servers ignored the beautiful girl parked on my hip. After I got my coffee, I ankled around the corner to Magus. I pushed open the glass door and entered a room of enormous tallness. The bookshelves went up up up ten feet, and then there was another expanse of ceiling above that, filled with dust motes drifting like the stuff of thought itself. It was as if the books were dreaming, and their dreams floated into the air above, just barely visible.

I took a token stroll through fiction, my homeland. It was against the back wall. I didn't really belong in the Eastern Religions section, or wherever it was I might find the yoga sutras. Maybe self-help? Or maybe physical fitness? (The eternal conundrum of yoga.) These were not the books I read. When I needed information, I went to the source: novels. That's where they keep the feelings. Religion and self-help books were merely diagrams. Novels were the full picture.

I reluctantly headed out into the vast reaches of nonfiction. The Eastern Spirituality section, halfway along a high shelf in the middle of the room, required the recruitment of one of those cylindrical metal step stools that look like they've rolled straight out of the 1950s. I set Lucy on the floor next to me, with a pile of books. Bhagavad Gita, *The Prophet* by Kahlil Gibran, *Tao Te Ching*, Upanishads. No *Yoga Sutras*. I looked on the shelf below. There was a pamphlet down there, more of a stapled folio than a book. I pulled it out. The paper was thick and yellowing. The print was indented in a way that suggested the thing had not been printed in the United States. I checked the copyright: Bangalore, 1972.

There was no introduction, no foreword, no preface. Just the sutras, which were numbered. What was a sutra anyway?

Number 1: "Now, the teachings of yoga." This cracked me up a little. It sounded like Don Pardo. I read on.

Number 2: "Yoga is to still the fluctuations of consciousness." I understood this just from practicing asana with Fran, the notion that when you presented your body with a series of challenging movements, you were also training your mind to be quiet, to endure and overcome difficult situations.

On to number 3: "Then pure awareness can abide in its very nature." This seemed unlikely, and things just got unlikelier from there.

The more I read, the dustier Patanjali's *Yoga Sutras* seemed. The words did that thing where they became so dissociated from the world, and from concrete meaning, that they didn't even seem like words anymore. It was like reading Kant. I flipped through the pages of the folio, looking for something to jump out at me and explain me to myself.

I wanted the sutras to pull me in emotionally, like a novel, and explain the world gently, by example. I wanted to escape into them as into a fantasy of another life.

But this wasn't that kind of book. It wasn't a novel. It wasn't an escape. Hell, it was hardly even a book. It was a tract, and some of it appeared to be crazy. For instance, sutra 3.40: "By mastering the flow of energy in the head and neck, one can walk through water, mud, thorns, and other obstacles without touching down but rather floating over them." If I wanted poetry, I'd be in a different section.

They were brief, yes, and looked aphoristic, but reading them was not like reading Oscar Wilde. It was like reading bread, or grass. Impossible.

Still, I rummaged around for a while, looking for words that might make sense to my eye. The philosophy of yoga was a series of rumors to me, and as I moved through the sections, I spotted things like the eight limbs, a term I had heard repeatedly but sometimes got mixed up with the eightfold path of Buddhism. (Maybe this is how Americans pick foreign religions—we like the ones with lists. Maybe it's the same impulse that drives us to pick up magazines that promise us ten steps to a new you. It makes sense—the kind of people who would try a new religion are likely the same kind of people who pursue self-improvement.)

I paused on the eight limbs, thinking they might contain the prescriptive information I sought. They looked more concrete. I found a cracker in my purse and gave it to Lucy to gnaw on.

The first limb was composed of the yamas, which were the ethical guidelines of yoga: non-harming, non-lying, non-stealing, sexual abstinence, non-greediness. All of these seemed doable and reasonable, except of course the one that was totally out of the question. I had a moment's pause—why should I even consider exploring a religion that asked me to do something I would never do?

The second limb was the niyamas, which were more devotional: purity, contentment, austerity, self-study, and surrender to god. The third limb was asana; the fourth pranayama, the yoga of breath. The fifth was pratyahara, the inward-turning that Fran had tried to teach me; the sixth was dharana, or concentration. The seventh was meditation. And the eighth was samadhi, or ecstasy.

The instructions were laid out before me, but I had no intention of following them. I mean, it was one thing to read about stilling the fluctuations of consciousness but another thing entirely to do it. Beyond that, I liked the fluctuations of consciousness. I made a living off the fluctuations of consciousness. I didn't want to be less conscious. I wanted to be smarter than I was, and maybe to have a cleaning lady. Unconsciousness would not help with either thing.

There was, as always with yoga, that weird disconnect. These looked like rules, but seemed impossible to follow. The eight limbs demanded not to be read but to be studied, and not to be studied but to be lived.

I bought the book anyway, with my Visa card, at the tall wooden counter, where there was a *Far Side* day-by-day calendar. I went back to get my coffee, which I had left on the shelf. Its taste was bitter and so very reassuring. I shifted Lucy from one hip to the other and left.

———

I was troubled by what I perceived as the inauthentic nature of my yoga practice. I had a feeling that doing yoga in a class, without knowing the philosophic and historical underpinnings, made me kind of a jerk. I had begun to notice that I felt guilt whenever I met a person of Indian descent.

I was, after all, a book critic. I needed more information by means of the printed word, which was my means of choice.

I read more about Patanjali, about whom little is known. He's usually referred to as a sage, which makes him sound like an avatar in a role-playing game. His was the earliest text that attempted to compile the teachings of yoga, almost two thousand years ago. Far from inventing yoga, he simply brought together teachings that were already ancient when he wrote them down. *The Yoga Sutras* gave rise to what is sometimes called classical yoga, and sometimes called raja yoga. At any rate, it is the only text that scholars call orthodox.

Patanjali drew on centuries of storytelling and mythologizing, which had slowly coalesced to create the tradition that he codified. These texts weren't somehow labeled "yoga." They were integrated into the massive literature that makes up early Indian culture.

A little research revealed that the earliest text referring to yoga was the Bhagavad Gita. The Gita—as groovy, in-the-know types call it—is but one section of the massive *Mahabharata*, which is said to be the longest epic ever written, though this seems hard to prove. I feel certain that some crazy would-be postal bomber in Wyoming or some hut dweller in the farthest reaches of Greenland has written one longer.

The Bhagavad Gita was easy to find. It was like the books of James Patterson; not something you'd really like to read, but once you had your eye out for it, it was everywhere. I had one on my very own bookshelf. How'd that get there?

The *Mahabharata* tells the story of Arjuna, a warrior who can't quite bring himself to kill anyone. Krishna, who is both Arjuna's charioteer and his god, has a long talk with Arjuna about serving god. The Bhagavad Gita is that conversation. It is also the first time that yoga is explained in any comprehensive way in a text.

Krishna explains to Arjuna that yoga is a matter of devotion, and that Arjuna might serve god by killing, since he would be practicing karma, or the yoga of action.

If it seems confusing that yoga, with its tenets of non-harming, might promulgate killing in its original text, well, that's yoga for you. The more I read, the more infinite it seemed. Commodious might be a nice way to put it. All over the map might be more accurate. There were so many historical yogas: hatha yoga, of course, and karma yoga, and raja yoga, bhakti yoga, Jainist yoga, and on and on. I felt hopelessly fettered by my lack of knowledge of Indian history; it seemed impossible to move through yoga's central ideas without it. My confusion was not unique. Even Arjuna says to Krishna, "My mind is in confusion because in thy words I find contradictions."

I read through Krishna and Arjuna's conversation. I read as a child reads a grown-up novel, looking for the sexy bits. I was looking for talk about the poses. This was the part of yoga I knew and understood, the place where I might insert myself into this weird and ancient story. I found nothing. There was a little talk about sitting and about meditation—at least here I could understand what was being discussed. And I found commonsensical elements I could understand. For instance: "Set thy heart upon thy work, but never on its reward. Work not for a reward, but never cease to do thy work." You could do pigeon forever, seeking some ultimate expression of the pose, but was that really the point? Wasn't there something to learn from the mining itself? Wasn't that enough? In fact, wasn't it everything? If you hoped to have perfectly free hips, you were hoping in vain. It was a horizon that you would never come to. Instead, never ceasing, do thy work.

Like a good student, I went next to secondary sources. In fact, I was intimidated by the primary sources. I thought maybe some Western scholars might come at yoga history from an angle I could better understand.

When I tried to figure out which were the most reputable and important yoga books, two names emerged as the leading Western students of yoga: Mircea Eliade, the Romanian historian, who made a decades-long study of yoga in the first half of the twentieth century; and Georg Feuerstein, a scholar of Hinduism who was nothing if not prolific.

Eliade and Feuerstein led me to a slew of lesser-known scholars, and soon I was up to my eyeballs in complicated strands of Indian history and Hindu philosophy.

And here is what I learned from these scholars: Don't think that because you're doing poses, you're doing yoga. In fact, many Western historians seem positively affronted by the spectacle of white people in their millions practicing asana, and go out of their way to explain that hatha yoga is not at all the same thing as raja yoga.

Raja yoga is the yoga that has been practiced by mainstream Hindis for centuries, with a supple and rigorous theology that has nothing to do with what happens in your local yoga studio. Raja yoga is the attempt to know god, or to abide in perfect consciousness. But who is this god, and what is this consciousness? That is harder to say.

God and the self are easy to understand in Western religion (at least to Westerners). Western religion is determinedly dualistic; there is god, and there is us, and the best we can hope for is to please Him.

There seemed to be some disagreement as to the role of dualism in yoga. On the one hand, yoga is non-dualistic in the sense that god is not there; he is, instead, in here, or, on the other hand, in everything.

There are too many yogas to pinpoint how dualism works in all of them. But in the case of Patanjali's yoga, or classical yoga, or raja yoga, there's a finer point to be made. Dualism does in fact exist—it's the distinction between matter and spirit. This sounds simple, like something your Lutheran pastor might discuss, but becomes less so when you realize that "matter" includes plain old consciousness. Thought. The ego. The mind. Whatever you want to call it. Thinking itself belongs in the same category as other matter. In yoga, matter is any object that pure awareness can rest upon.

Thought itself becomes something that is observed, something to become aware of. In this way, it fulfills the same role as a dog or a cup. Thought must, through practice, be transcended, just like everything else on earth. This transcendence is the job of the yogi; this is what is meant by knowing god.

At the same time, thought is potentially more disruptive to transcendence than a dog or a cup. Thought is kind of the problem child of yoga. It can obstruct the way. Westerners are comfortable using our minds to understand god; yoga shows us specific ways that our minds prevent us from knowing god.

The texts of yoga are full of categories and explanations for the way the mind and its habits prevent the practitioner from transcending the self. When Patanjali says that yoga is the stilling of the patterns of consciousness, he means that thinking can't help us and might be hurting us.

What I took away from my readings was this: I was, according to these scholars, not doing yoga. I was doing asana, and the origins of that were quite suspect. Over and over I read that mainstream students of yoga in Indian history did not perform asana; that asana was the realm of charlatans, of soldiers of fortune, of outcasts. People who focused on asana were straying from the classical yoga path.

Back on my mat, bent and pinned into pigeon, I wondered: What was I doing, then, laboring in the yoga studio? I thought of Krishna, telling me to set my heart upon my work. Somehow I had to believe that doing some work, in a wrong way, was better than doing no work at all. I was deeply interested in how far I might go in pigeon, how deep the tension was, and whether or not I might release some of that tension. I would keep doing that work.

I didn't know it at the time, but it was at this moment, when I decided that I couldn't be bothered to learn the right way to do yoga but that I would instead continue doing it, following my teacher and doing my work to the best of my ability, that I began to reap the fruits of yoga. Submission, trust, transmission from teacher to student, imperfection, the release of the ego—these were the things that would save me from myself, even if they were as unfamiliar as Krishna with his blue face. You can't go deeper and know what you're doing the whole time.

6. CHILD'S POSE 1

I pulled back into child's pose. I thought what a strange thing this posture was. You folded into yourself; you were closed off from the world and entirely self-sufficient. This is the opposite of how we normally think of children. We like to think of them as free, moving, open; we picture them skipping or marching or dancing or reaching their arms toward us. My own child did all these things, except when she did not.

Children are often not what we want them to be. They are not free-spirited or unfettered or even happy. They get depressed and sad and lazy. They get burned out and they get crabby.

Before my husband and I were married, we fell sort of in love with a little girl we met while we were on a short trip to Hawaii. We were staying in a complex of old plantation cottages on the sleepy west side of Kauai, a place where the nothingness of the days was vast in scale. You could spend quite a lot of time looking at brown waves and imagining Japan out there somewhere. Encountering a giant palm frond was something of an event. The place was small in scale, with little wooden houses dotting the grounds, dwarfed by banyan trees. In the cottage opposite ours a girl, probably about four years old, was staying with her parents. She came dancing out of her house in the mornings and greeted us where we sat drinking coffee on our porch. She had long brown hair that hung in lank curls down her back. She may have owned clothes; we saw her only in a swimsuit.

She had a genius for being the kind of child adults want children to be: She danced on the lawn, she dangled flowers from her ears like earrings, she solemnly told us that she intended to become a mermaid when she grew up. We called her "The Sprite."

One morning the Sprite didn't come dancing out of her house as usual. Well, maybe she had left. We felt a little let down, but this is what happens on vacation, these unsaid goodbyes. After we drank our whole pot of coffee we headed to the beach. As we passed the Sprite's house, we saw her stretched across the porch steps. Her head dangled to one side.

"Good morning," said my husband.

She rolled off the stairs and looked at us with a cold eye. She said, "Go away." She slowly, sadly climbed the porch steps and curled herself into a ball.

This was child's pose.

The Sprite didn't look quite the same to us after that.

We want children to embody lightness and joy because this is how we would like to remember our own childhood. We really want to believe that our childhood was just right. When I was a child, the adults around me wanted me to be a Sprite: cheerful and unfolded and happy. Above all, they wanted me to be happy.

1973

When I was six, I didn't have a bike, and neither did my best friends, Bridget and Marie. Their mom was Margaret, my mom's best friend. Our grandmas—my mom's mom and Margaret's mom—were also best friends; they lived on Northeast Eightieth Street, in what had been the epicenter of Irish Catholics in North Seattle. Now the Irish

Catholics were moving all over town, to whatever neighborhood they pleased. Being Irish and Catholic was no longer the defining fact of existence.

Margaret had a lap that was always available, even though she had six kids. Bridget and Marie lived a couple of blocks away in Laurelhurst, our leafy neighborhood filled with stern Tudor houses and pretty brick houses and big frame houses set on elegant lawns. We walked back and forth between our houses, looking for more toys and better snacks—when we'd exhausted the resources of one venue, we moved on. My mom could be crabby; their mom could be harried; we toggled back and forth.

Starting when I was four or five years old, we roamed over to Condie's, the corner store on Sand Point Way, where THE CANDY YOU TOUCH IS THE CANDY YOU BUY. Marie was a couple of years older than Bridget and me, so she was in charge.

We always took the shortcut through the think tank (really!) that lay between our houses and the store. It was filled with lawns and ponds, and bounded by woods, where the older boys left behind *Playboys* in their crappy ill-hidden little forts.

We walked along in the hot sun. The curved pathways and drooping willows of the think tank were designed to promote thinking, I would imagine. In my case it wasn't working. But Marie was thinking, thinking, thinking, relentlessly, in the way that children older than you always were. They were full ideas and notions and plans. Next to these paragons of ingenuity, these wicked planners, you, the younger sibling, the younger child, were as dumb as a rock, a stick, an infant.

It was time to choose bikes, Marie said.

Marie was the oldest, so she got first choice. "Mine is purple, with sparkles and a banana seat."

Bridget chimed in quickly. "Mine is red-white-and-blue"—in the 1970s, this was a single color, which would eventually reach its apotheosis in the stylings of Evel Knievel—"with stars on the seat. A banana seat," she hastily added.

Those were the two most desirable bikes. I had to think for a long time. "Sky-blue. Sparkles. Banana seat. A basket with flowers." It was a little weak, but what could I do? My hands were tied. Purple and red-white-and-blue were taken; everything else was less-than. Of course, now all middle-class children have bikes. In those days, it seems incredible to recall, you had to wait for your older sibling to outgrow his or hers before you could ride it.

We were walking uphill, so rather than riding our invented bikes, we pushed them. Our dads were at work, working. Our moms were at home, smoking. Our brothers were in the woods, looking at water-logged porn. We thought it would be like this forever.

Here's how I remember it: One day my dad was there, painting the french doors in the den. It was a sunny Saturday afternoon, the kind of day made to be wasted lying on the couch reading *Archie* comics. My dad was wearing his fishing hat, a stained and worn Gilligan-type affair, and my mom was leaning out the back door of the kitchen for a kiss. Looking back, I suppose this kiss must have been unusual because my heart gave a kind of ping of joy. A kiss. It seemed a great, notable thing to me.

I don't know how much time passed—it could have been years or days—but one day my dad was gone. He had been spirited away. He was no longer there to call me "Dairy Queen" when I ate butter straight off the stick on the butter dish. He had taken his lankiness, his gentleness, his tallness, his darkness, his diffidence, his smile and gone elsewhere with these qualities that seemed so essential to our household. They were like milk or clean, folded laundry: things I needed but had not imagined I'd have to do without.

He called me up on the phone. This, like the kiss, was wildly novel. My dad on the phone, inside the phone. That was not where he belonged. I sat at the little wooden table in the kitchen and took his call like a grown-up.

"Where are you?" I asked.

"I'm staying in a hotel for a while," he answered, in his calm, slightly throaty voice.

"Oh." I didn't think to tell him I missed him.

He did, though. "I miss you."

I thought about that for a minute, and then asked, "What did you have for lunch?"

Before, when he lived with us and was my regular father, every day at dinner I asked him what he had eaten for lunch when he was downtown at his office. He always made a little story of it: He had gone to a fancy restaurant with the president of his public relations firm. He had eaten a ham sandwich and a cookie at his desk. He had found a new hamburger place. He was that kind of person, the kind of person who responded well to a specific topic. Maybe this was why my mother left him. Or had he left her? It wasn't clear. In any case, I wanted to know what he had been eating for lunch.

"I went out to lunch with a client and I had chicken."

"OK."

We said "Love you"—the first of hundreds, maybe thousands of "Love you"s exchanged over the phone—and hung up.

The only hotel I could picture was the one right off Highway 99, by the Battery Street Tunnel. It had a blinking neon palm tree and was surrounded by very rectangular brick buildings. It looked shabby, even to me. This worried me.

My dad did not move back, as I had not very secretly hoped he would.

Then it was summer, and as we did every summer, we moved to a rental cottage with Bridget and Marie's enormous family and a retinue of hangers-on; in my memory's version everyone, even the two-year-old, is clutching a jug of wine. Every year we went somewhere different. The particulars changed but the generalities were eternal: a single, teeming bunk room for the kids; lots of wine drinking and singing for the grown-ups; a fire every night; desultory arguing over the toy in the cereal box; entire days spent on blow-up floats in the freezing water of Puget Sound. There was always a physical challenge that defined the summer's arc. Either you would perform this challenge or you wouldn't. Your failure or success determined how you would remember this particular summer. The previous year it had been a porch railing high above the ground that you had to walk. Bridget was good at these challenges. She was also good at making a fist and punching the boys. Her big brother called her "Lil' Harmer."

This year we moved to Bainbridge Island; we were living in a house we all called "Shiver Me Timbers," for no particular reason that I can recall. I suppose it was a play on words.

It was the summer of "Kodachrome," the Paul Simon song. Bridget and Marie and I spent a lot of time standing underneath an enormous cedar tree on the lawn, singing "those niiice bright colors . . . the gree-uh-eens of summers," our arms wrapped around each other's shoulders, our mouths open wide. Bridget and Marie might have been extensions of my own body.

We discovered a bulkhead taller than ourselves, and we jumped off of it. That was our challenge for the summer. My dad came to visit and took a picture of me, flying through the silvery sunlight, my hair lifting with velocity.

Partway through the summer, we drove over to Port Gamble to visit the green-eyed man with the mustache whom we had met at the pig roast. Larry. He was twenty-four. My mom was thirty-two, a matron with a large house and a lawn and an Irish housecleaner who tippled from the liquor bottles on the high shelf of the pantry. My father was forty. The three of them, with their cascading or ascending ages, were lined up like dominoes, ready to fall. Larry was kind and quiet. His house was not filled with hippies. Just the one: him. He promised that "next time"—next time?—he would take us to Crazy Eric's drive-in. It was going to be great. The best shakes. The greasiest fries.

My mom took us to the Bainbridge Island Street Fair. (A 1970s trope: My childhood was rife with street fairs.) At the street fair, I glazed a tiny pottery bowl. I begged for a black-and-white kitten that was being given away outside the Town & Country Market. I named her Daisy. She was the meanest cat ever. Over the years, I've realized this: If your mom lets you get a cat, your parents are splitting up for sure. Sorry, kids.

Daisy ate bees and scratched my arms. She was so mean.

Larry came to pick us up in his little Porsche. (Another 1970s trope: Sports cars were the very emblem of freedom. No room for the kids, that's why.) He had love beads! We were going to Crazy Eric's. It will come as a surprise to no one when I report that I ate too many fries and vomited all over his car.

7. COBBLER'S POSE

Lucy sat in her high chair, chewing a piece of apple. She kicked her feet against the chair and chatted away. Bits of apple speckled her T-shirt; I had failed once again to locate a clean bib. Green snot bloomed in her nostril, and she coughed occasionally as she ate and prattled. It was a November evening, not quite dark yet. Rain was misting down. Bruce was working in the office out back. I could see him through the window, hunched over the computer, his black eyebrows beetling. I stood on the back porch and waved extravagantly: Time to come home from work.

I left Bruce and Lucy in the cozy, tiny kitchen, with its red Marmoleum floor, which we had installed because the Environmental Home Center had told us that marmoleum was sustainable and nontoxic.

I had missed Fran's early-evening class and was headed for Jonathan's later restorative class. When I arrived at yoga, the air was hushed and the studio was murky. Jonathan liked to keep the lights low when he taught his evening classes.

We went through our opening-of-class motions. Then very slowly we went through a series of poses: warrior I and II, high lunge and low lunge, forward bend. We did forward bends and we did a gentle version of bridge, pushing up from the floor into a small backbend. It felt good to be moving. I didn't think of it as an escape; I just felt the relief of moving and not thinking. There was also this relief: It was a room I didn't have to clean. It was a like an hour-and-a-quarter visit to a hotel. It had that same visceral thrill: I will never vacuum this floor. I will never dust these baseboards. Never.

Toward the end of class, Jonathan asked us to sit in cobbler's pose. He told us its Sanskrit name: baddha konasana. The pose was very simple: You sat with your knees splayed out and the soles of your feet pressed together. It was nice to feel sole pressing against sole, a kind of not-quite-tickle.

"This was one of the poses the yogis used for meditation. This, or lotus. The rest of their asana practice was designed to loosen and strengthen the body so they could sit for long periods of time in meditation."

He hopped up and crossed the room to the light switch. At the end of class, he liked to dim the lights until they were mere yellow pinpricks. It could get a little creepy in there. When we lay in corpse pose, the shadows seemed to come alive. It was too quiet. Anyone who's ever watched a horror movie knows that when it gets really quiet, nothing good can happen. Sometimes when we sat there in the silent almost-dark, I felt as if we were meditating underneath the bed, where they keep the monsters.

When he had the light level roughly equivalent to that of a medieval beer hall, Jonathan sat back down and said, "Tonight, rather than lying in savasana, we'll try sitting as the yogis did. Simply continue sitting in cobbler's pose. If that's not available to you right now, come to any comfortable seated position."

We moved around a bit until we were all comfortable, or some approximation thereof.

When we'd stopped fidgeting, Jonathan said, "Being still can be the hardest thing you'll do in yoga. If you find your mind racing, just return to the breath. You don't have to breathe any special way, but just observe the breath. Don't try to control it. Don't try to deepen it. Just watch it go in and out, and see if that helps your mind to quiet."

I felt grumpy. I was here for a workout. I wanted to improve. That certainly wasn't going to happen when I was just sitting here.

We sat for a while. Long enough that I felt Jonathan had really made his point. Sitting was hard. Got it. I snuck a peek at the clock. There were still, like, ten minutes until class got out! Did he expect us to sit here the whole time? Jonathan himself sat there looking almost show-offily serene, like he could meditate all night. I willed myself to shut my eyes again.

Jonathan's incessant voice had kept the creepy shadows at bay during class, but the longer I sat there silent, the closer they crept.

I tried to breathe, tried to remember all the stuff you're supposed to remember when you're meditating. But something was pushing up from below the surface.

Before I knew it, I was crying. Tears were streaming silently down my face. I was losing my shit.

Good lord. I opened one eye. No one was looking at me.

What was the deal? I couldn't figure out why I was crying. I wondered why I was crying; I cried; this went on in a loop for a while. Then an image flashed into my mind: Lucy, and her stuffy little nose, and her minor cold. I sobbed more. Every time I saw her sniffle, every time I wiped her nose, I remembered her catastrophic birth and the terrible months that had followed.

It was a gray December morning, the worst kind of Seattle weather, where the sun won't shine and the rain won't rain and there's a kind of high, bright, headache-inducing light that makes you want to go to the movies for the rest of the day, or maybe the rest of the winter. I was nine months pregnant; it was the day before my due date. I got up, donned my tentlike garment, and drank my single cup of coffee. Bruce and I were sitting at the table reading *The New York Times*—it was Tuesday, Science Times day—when I got the feeling, the well-documented, giant-desire-to-crap feeling, and phoned my doctor, Chick. It was good to have a doctor you called by his nickname. Chick had been my babysitter when I was a little kid and became my doctor when I was fifteen. Now he said, in his gravelly, calm, laid-back voice, that maybe we ought to head off to the hospital. I hung up and told Bruce it was time to go.

We read these numbers on the baby's oximeter:

72

69

88

77

80

62

The baby, unnamed and not likely to live, had become distressed in utero and aspirated a lot of meconium. In other words, her lungs were filled with her own feces while she was still inside the womb. The birth, a C-section, had been . . . how many days ago? Two? Three?

We were living that secret life that goes on around all of us all the time, the life of the hospital. We sat in the NICU and watched as our baby grabbed for breath, in tiny sharp intakes, bringing air into the little bit of lung that wasn't clogged. She was powerfully focused on breathing, and yet very bad at it. She was an imperfect machine that had only one function: to breathe. She faltered at her task, but she never entirely failed.

The numbers were bad. We were waiting for the oximeter to say 90 or, beyond our wildest dreams, 95, which the nurses said was the lowest rate of normal oxygenation. We kept reading 82. And 77. It went up to 87 and I called for the nurse, excited. She said quietly, "That's not high enough." She rested a hand on my shoulder.

We watched and watched: the baby, the machine. No one would say the words we wanted to hear: "She's going to live."

She lay in her incubator, taking her tiny gasps, flailing her fist in the air. We took to calling her Braveheart. The baby was visibly fighting for life. You could practically see the will to live coursing in her. You felt that if she had a standard, she would have waved it. She was proof of something that seemed unprovable: the existence of the life force. In her, life was something as definable as chlorophyll in a leaf, green and necessary.

Time was a continent we walked across. Somewhere in the morning of the second day, my mother came into my hospital room and found me sitting on the floor in the bathroom, banging my head against the wall and saying over and over, "I'm so scared." Or so she tells me. I remember only patches; my memory is piebald, calico. Somewhere in the middle of the vastness of the third day, Bruce snatched a pen and wrote "Lucy" in the still-blank spot for "Baby's Name" on the paper label at the foot of her clear plastic condominium. Lucy, not quite lucky.

Bruce and I bound together furiously. When other people talked about the baby, it was like listening to a bad cover song: tuneless, depressing, wrong. Only Bruce and I were completely without hope and were completely hopeful. It was a terrible knowledge we shared, the knowledge that the baby would certainly make it and that she would certainly die.

I was released, to my sorrow, from the hospital. I would have to sleep across town from the baby. My friends and Bruce had transformed the room with the TV into a bower for me: beautiful sheets on the bed, flowers, everything exquisitely clean.

At home, I set to work at my new task: pumping. A woman from the La Leche League had appeared like a vision at my bedside in the hospital and told me I had to pump every three hours or my milk wouldn't come in. So I did. The hospital gave me an electric pump, and when I say I pumped religiously, I mean it in every sense. It was the one thing I could do for the baby, and I did it perfectly. If I did it, maybe she would live. I certainly wasn't going to risk the alternative.

My mother attended me while I pumped. A fastidiously neat woman, she has always had an out-of-character fascination with body

functions. She was the only person in our house utterly unembarrassed by the breast pump. I myself could barely say the words. She
would chat with me while I pumped, then whisk the filled cylinders
away to the freezer and make sure they were delivered to the hospital
for such time as the baby might take a bottle. She cheered me on
when I produced in volume, noted the diminishment of colostrum
over time, and, observing the comparative output of my two breasts,
pronounced, "Rightie is the champ!"

The Sunday after her birth. The oximeter read:

88
77
89
90
91
91
92
95
95
95

"She's going to make it," said a red-haired nurse, becoming my
favorite in that moment.

I breast-fed her at last, sitting in a rocking chair behind a curtain
in the NICU. That night I baked chocolate-chip cookies for the
intensive-care nurses.

When a baby had lived at the hospital for a while, as Lucy had, you
couldn't just take her home. You had to go to a meeting first. We went
to a meeting in a windowless room with a bunch of other terrified

parents getting ready to take their off-brand babies home from the hospital.

The nurse leading the meeting talked for a while about caring for our weird little babies. As she talked about breast-feeding, she interrupted herself and peered at me and Bruce.

"Are you the people who are going home with an oxygen tank?"

"Uh, no, I don't think so," I said. I wanted to quash this talk immediately.

The nurse glanced down at a clipboard and then back at us. "Lucy? That's your daughter?"

"Yes, that's her."

"You'll need to stay after class. Just stay and I'll go over some details with you."

Everyone in the gray room turned their gray, sad faces to look at us, the people going home with an oxygen tank.

My mind surged and bounced. Would she always be on an oxygen tank? Was there something wrong with her that they hadn't explained? Were her lungs permanently broken?

After the meeting, the nurse assured us it would only be for a while, just to be on the safe side. What was "a while"? The safe side of what?

We took her home, feeling like we were stealing her. She had a cannula taped to her nose. This was attached to an oxygen tank that followed her around like it was her familiar. We found her cannula adorable. We found her oxygen tank lovely. We were home and happy and terrified and in love.

We had been given strict instructions: We were supposed to keep her in quarantine for at least five months. It was flu season, and she absolutely must not catch a cold. We could not take her anywhere.

The first day she was home was an unseasonably warm December day. My mother came over and held her and watched while I washed her in a little plastic bathtub, first carefully removing her cannula and then re-taping it when she was dry.

And then my friends arrived, with food and children and flowers. Our old Phinney Ridge bungalow was filled with sunlight. We propped open the front door and let the good smells of outside come inside. A fire burned in the fireplace, its light added to the sunlight, a surfeit of light.

Chick dropped by to check on me. He walked around the house, taking in the whole thing: the bustling friends, the beautiful toddlers, the fire in the grate, the open door. He took me aside and said, "Not exactly what we meant by quarantine." I had pictured quarantine as a six-month house party, but this was not to be.

Grandparents were allowed, along with one or two childless friends. We were not to take her anywhere, except for walks. He sent everyone away, and so began the season of our isolation.

When they came to take away her oxygen tank, it was as good as— better than—the day she was born.

When I lay down to sleep, I placed her basket on the side of the bed away from the door. If something or someone came to take her away (again), they would have to get through me first.

When people came to see her, we held her up in the dining-room window. Our relatives trooped into town from the suburbs, from their neighborhoods. We held her aloft in the window.

When I couldn't stand the house any longer, I took her for long walks. There were not many blocks in Seattle unknown to me. I sought these out and walked them, for hours. I grew thin. She grew fat.

The quarantine ended. Slowly I began to forget.

Jonathan called us back to attention. I wiped my tears away silently.

As everyone else in the class drew their knees together, I stayed on in the pose, an unusual, small incursion against the rules. I thought about Lucy's quarantine. I thought about what it had taught Bruce and me. I had been trained to try to do everything exactly right. Even more than my friends, I had a reason to try to follow all the rules. I felt I had made a very real bargain when I stared at the oximeter and pumped every three hours and spent every possible minute at the hospital. The bargain was this: I will do everything perfectly and avert disaster. My idea of motherhood grew from this bargain.

This had all happened a year ago. And now I had this small person living in my house, not an infant any longer. Not attached to my breast. With a head cold that left me confused: Should I be scared? How scared should I be? Day by day I kept the shadows of her birth at bay—how else could I function? But all it took was these ten minutes of silence, with these strangers in this room, to bring it all back. I was scared for my daughter when she sneezed. When she sniffled. When she breathed. I was so scared that sometimes I forgot to breathe.

While I sat there in that dark room, remembering to breathe, I recognized an inherent inauthenticity in my mothering: I was resolute and cheerful; I was scared all the time. What I felt had nothing to do with how I acted.

See, this is why people don't like to meditate. This is why, as a culture, we don't sit in silence. This. Who knows what's in there?

I had read in the Bhagavad Gita: "For concentration is better than mere practice, and meditation is better than concentration; but higher than meditation is surrender in love of the fruit of one's actions, for on surrender follows peace."

I could muster neither concentration nor meditation, and certainly not surrender. On the contrary, constant vigilance was my watchword. I existed in a state that was the opposite of surrender. The sutras teach that in meditation, perception settles on an object and the meditator becomes absorbed and enters a kind of flow. But, in truth, I could not lose myself in concentration on an object because my sadness and fear were there lurking beneath the surface. When things got quiet, my fear swam up and made itself known, like a giant manatee. I've been here all along! It was shocking to think that this beast was always lurking beneath the surface.

I slowly drew my knees together; my groin was sore from sitting with my legs splayed for so long. I said, "Namaste." Jonathan smiled at me. He liked it when people didn't follow the rules, I had noticed.

I went home, and Bruce met me at the door. The baby sat behind him on the living-room floor.

"Hi!" he said. "How was it?"

"It was weird. I got all obsessed with Lucy's birth, and I cried right in the middle of the studio."

I hefted her into my arms.

"Huh. Do you still think about that a lot?"

"I guess I do. I still get nervous that someone is going to steal her."

"Who in their right mind would ever steal a baby? There's some spaghetti on the stove if you want it."

I frowned an interior frown. I disapproved of Bruce's inefficient method for keeping spaghetti warm, which involved setting the cooked spaghetti in a colander on top of a big pot.

We had started out fused together, bound by giant terror. I had thought it would always continue this way, but I was the only one who was still spooked.

I ate some spaghetti, sticking it in the microwave to get it properly warm. And then I donned the mantle of cheerfulness again. It was easy because Lucy was wearing a pair of lavender footie pajamas. It was hard because I had remembered my fear.

I sat in the rocking chair in her little room under the eaves and read to her until it was time to go to sleep.

8. HEADSTAND

At Thanksgiving, Bruce and Lucy and I went to my mom's house, along with a bunch of my cousins. I had so many first cousins that I couldn't count them on my fingers. I needed to use my toes as well. When I sat in my house in Phinney Ridge, my cousins surrounded me in a giant invisible web of usefulness: a public defender, a dogcatcher, a fireman, a floor guy, a banker, and on and on. If you needed it done, one of my cousins could do it. Mostly they just made me laugh. In my experience, cousinship is the perfect human relationship: Like siblings, cousins will be with you forever, no question; unlike siblings, cousins adore each other and forgive each other always, no question.

Anyway, I was telling my cousin Brad, the fireman, that I had taken up yoga. With the frankness of a cousin who has a beer inside him, he said, "Yoga is just gymnastics for uncoordinated people."

"You say that like it's a bad thing."

My cousin had in fact hit on a problem: I still wondered what yoga was, exactly. In America, was it just a gentle way for dorks like me to get in shape? These poses, honed and refined over thousands of years, were like a safe harbor. I didn't know exactly what yoga was, but I knew that for one of the uncoordinated people, it felt like a haven.

At least that was what I thought until Fran announced that we were going to do headstand. I was filled with a terror so complete that a kind of veil of unknowing came over me. Like a zombie I moved around the room, dragging my mat to the wall, setting up for my headstand, as though for an execution. I was certain that I would break my neck.

Once our mats were set up, Fran showed us how to place our forearms on the floor and clasp our hands a few inches from the wall. We were to angle our forearms to make a kind of base, with our elbows no wider than our shoulders. Then we were to lift our rear ends into downward dog, and walk our feet toward our hands. Then we were to kick into headstand.

Still veiled in my denial of what was about to occur, I followed instructions. Headstand wasn't a pose like warrior or triangle or lotus. These were poses that belonged only to yoga; they were part of yoga's secret, studio-bound world. Headstand belonged to the world. Headstand was a one-way ticket to elementary school, to little girls with no pudge on their waists and demon moves on the monkey bars. The closest I ever came to the monkey bars was the ground a few feet away, where I would sit composing a poem or reading a book. I didn't like it up there. I liked it down here.

Still, I would try. Kneeling on my mat, facing the wall, I clasped my hands and set up my forearms. I raised my bottom into downward dog and walked forward so my center of gravity was over my arms. I kicked. My legs felt like they weighed a thousand pounds apiece. I kicked again and again. I had a secret: I didn't really want my legs to go up.

"Claire." Fran appeared next to me, speaking quietly. "You can do this. I know it."

It was so simple. I had just been waiting for her to say this thing to me. She stood there, with her pants rolled up. This was her way, to roll up her pants when she got really excited about what was going on in class. Who knows why. She stood there, a benevolent witness, and I rose back into downward dog, and I walked my feet toward the wall, and I sucked my gut tight to my spine, and I kicked easily up to headstand.

"Keep your stomach pulled in," said Fran, in a voice that was glad. "Reach up with your feet. Don't let your hips sag back. Relax your neck. Breathe."

I did all these things, and felt my legs shooting toward the sky, where they had never been before.

It might be that my cousin was right. It might be that yoga was just a safe, womb-like place for onetime dorks to relearn the lessons of gym class. But. Here I was, a different person, a person who could do a headstand. It seemed a significant change to me. Not as big a change as getting married or having a baby, but maybe as big as seeing my byline in print for the first time. In a moment, in the kick of a heavy leg. Different.

We lived in a strange state of busy isolation. The essential journey of the American family—the retreat behind the four walls, the apoliticization, the dropping out from the life of the city—had been almost entire for us. We stayed home and took care of the baby and worked on our writing.

Our families popped in constantly. There was not a day of the week when a grandparent was not at our door or we weren't at their houses. Once in a while we'd get a day off, but phones were employed. Our lives were very public, in that people were there all the time, watching us. Judging us? Maybe. And at the same time, our lives were entirely private. We were creatures of the domestic sphere: in the backyard office, in the kitchen.

That week, we had a typical day at home. I was expecting my dad at noon. I liked to give him a meal once a week.

That morning I was trying to wedge in a little work while Lucy napped, and trying to get lunch ready for Dad as well. Lucy was a light sleeper, so I gently opened and closed refrigerator and cupboards, getting a couple of chicken breasts into the oven to bake. Finally I set-

tled at the kitchen table with a cup of coffee and the book I was supposed to review by day after tomorrow. I felt like listening to a little
music but didn't dare risk the stereo. An hour. I was on page 13 when
the doorbell rang. I sprinted across the house and saw my mom standing there. I opened the door.

"Lucy's asleep," I whispered fiercely, not bothering to say hello.

"Oops! I just wanted to drop off this mail for you. It looked
important." My mom occasionally received mail for me at her address.
"Do you have time for a cup of coffee?"

I looked at the mail in her hand. It was nice of her to bring it over.
"Sure. Dad's due for lunch in an hour."

I got her a cup of coffee and we sat at the kitchen table. She picked
up my book. "What're you reading?"

"For review."

"Oh. Your garden looks good. Have you thought of moving that
mallow? It's sort of taking over the front yard."

I looked at her as though she was insane. I was trying to work and
had a one-year-old. I wasn't moving any mallow.

"I'm not moving that mallow."

"Well, maybe if you just cut it back. And I think a couple more
rosemary bushes, to kind of anchor the front bed?"

I ran through a list of grievances in my mind: She assumes I have
time for this. She assumes I have money for this. She assumes that
because she cares, I ought to care.

We talked about my garden for a while and gossiped about a couple of cousins. She was clearly hanging around waiting for the baby to
wake up. Which the baby did, and my mom was off like a shot,
snatching her from the crib.

She was giving Lucy her bottle at the kitchen table when Bruce
came in to get some coffee.

"Hi, Bruce," said my mom, in the voice she used for managing
difficult personalities.

"Hi, Donna," said Bruce, not looking at her.

"How's work?" asked my mom.

"It's good, good," said Bruce, eyeing the door. He thumbed his intention to head back out to the office. "Gotta hit it!"

My mom folded up her face, silently asking, Why won't he talk to me? Bruce headed out the back door, silently replying, These people expect me to be social, and I'm at the office! Trying to earn a living! I don't have time for this.

My eyeballs toggled nervously between them.

My mom was cuddling Lucy in the living room when my dad arrived. Mom handed Lucy to me and the two of them huddled for a minute to talk over an upcoming meeting with some financial person or another; they were always putting their heads together over such things.

My mom reluctantly shoved off, I stuck Lucy in her high chair, and Dad and I sat down to lunch. He was losing his hearing, and as often happens with the semi-deaf, our conversation quickly turned into him talking and me listening. Simpler that way. He told me about his recent fly-fishing trip and what was new at FIFA, the organization that oversees international soccer. We talked about my brother's work and a bit about an article I had written recently. My dad demanded a certain level of attention. He wanted to talk. My daughter, too, demanded a certain level of attention. Finally I got them set up on the floor with some blocks and went to put the lunch dishes away.

My dad sloped off awhile later, taking the last of my energy with him. I tried to get Lucy to nap but gave up and read her *Bibs and Boots*, which I will be able to recite until the day I die.

As we read, Bruce's dad came by in his truck. He had quit his office job a few years back and started a business selling candy outside Mariners games. He was a baseball nut. He had worked a game today, and was bringing by a box of candy for Lucy. I was immediately annoyed—who brings candy to a one-year-old?

Bruce came in for more coffee and encountered his dad standing in the kitchen. I glared at Bruce: It's your dad! Talk to him! I'm not in charge of him! He's not my dad! Bruce glared back at me: I am in the middle of my workday! Not my problem! I have to WORK! Mortgage! Mortgage!

I chatted awhile with Bruce's dad—a deeply nice man—until finally I had to start cooking dinner.

"Want to stay?" I asked.

"No, no, Mary's waiting for me in Everett."

He smooched the baby and headed out the door as the phone rang. It was Mary, Bruce's mom. She had a couple of new books for Lucy—could she bring them by tomorrow? Of course, I said, mentally slotting her between preschool in the morning and the babysitter in the afternoon. It would've been nice to have had a few quiet minutes alone with Lucy, but Mary wasn't asking for the world, just a few minutes with the baby.

It should have been nice—all these loving grandparents dropping by. It sounds idyllic, when you put it that way. But picture it happening every day. Every single day. And add in cousins' birthdays and Mother's Day for all the mothers and a few Easter egg hunts and two Thanksgivings and a special corned beef dinner on Saint Patrick's Day and you have yourself a situation.

The day after *that*, I was finally able to get to my book review.

I was out in my office, drinking coffee, reading e-mail, and trying to settle down to my writing, when I had a call from Isabel.

She was calling to make sure I knew about her opening on Thursday. She had a solo show.

"Of course I'll be there. We're all coming. Lucy has a new dress to wear."

"A new dress. That's what I need! Maybe I can borrow hers. OK, so are you going downtown to the WTO protests today? My mom is going this afternoon and I want to go with her."

I had heard something about this on the radio. I couldn't quite follow what the WTO was, or why I should be against it. Lying in the bath the previous month, I had consumed a whole *New Yorker* article on the subject, but the information had gone straight down the drain with the bathwater. Don't ever let anyone tell you that you'll be the same woman, with the same brain, after having a baby.

"Oh, man, I heard about that. I should probably go. Your mom is such a pinko."

"You should totally go. Louisa"—for she called her pinko mom by her first name, Louisa—"says you should go." Louisa was a retired librarian and had taken a somewhat proprietary interest in me since I became a book reviewer.

"I've got a deadline, and then the babysitter has to leave."

"Well, bring that fat little baby with you, too. Just stick her in a stroller," said Isabel with the blunt pragmatism of the childless. (And this pragmatism is usually right, too. We probably ought to listen to it more often.)

"Maybe. But probably not."

"You'll be sorry."

And I was. That night Bruce and I sat in the TV room, which we never called the TV room, and watched the images from the WTO demonstrations. There were people in the streets of our very own city herded against building walls, being arrested. It was hard to get a hold on exactly what they had done wrong. Dressed up like sea turtles? It appeared someone had broken the windows of the Gap, the windows of Niketown. I had to admit some sympathy with these window breakers, even when the local news smugly zoomed in on an image of one such breaker and showed that he—hypocrite!—was wearing Nike sneakers. This seemed to me simply to prove the window smasher's point.

But I didn't get to share my opinion, except with Bruce. I was at home. Not rioting, not watching, not writing. I watched like someone would watch in Omaha or Brussels—as if the WTO riots were happening a world away. But this was happening just a couple of miles down streets I knew by heart—beyond by heart: by cell. We, two journalists, weren't writing about it for the local paper, we weren't living it, we were just watching it on TV.

———

The next morning, at around eleven, Lucy was eating her lunch: toast, raspberries, cut-up chicken. I was reading *The New York Times*— Wednesday, food section—and watching her fling her raspberries around. Bruce was out in the office working on his interminable story about dams. Lisa appeared at the door, spare of frame and fiercely pretty, her yellow hair scraped back from her face. She wore a sling around her neck and a baby, her fourth, in the sling. The baby was impossibly cute, with a giant round pate and shiny green eyes. Her older children were at school.

"God, why do you always lock your front door?" she asked, kicking the back door wide open and walking into my little kitchen, which seemed barely to contain her.

"Bruce is nervous about unlocked doors," I said.

"We never lock ours. Hi, Lucy." She took a piece of Lucy's toast and ate it. Her baby, Sam, grabbed for the toast but she held it away. "Do you want to eat? Do you? Well, let me sit down." She sighed, sat down across from me, pulled out her breast, and held Sam's funny head to it. Everything abided as Sam began to feed. The world simply stopped for a few moments.

Lisa stared for a moment out my window, where there was nothing to see, just the windows of the house next door. Every group of friends has a Lisa: the one who gets married first, gets pregnant first, and leads the way into the world of parenting and adulthood. It's a funny job— the Lisas of this world get to be gods and dogs, alternately. We were awed by Lisa and her husband, Steve, and their incredible baby-having. We were hopelessly in love with their children. It didn't hurt that her babies were truly beautiful, with firm chubby limbs and those giant marine eyes.

At the same time, the person who goes first has to learn everything by herself. She has to make all the mistakes. She has to learn miserable words like "Pitocin" and "mastitis," and then wait years before it's time to teach them to all her friends.

This role suited Lisa. She was an older sister, and—with her confidence and her scattershot pronouncements and her reproductive prowess—had become older sister to the rest of us as well.

I lifted Lucy out of her high chair and began to sponge off the smeared butter and raspberries. It didn't take long to clean up my kitchen; it was very small. Lisa watched me work, telling me about an argument she'd had with her sister, who was just about to get married. She paused mid-story and sighed as she watched me clean. "God, this is such a one-child household."

I looked darkly at her, disliking her implication that I only kept my kitchen clean because I had just the one child. Troublesome undercurrents flowed between us at all times, and indeed between myself and all other mothers.

I judged Lisa and any other mother who came within my range. The next-door neighbors put their kids to bed too early; the people down the street put their kids to bed too late. The friend who lived near Green Lake was overly fussy about organic baby food; the friend on Queen Anne Hill was not fussy enough. Friend A dressed her baby in designer clothes, which was ridiculous. Friend B let her kids go around looking like slobs. I felt there must be a happy medium to parenting, and I felt that I was the very barometer of that happy medium. Anything that someone else did that I did not do was, to me, excessive and probably crazy. My strongly held opinions about parenting were like an elaborate carapace for my insecurities.

Bruce called it "the loathing of the half degree." You despised or looked down on or envied those who were most like you. The moms who were like me, just a tiny bit different: I hated them! They infuriated me.

Bruce seemed to take my motherhood travails quite lightly. In fact, Bruce was not getting with the program as I might have wished. He did not always buy organic milk. He had vetoed cloth diapers. And there would be no sharing of the bed with the baby on his watch. These were political, moral, and ethical stances for me. For him, they were inconveniences.

Ideology, in my experience, had always been unmoored from real life. The activist or political movements of my youth were to me somewhat abstract: support for the guerrillas of Nicaragua; shanty-towns built on the college lawn that were meant to urge the administration to divest their holdings in apartheid-era South Africa. However worthy these issues might have been, I didn't have the political imagination (or the compassion) to connect them to my own movements. They affected not at all what I ate, where I slept, what I did all day. This is what I learned: Politics are for talking about. Politics might affect people who live halfway across the planet, but they will never, ever affect you.

Until you have a child. Then, all of a sudden, ideas are tightly zipped to action. The personal becomes unrelentingly political, whether you like it or not. It starts with pregnancy: Do you hit the KFC or do you eat bulgur? It moves on to birth: Do you believe in natural childbirth, or are you flipping open your cell phone right this minute to schedule a C-section? Home birth or hospital? Circumcise or not? Breast-feed or bottle-feed? Continue working or stay home? Let the baby "cry it out" or sleep with it in your bed? Stroller or sling? TV or no TV?

Regular life seldom presents us with dichotomies, especially dichotomies that are so fraught with philosophical underpinnings. These choices could be overwhelming. A huge number of the parents I knew were mostly reliant on a single approach that solved all these problems and answered all these questions: attachment parenting. There were many ideas extant about parenting, but you wouldn't know it to visit North Seattle (or, based on friends' reports, West Los Angeles or Brooklyn or Portland, Oregon, or any other liberal bubble town). In North Seattle, there was attachment parenting, and that was about it. North Seattle was like Isaiah Berlin's hedgehog, a creature caught in the maw of a single notion.

Attachment parenting—the general name given to the kind of parenting that involved co-sleeping and breast-feeding on demand and toting your baby around on your person—had the mothers and fathers of North Seattle in its grip. Exhausted greasy-haired Dansko-shod mothers stumbled into cafés with their babies snugged to their chests, anxious about drinking still more coffee—how much caffeine made its way into breast milk anyway? No mother within a given set of zip codes had had a full night of sleep in years. We walked into things. I'm surprised we were allowed to drive and that, once driving, we didn't run into each other all the time. It was a crisis, really.

Attachment parenting was like a constant reminder that the other mothers were better. No matter how consumed I was, other mothers were more consumed with their babies. Although I didn't practice attachment parenting, it had a powerful hold on me; the idea of it hovered around my parenting like a cloud.

Even its name was a taunt. It implied that the rest of us didn't care if our kids became attached to us or not. (In college, my boyfriend railed against the group that named itself Students Against Rape. "Because clearly the rest of us are for it!" he would say.) And so I hated the attachment mothers and suspected that they were judging me.

Lisa's attachment parenting was one of her defining characteristics. She was an attachment parent par excellence. Her saving grace was the fact that she was voluble. Her frankness was very restful. She didn't silently judge me when I moved Lucy into a crib, or look on disapprovingly as I switched the baby from breast to bottle. No, she said what she thought: "You're crazy! A baby needs to sleep with its parents." "Well, you know, I would never wean my child before a year, and I really think they ought to nurse until they're two." And so on.

Lisa's baby, bored upon his mother's knee, began crying, with a piercingly effective mewling sound.

"You dork," Lisa addressed the baby. "You ridiculous little dorky dork." She stood up and began to move the baby fluidly around her body, like a basketball player doing tricks. With her long dancer's limbs, Lisa seemed to have more places to put a baby than other people did. She had secret holds: upside-down patting positions, behind-the-back snuggles, daring over-the-shoulder suspensions that could produce a burp from any baby within seconds.

"Did you hear that the riots are still going on?" I asked.

"What riots?"

"The thing about the WTO."

"Oh, I think I heard something on the radio this morning when I was driving the kids to school."

"Don't you kind of wish you were down there? Just to, like, see what's going on?"

"I've got to pick Sarah up from preschool," she said simply.

"Yeah, I guess I probably won't go, either. You going to Isabel's opening tomorrow night?"

"I doubt it. Maybe by myself. I don't want to take the kids downtown, it's just a huge hassle."

"We're definitely going. Lucy has a new stripey dress that is very arty."

"Lucy is ridiculous," said Lisa, kissing the top of Lucy's curly blond head. "The most ridiculous perfect girl ever."

Well, it was true.

"Hey, wanna see something cool?" I asked. Nervously, I dropped onto the floor. I clasped my hands together near the wall and spread my elbows. With a knot in my stomach, I lifted my rear into a downward dog. I walked my feet forward and here came the crucial moment. I kicked up once and came back down with a thunk. I kicked up again and amazed myself by staying up. I held headstand while Lisa clapped.

I kicked back down and she gave me an appraising look. "Lemme try that."

She handed me the baby and without hesitation clasped her hands, set them on the ground, and kicked up against the wall.

"Huh," she said. "That's fun."

Downtown was closed—who knew they could do that? The mayor had ordered that the center of the city be roped off. On television, he warned the citizenry to stay away.

We nervously drove down Bell Street with the baby in the backseat of the Volvo and parked outside the flimsy yellow police cordons. It seemed crazy to be taking a baby past police cordons, but it seemed crazier still to close downtown, to miss a friend's important event because of some yellow plastic tape.

It was early evening, but black the way Seattle is in December. In December the city asserted its urbanity. In the summer, Seattle—with its showy, shop-window views and its omnipresent arboreal floor show—was a city that tricked you into thinking it was wild, or at least somewhat pastoral. In the summer, in Seattle, you could sit under a tree, near the water, and forget you lived in a city. In the winter you remembered. Seattle lay there in the dark, wedged between mountains and salt water and yet utterly unrelated to them. Its rain and wind had to do with traffic and overcoats, not with tides and snowdrifts. The city became a series of windy, ill-lit parking lots.

Which is to say, winter in Seattle was pointless without glamour. Winter was bookshops and rock shows and art films and woolly black overcoats and rainy afternoons spent in the back room of Hattie's Hat playing cards. None of these are things you can do with a baby, except maybe wearing an overcoat, but an overcoat needs to be dry-cleaned if it gets spit-up on it, so just forget it.

This glamorous Seattle was occurring all around us, but we had forgotten about it on account of never leaving the house. Now we hefted the baby out of the backseat into her stroller and pushed underneath the caution tape, off into the black night of car-less downtown. The streets were empty. It was strange to walk up the center of Second Avenue; we kept herding ourselves to the sidewalks.

The plate-glass windows of the gallery showed the urban winter glamour we had forgotten. The room inside was crowded with pink-cheeked people doing their best to create an atmosphere; there were dresses and tall black boots and ironical pin-striped suits. There were careful hairdos and lipstick. There were people who were out, out in the world, and absolutely up to the occasion.

I took the baby out of her stroller and held her cushioned weight to my chest. I dived into the room, into the crush of dog-smelling wet wool. Round happy faces greeted me as I made my way around the room, looking at the work.

Isabel had made graceful paintings for many years, but all of a sudden she had exploded into minimalism, if such a thing is possible. Her work was austere and almost frightening. She made spare lines, over and over, with pencil and paint and rubber bands and pieces of tape. These lines, looping and intersecting, seemed like maps of the landscape of her brain. There was something alarmingly naked about them; I couldn't quite believe she was going to exhibit them. At the same time I was envious of the way she had made her private world so beautifully public.

Isabel hugged Bruce and me and her tall handsome punk-rock husband gave us his jack-o'-lantern grin. I wandered around kissing people and smiling. It was great to be out of the house.

I found Isabel's pinko mom. "Hi, Louisa!"

"Hello, Claire!" said Louisa. She was a tiny birdlike woman, with glittering eyes and flying gray hair. She looked like a librarian in a children's book: kind, but with standards. "Oh, we missed you on Wednesday. It was really something. And how is baby Lucy?"

"She's fine." I looked down at Lucy. Her face loomed into mine, like a small moon. She was safe as houses there in my arms. Her father was roaming silently, one of the few people looking at the art.

"How was it? The WTO thing? I'm guessing you didn't get arrested?"

"Oh, it was so good to see people out there. It made me feel so much better about the world, about young people, you know? To see so many of them out there. Of course I left before the police came. I just got on the bus and rode away."

I had been ridiculous to think that somehow we would be met downtown by jackbooted youth or by storm troopers. Louisa was braver than I was. It was a strange thought.

I looked at Louisa there, with her beautiful silver hair drifting around her head like Easter grass. I thought of Lisa at home, with her baby held to her breast. I felt strangely caught between the two.

It had come to seem normal and right to be dissociated from the life of the city, to think all the time about feeding schedules and bedtimes and babysitters. My world had telescoped down to the few rooms of our house, and that was the way it was supposed to be. It was right for me to spend my energy thinking about my house and my yard and my child and my husband. Wasn't it? Seeing Louisa, out here in the world, her eyes so alive, made me wonder.

I stood and listened as she told me about the march. I set Lucy on the gallery floor and she played with my shoelaces and mewled a bit. Bruce came over and leaned against me and listened, too, as Louisa told us about marching up Pine Street and watching as kids peeled off and scaled the walls of the Gap and climbed the lampposts. She told us about the realization that the situation might be dangerous, and taking the bus home, feeling like she might be missing something, and watching the arrests on TV that night, plagued by guilt and relief.

But then I went home and forgot all about it.

Lisa, now, ventured out of the house as well. A headstand veteran after one go, she took herself to gym yoga. The first time she went, she came home thrilled.

"Well, you didn't tell me how fun it was going to be. It's so fun. Come with me! I have the best teacher."

It was just like Lisa to have the best teacher, at her scrubby gym, after attending one class.

I went with her, feeling snobbish as we carried our mats through the forest of weight machines. We went into a room with windows and a glass door. I worried about sniggering jocks watching us as we did our yoga. None appeared, but still. While I was standing there in prayer position, which was uncomfortable enough for an atheist, I could imagine them out there: the jocks, in their sweaty gray UW Law T-shirts and their big white shoes. Doing yoga at the gym made me feel prissy, like the smart girl who always raises her hand in social studies. Like I was at Young Life while everyone else was headed to the kegger.

The other thing I noticed at gym yoga was the affronted look on the faces of the other students. The mood was this: I've heard about yoga; I'm trying it; it's fucking crazy. Lots of surprise and verbalized irony, of the "Yeah, right, like I'll be able to do that!" variety. Of course there were new people at the yoga studio all the time, but they weren't affronted. They were nervous and uncomfortable and excited.

Lisa, along with a few others, was excited to be there. I hadn't known she was capable of such riveted attention. The teacher was good—gentle and thorough and articulate. Lisa stared at her unflaggingly.

After that, Lisa seemed to be at yoga all the time. At yoga. It was an interesting prepositional phrase. Yoga had become a place to go to, a destination. The kids stayed with Steve, or a teen sitter, or me, and Lisa fled. She had found somewhere to go. Somewhere she couldn't resist.

Yoga for me was an attempt to fix something that was wrong with me. This anxiety that I didn't understand, that seemed to come from nowhere. For Lisa, yoga was a flight, out of the house and into the world. She was good at it and she thrilled to it. Lisa, with her competence and her children and her collection of cookbooks, was not a mother at yoga. She was something else. She found this experience—of being a body in space; of being a character in the drama of a studio class; of becoming a yogi, a word she used freely—irresistible. How could home compare with being at yoga?

9. CHILD'S POSE 2

In 1973, our life, quite suddenly, became a series of ferry rides across Puget Sound. The ferries of Washington State glided back and forth, east and west. Massive white oblongs, from the outside they had a weirdly charming gracelessness, as though they were made by a child from a shoe box and set afloat. On the inside, they looked as boring as school lunchrooms. Nothing ever happened inside the cabin of the ferry. It was an eternal place, calm and uneventful. The weather outside might be hectic with wind-driven excitement and wheeling, hoarse-throated, desperately calling gulls. Storm clouds might be clustering over the faces of the downtown Seattle office buildings. The ferry would cast off into this big wet mess of rolling waves and whitecaps, and you, in the cabin, would feel exactly . . . nothing. It was the rare, once-every-five-years wave that even got your yogurt to slide across the table.

When summer was over, my mother decided that she and my brother and I would stay on Bainbridge Island. "Everything is OK," my mom told us. "Your father and I are separated but not divorced. We're still a family. We just don't live together."

We moved into a gray house on gray Manitou Beach. I don't remember the sun ever coming out. My mother made the house cozy. We roasted pumpkin seeds and sat in the gray kitchen window and played cards and looked at the gray bay. You could see the houses of Seattle across the sound, and I knew that that was my proper home.

Ms. Roberts, my first-grade teacher, was chipmunk-cheeked and wore her hair in a mod black helmet. She gave me, and only me, free rein in the library, which made me think that libraries were a privilege, and I was the one who deserved the privilege.

I am not exaggerating when I say that the proudest moment of my childhood was when Ms. Roberts wrote me a note telling me that I was "cheerful."

I didn't really know what my mom was talking about when she said that she and my dad were not divorced, that they were separated. I didn't know what it meant to be a family but live in different houses, on different landmasses. I didn't get any of it. But I knew one thing: I was supposed to be cheerful. That was coming across loud and clear. Maybe Ms. Roberts had no idea about any of this. Or maybe she saw me as a tragic child of divorce. I don't know.

When Ms. Roberts wrote me that note, I was six years old. I lived with my brother and my mother and had misplaced my father. My brother and I had to walk past the old folks' home to get to school. Old people, most of whom appeared to be entirely insane, roamed the lawn in their bathrobes. We had assigned seats on the bus. Mine was behind a girl who never washed her hair, and she smelled as sour as my mood.

My best friend, Bridget, came to Manitou Beach from Seattle for a sleepover and we decided to take a bath together. As the tub filled with warm water, Bridget sat splashing and chatting. I slipped out of my clothes and stood in the bath. I started to pee.

Bridget yelped, "Clairesie!" For this was my unfortunate nickname. "That's yucky."

My mom came rushing in. There would be no yuckiness, not on her watch.

"Claire, stop it right now."

I stood there and peed on and on, a yellow stream, its warmth running down my legs. It felt great.

"Stop it!" Everyone was furious at me, and I wasn't too crazy about them, either.

On weekends we rode the ferry to Seattle to see my father. My mother released us like pigeons at the terminal on Bainbridge Island; we rode across alone; my father received us on the other side. They continued to tell us that they were married.

My mother set a table by the fire for my brother and me.

"We're having dinner by the fire," she said brightly. "It'll be fun, a change of scene will do us good."

I'm sorry, but weren't we already having a change of scene?

Mom walked around the living room, turning off most of the lamps. The fire was lit and dinner was laid neatly on the coffee table. We sat down on the floor to eat. The floor! For my mother, this was a radical departure.

By our plates were little dishes of stewed tomato. That's what my mom said it was, anyhow. They looked like dishes of lumpy blood.

"Just a bite," she said.

"No."

"A tiny little bite."

I forked a stringy, wet piece of the alleged tomato, placed it gingerly between my lips, and vomited all over the hearth. My brother immediately vomited as well, like a person who answers a question without taking even a second to think about it. For a moment, it was like being in a horror movie: the dark room, the red fire, the vomit.

When we were done vomiting, we felt great! We brushed our teeth in the crowded tiled bathroom and leaned on each other and giggled, while my mother toweled up the hearth and cleared the dishes and put some bread and butter and milk out for us on the kitchen table, as if we were kittens. The little waves crashed against the bulkhead, a gray sound in the night.

This story has assumed different guises in my memory. For a long time, I simply thought it was funny: We barfed. Then it was a story about how my brother and I used our bodies to tell the truth about our feelings, which could be described as: upset, very. I had vomited so recently in Larry's car, and now I had let loose again. I had something I had to get out, one way or another. We were not allowed to talk about our parents getting divorced, what with their insistence that such a thing was not occurring, so we got our feelings out a whole nother way.

But there is another story, too: the story of my mother building the fire, setting the coffee table, making the dinner, turning the lamps down, inviting the children into the living room for a special evening, a special treat. When I think about this story, the story of my mom in the gray house on Manitou Beach trying to make something new and pleasant and fun, my heart breaks a little.

We sat at a long table, which like all the tables on the ferry was secured to the floor with bolts. The ferry moved quickly and silently and massively, like always. Dave set up a soccer game: At each end of the table, he placed two little cylinders of half-and-half, with about six inches between them. These were the goals. Then we flicked another half-and-half container back and forth across the table, trying to score. We were bored in the weatherless timelessness of the ferry.

My mom read her book, or smoked, or chatted with us, or marveled at my brother's ingenuity. We were going home. We were moving back to Laurelhurst. We were done with Manitou Beach. The experiment had failed.

By the time we got back, Bridget and Marie had moved away, to a town in south Puget Sound. It seemed like everyone was not where they belonged. Even though we were back, nothing was the same.

My dad, confusingly, moved into the Manitou Beach house, and then farther west, to Lemolo Bay on the Kitsap Peninsula, to a tiny house underneath a madrona tree next to a gloriously flat beach perfect for throwing rocks. The memory of our months at Manitou Beach became a handful of images: the gray beach, with the water hitting the seawall; walking to the school bus with my brother and hoping the crazy old people wouldn't be out roaming the lawn in their terrible bathrobes; the feeling of pee running down my legs into the bathtub, the feeling that I was letting something out that was supposed to be inside, the feeling of joy when I let it go.

Back in Laurelhurst, Larry moved in. He slept on the living-room couch. (What insane niceties ruled these people? What bizarre, neatly spliced gradations of respectability and acceptability governed my mother's mind? On the other hand, I have slept on that couch myself and it is very comfortable.) I picked up the essential lesson: The way things seemed, the way they appeared, was not the truth. The truth was what my mom and dad kept telling me: They were not divorced. We were still a family.

Three doors down and across the street at my friend Bobbi French's house, I sat at the strangely formal kitchen table. Cloth napkins? For a snack? I ate grapes, explaining that they were not allowed at our house because of the boycott. I was hanging out with Bobbi a lot more now that Bridget and Marie had left town.

Bobbi popped a grape in her mouth. "Let's stomp on some ants." She was my most destructive friend. She did not have an unmangled Barbie to her name. She owned a pair of white vinyl go-go boots she put on when she felt like stomping on the ants in the basketball court behind her house.

"Let's go find the cat," said Bobbi. This did not bode well for the cat.

"Just a second," I said. I was methodically making my way through the bowl, denuding the tiny branches of their fruit. Bobbi went upstairs to her room.

"Who's that man I've been seeing at your house, dear?" asked Mrs. French.

"He's the handyman," I said, without missing a beat, without thinking, the way my brother had vomited in response to my own vomit. "He lives over the garage."

"Really? I didn't know there was an apartment in the garage."

"There's kind of a little attic place, he sleeps up there." I was almost done with the grapes.

Bobbi appeared in the kitchen doorway, wearing her go-go boots. Time to kick some ass.

These were the early days of our new life. Our story was unremarkable. We lived with my mother and her boyfriend. My father got us every other weekend and Wednesdays. He took us away in August. Our story is the story of every child of divorce. And lucky. Look, everyone wanted us. All three adults loved us. My mother, passionately. Larry, in a distant big-brother way. And my father. He loved us. He told us so every time he talked to us on the phone, just before we hung up.

1974

I turned seven. Things weren't so bad. We spent a lot of time at Port Gamble, in the cabin where my mother had originally acquired Larry. My mom laughed a lot when they were together. In spring, trilliums starred the wooded drive; Larry helped us find them.

Some hippies lived nearby in a cluster of houses on a windy point. It was a sort-of commune they called, not very imaginatively, the Point.

One day we went to visit one of the couples who lived at the Point.

"You'll like them," said my mom as we drove out the peninsula. "Their names are Stan and Mimi. Mimi's hair is so long she can sit on it!" My mother had a genius for the right detail.

We parked our car and stood in a dark copse of trees, where we were greeted by Stan, who had a strong laughing face and a long wiry mass of bushy hair, and his girlfriend, Mimi, whose silky hair was indeed very long. I craned my head around as politely as possible, trying to see if she could sit on it. Finally I simply walked around her to have a look. It hung to the backs of her knees.

Stan was a wood-carver. That is the kind of profession people had in those days, professions that belonged in fairy tales. Mimi was an embroiderer. She had made a shirt for Gordon Lightfoot.

Stan said, "Hey! Would you guys like to see Bighorn?"

"Stan," said Mimi, "no one wants to see Bighorn."

"Sure they do," said Stan. He had a funny nasal voice, the very voice of "Why not?"

Bighorn, it turned out, was an old-fashioned panel van parked underneath some sheltering cedar trees. It had BIGHORN painted beautifully on the side in art nouveau lettering. I knew this because Stan said to me and my brother, "See that lettering? It's called art nouveau."

Bighorn, it transpired, had been the name of a band Stan had managed in Seattle. He was the manager because he had the van. Now the band was broken up, but the van kept the name. I was moved somehow by this story of transformation. Bighorn was a band, and then a van. Stan seemed magical to me, as if he had literally turned a group of hairy men into a hulking piece of metal.

When we had seen enough of Bighorn, we visited Stan and Mimi's house, which was a tiny structure, delicate even, built entirely out of wood they had found on the beach. The house was constructed atop a barge, but mostly it sat beached. Only occasionally would the tide come in far enough to lap at it.

Every day after that I begged to be driven to the Point, where Stan and Mimi's houseboat was docked, or really beached. My mother would drive me down there, sometimes holding me in her lap and letting me drive: It was a straight and empty road. I climbed up the narrow driftwood staircase to the deck of the barge, then down the smooth, polished wooden stairs to the plush little cabin that was held between the sides of the hull. Light streamed into the room, illuminating the woodwork that bore signs of Stan's genius and the rich upholstery that showed Mimi's. I chatted politely with Mimi for a moment, passed through the tight, neat galley to Stan's tiny shop, fitted in the stern of the boat. Golden wood shavings curled in his hair and sawdust blew.

"I'm here!" I said.

"Oh, good," said Stan. "I could use some help."

I wedged my podgy seven-year-old self into the space and cranked the handle to the vise, which held a piece of mahogany in place for cutting. Stan cut, and thanked me.

I helped him in this manner for a while, with very little talking. After a bit, I went to find Mimi, and together we made chocolate-chip cookies, leaving the nuts out. The tide came in, and the water moved against the hull. You could hear it.

Mimi got pregnant. Her smile, sharp as a dagger, grew more radiant. I hated leaving her and Stan and going back to Laurelhurst, to the city.

In my bedroom, sitting on the red shag rug, I made a ring for the baby out of pipe cleaners. I made it very small, the way I imagined a baby's finger.

"Honey," said my mom, "it's beautiful, but it's too big."

"No! Really?" I couldn't believe it.

I made the baby a quilt instead, a small square of green velvet with little swatches sewed atop it. I thought the baby would like to feel the different textures with its fingers. I worked carefully with all the jewel-colored swatches, wanting to match Stan and Mimi's careful handiwork.

The baby came. It was a beautiful baby girl. They named it Sunny. I learned of Sunny's arrival with some trepidation. What if Stan and

Mimi weren't fun anymore, with a baby? What if they didn't want me to come? On the other hand, a baby! It was truly thrilling that my two favorite people could make a third, new person.

We drove out from Seattle to meet Sunny on a rainy November day. We took the ferry from Edmonds, just north of the city, to Kingston. When we got off the main road, my mom let me climb onto her lap so I could drive through the downpour—"dodging rain-drops," she called it—to the little houseboat. The sun did not stream in the windows as I silently watched Mimi feed Sunny. Then she brought the baby to me where I sat on the window seat. She laid the baby in my arms, and I felt a perfect contentment. I had never known weight could be delicious.

I felt the opposite of a premonition. The fairy Blackstick comes to Sleeping Beauty's bedside and spreads her ill omens for the baby. I felt, instead, a kind of glad tidings, not just for this little family but for myself. I felt strangely that some part of me was in this baby. I felt almost as though I was holding myself, that I was this baby who had been born to Stan and Mimi, and that I was going to have a good life in the tiny beautiful houseboat with my beautiful parents who loved each other so much that they would never, ever leave each other.

1976

Larry bought a sailboat named *Nawitka* (Chinook for "yes") and our lives took on a new pattern. School years in Seattle; summers living on the boat. August was for my father and hiking. Dave and I slept in the bow. We had little hammocks above our beds for keeping our stuff from falling all over the place. The string netting mashed together my *Archie* comics, my rag dolls, my Betsy-Tacy books, my magnifying glass. We lay up front on our bunks, trading limp issues of *Richie Rich* back and forth. Everything was damp.

We went to a lot of parties, me and my brother. We were taken to them, really, dragged along by my matron-gone-wild mother and

Larry. But even we, with our pretty vast knowledge of parties, could tell this one was special. For starters, it had a title, like a book: Spike Africa's Potato Party.

Spike Africa was the person throwing the party. Now that I'm an adult, I can see that calling yourself Spike Africa is a ridiculous affectation, but as a kid I thought it was the best name I ever heard. Spike Africa was some kind of sailing pooh-bah, one of those been-everywhere, seen-everything people who are so excellent in theory but often turn out to be tiresome in reality. By this time, I had met many of these people, in obscure harbors and drunken marinas. They took it as a personal insult if you read your *Archie* comics during their interminable stories.

Except that Spike Africa wasn't tiresome. When we arrived at the party, someone seized my hand and led me down to the water, where the old man was seated on a dock hovering over Lake Washington. I was presented to him as at a royal audience. He wore, you guessed it, a Greek fisherman's cap, and under the cap he had what I was always reading about in books but never saw in real life: twinkling eyes. No shit. They looked right at me, in the way grown-up eyes did not, and when he told me that he was happy I was there and that I should eat all I wanted, I believed him.

Then he was done looking at me. I had enjoyed my moment in the full blaze of his attention, and now it was time for me to eat potatoes. I made my way up the lawn, through clumps of people. Joints and cigarettes sparked in the fading bright of the afternoon. The smell of the lake rose up: part metallic algae tang, part mud. It was a smell that contained both acid and base.

I wandered into the yellow-glowing house, where it was all spatter and fry. A couple of pots bubbled on the stove and three long-haired women seemed to be involved in an eternal loop of mashed-potato-making. Boil, drain, mash; boil, drain, mash. A mustachioed man pushed through the group. He pulled open the door of the oven, which was filled with baked potatoes, softening in their skins as they waited like orphans to be chosen.

Next door in the living room was an electric deep-frying pan, tippily set up. I remember the pan as being balanced atop a metal filing cabinet, though surely this is memory's exaggeration of a more stable, but still contingent, arrangement. A young couple was merrily making potato chips by hand. The man, or boy, was slicing potatoes with what I realize now must have been a mandoline. The skins were on. The girl was dunking the slices in boiling oil, scooping them out with a slotted spoon, and dumping them on paper towels. I drew close, and stood watching.

The couple smiled at me and motioned me closer. Someone had to start eating, they said. The boy handed me a salt shaker. I salted, and bit tentatively, and tasted a perfect combination of wet crispy fat and dry fluffy potato. Salt coated my lips. All of a sudden, it dawned on me like a revelation: Potato chips were made from potatoes. Here was the chip, deconstructed and laid out in its concomitant parts. Potato, fat, salt. It was like magic, the idea that such humble, kitchen-y ingredients could produce a food so heavenly. It was the best thing I'd ever eaten, literally.

They ran out of potatoes and sent me to dig some up. I scrabbled in the potato hill behind the house, got a small armful, and brought them back with me. I washed the spuds, and they fried, and I ate, and we repeated this over and over. Dig, wash, fry, eat.

My brother found me after a while and joined the vigil.

Dave and I had an adventurous childhood, which sounds like, and sometimes was, a Chinese curse. Possibilities proliferated ahead of us: more parents, more homes, more adventures. More parties. Unfortunately, these are not necessarily things children want. Fortunately, we had each other. And sometimes this adventurous childhood brought a perfect moment, salt and fat coating our lips, the mysterious smell of water around us.

10. SCALE

After only a couple of months, Lisa found her way to a yoga studio that I had been assiduously avoiding. Frankly, I had been intimidated. It was reputed to be the most serious in town. Its owners had studied with David Life and Sharon Gannon, at their New York studio Jivamukti, where chanting and devotional rites were integrated into a rigorous physical program. Jivamukti means "liberation within this lifetime," and Lisa's studio, I had heard, took this goofy-sounding notion very seriously.

Fran had headed to Italy for a vacation, so I told Lisa I would check it out. She watched Lucy so I could try a class there. I entered dubiously. At first glance, the place seemed unthreatening enough. It appeared that Enya had been hired as their decorator. Lots of Eastern iconography and lots of purple. Altars. It looked almost stereotypically New Age-y, as though it would be filled with zaftig ladies teaching us to love ourselves.

But it was instead full of teachers and students who were almost frighteningly fit. All had interesting hairdos. The women had magenta streaks or dreads; the men had long, sheeny curtains that made them resemble creme-rinse ads from the 1970s. They all did yoga like they'd spent the last three years in India, or in Madonna's personal gym.

The teacher, a stringy woman with hair to her waist and dark purple lipstick, led us in a chant, which I did my best to follow. It circled around every once in a while to "Om shanti shanti, shanti om," and I would jump in there. It seemed to go on for a long time, at least ten minutes, and then at last we began to do poses. The poses were linked tightly together, one after the other. Later I would learn this was vinyasa yoga. Now it just seemed crazy. Around me the creme-rinse people moved smoothly and quickly, as if they were a bunch of gears that had been oiled just before class.

The combination of spiritual competence and exceptional physical ability gave the place a strange vibe, like it was a science-fiction dojo, turning out some new breed of humans who would go forth and teach humanity the word of god by chanting in Sanskrit and balancing on their forearms.

I was still baffled by the big question: Is yoga a spiritual practice? Is it exercise? How could it be both?

I suspected that many of the students around me would not be willing to listen to an aerobics teacher lecture them about Jesus. So how come they would listen to a yoga teacher lecturing them about Hindu religious practices? What was it that we were learning when we listened to these white people talk about Indian spirituality? Did my fellow classmates believe they were engaged in exercise? Or were they practicing religion?

I never questioned that American bodies needed yoga. Fran used to tell a story about her Indian guru, who came to visit her in America. He could barely stand to walk around the streets here because people's hips were so visibly tight. "American hips!" he would say in despair. American hips needed yoga. American hamstrings and psoas muscles and quads, contracted from sitting at desks and driving cars, cried out for yoga.

But what about American psyches? Was it really useful to adopt another culture's cosmology? Was there something inherently inauthentic about it? Were the scholars right? For all I knew, I was missing the point entirely. If I said I was a follower of yoga, what was I saying? No matter how long I studied, would I ever really experience yoga? What was it exactly that we were doing? Were we engaged in a massive national distortion? And if so, was it hurting anyone?

At the science-fiction dojo, they seemed untroubled by these questions. Asana and philosophy were tied together in a liberation project that seemed vital to them, if not very likely to actually occur.

Yoga has had a strange history here in the West. Popular perception holds that it exploded onto the American scene in the 1960s, along with sex and the Beatles (pace Philip Larkin). But it first really got a toehold in the late nineteenth century, when Swami Vivekananda came from India to America and then England to teach Hinduism, yoga, and Vedanta, which is the spiritual path drawn from the Upanishads. During his time in America, Vivekananda lectured first in Chicago and then in New England—where transcendentalism had softened the ground, Vivekananda sowed the seeds of yoga.

After Swamiji's appearances, yoga slowly grew in popularity. From the first, it was taught as a kind of combination of physical culture and psychic spirituality (enthusiasms of the age), and greeted with both enthusiasm and suspicion. This was perfectly illustrated in *Queen Lucia*, the wonderful 1920 comedy of manners by E. F. Benson. Lucia is the pretentious middle-aged queen bee of Riseholme, a village constantly caught in the grip of various genteel crazes: Elizabethan pageants, bridge, séances. When a guru comes to town, they all take up yoga.

The first activity Lucia tries at the knee of the guru is alternate-nostril breathing, which we did in yoga class with Fran: You held your right hand to your nose, held your right nostril shut with your thumb while you breathed in through your left nostril, held the breath for a bit, and then held the left nostril shut with your forefinger while you breathed out through your right nostril.

Says Lucia of this technique, "Upon my word, it does give one a sort of feeling of vigor and lightness. I wonder if there is something in it."

Soon the whole town is doing yoga in Lucia's back garden. It's typ-

ical of the era's attitudes about yoga that the guru is in due time
exposed as a fraud; he's not a Brahman, as he's claimed, but a curry
cook in a London restaurant. He further demonstrates his true colors
by robbing the Riseholmites of their precious bibelots. Even so, the
yoga students can't deny that the guru's lessons have had a positive
effect. Says Lucia, "About our studies . . . I for one should be very
sorry to drop them altogether, because they made such a difference to
me, and I think you all felt the same. Look at Georgie now: he looks
ten years younger than he did a month ago, and as for Daisy, I wish I
could trip about as she does."

The guru is revealed as a charlatan, and yet what he has to teach is
valuable. This mistrust of the unknown, of the brown-skinned other,
has informed yoga throughout its history in the West; right alongside
it is a ready, easy reverence for the product of a culture that is
unknown to most of us. Its vastness and complexity and ancientness
made it a kind of scrim on which to project whatever we like. Never
mind the bits that make us uncomfortable—the caste system in the
culture itself; the abstinence in yoga specifically—we can take what we
need from this well.

Midcentury American yoga teachers dealt with this Western con-
tradiction by excising the philosophical aspects of the practice. Yoga
was modeled closely on physical culture and gymnastics. It taught
calmness and stress relief, but it was largely not a theology or a spiritual practice.

The 1960s saw the beginning of a more widely spiritualized yoga
in the West, one that was disseminated by popular culture. Possibly
the most important moment in the history of yoga in the West was
the moment the Beatles' plane landed in India on their first visit
to the Maharishi. The idea of modern spiritual tourism was born in
that instant. A handful of Americans began to travel to India to learn
from the masters. They opened the way for Indian teachers to come
West.

In the 1970s, major yoga teachers either moved to the States or
paid extended visits: Iyengar, Kripalu, Krishnamurthi, Bikram, Jois.
As their students found their own students, yoga began its inexorable

crawl over the landscape, until it had become the de-weirded, non-threatening thing we see today. Old-time yoga students love to complain about the commodification of yoga, but in many ways it is one of the great word-of-mouth successes of the latter half of the twentieth century. It was called a fad at first, but it continued to grow steadily, teacher to student.

At the turn of the millennium, yoga was still closer to the physical culture teachings of the middle of the twentieth century than it was to a Hindu spiritual practice. But we now understood that it had a spiritual component. We just weren't quite sure what to do about it.

Emblematic of this inchoate desire for yogic spirituality was the puzzling dominance of Rodney Yee, the only true celebrity that yoga culture had managed to produce. Pretty much every person who had taken up yoga in the last decade had, whether they like it or not, a relationship with Rodney Yee, a very buff, eternally youthful Chinese American man with a long ponytail and a serene gaze (two characteristics which often seem to go hand in hand in the yoga world). In the late 1990s, he hosted the world's best-selling yoga videos, Living Arts' beginning yoga series. He wrote a shelf full of books, appeared on *Oprah*, and popped up like Waldo at yoga conferences.

Rodney Yee was many people's idea of what yoga ought to look like. Never mind that Yee was of Chinese descent and yoga was of mostly Indian descent. With our American genius for conflating cultures, we thought of him as Eastern and therefore an ideal yoga adept. Yee, as a cultural image, was like an embodiment of the mash-up that characterized yoga-studio spirituality.

We picked Rodney Yee as an icon because we could project our not-knowing onto him. He was a comfortable, vaguely Eastern, very handsome stand-in for that vast unknown quantity that was Indian spirituality.

Of course, not every teacher fit this mold. Yoga teachers were likely, now, to be white and female. But Yee represented our desire for authenticity, for some connection with the other that yoga seemed to ask of us.

The ostentatiously calm teacher said it was time for an arm balance. We did scale, that great-looking pose where you cross your legs or fold them into lotus, place your hands on the floor by your hips, push down, and lift the whole ball of wax into the air. I needed blocks under my hands to accomplish this—since my arms are short and my torso is long, there was no doing the pose otherwise. But with my props in place, I loved this pose. I had a sense of proprietorship about scale because it was one of the few arm balances I was really good at. And it suited me. I was, after all, a critic. A professional judge. I had rushed to judge these people: their hair, their bodies, their beliefs. What they were doing seemed, basically, bullshit to me. I didn't believe that they believed the stuff they were chanting. I didn't believe that they believed they would be liberated in this lifetime.

Still, there was something in their intensity that I . . . liked. Wanted. Envied. They weren't second-guessing what they were doing. They were committed. They were in.

The students here at Lisa's yoga *shala*—the studio used the Sanskrit name for "school" to describe itself—seemed a little overzealous, but maybe they were just being overt about what they were looking for. They wanted to understand Indian spirituality, but like me weren't going to India any time soon. We were all trapped on home soil. We'd have to figure it out right here.

After we'd finished scale, the teacher picked up a little book and read, "Salutation to Shiva, who expounded the knowledge of Hatha Yoga, which like a staircase leads the aspirant to the high pinnacled Raja Yoga."

She read on, but I couldn't hear her.

I had been unsettled by my previous readings about yoga, which suggested that hatha yoga was just a bastard child of raja yoga. Here was someone telling me that hatha yoga leads ("like a staircase"!) to raja yoga. Around me people were sitting in attitudes of silent rapture, their heads bent forward in prayer or tossed back as if to receive the reading. The teacher stopped and said with ostentatious simplicity, "That is from *The Hatha Yoga Pradipika*."

———

The Hatha Yoga Pradipika was not exactly easy to find, but finally I tracked down an old copy at the University of Washington libraries. I didn't have borrowing privileges, so I sat in a dusty Formica carrel and read. I hopped up every few minutes to photocopy another page. *The Hatha Yoga Pradipika* is the oldest known text about hatha yoga, written in the fifteenth century. On the very first page, it addressed me—or, OK, the reader—thus: "Owing to the darkness arising from the multiplicity of opinions people are unable to know the Raja Yoga. Compassionate Swatmarama composes the Hatha Yoga Pradipika like a torch to dispell it."

Well, *thank* you. You have to love a book where the author refers to himself in the third person and modestly lets you know how compassionate he is on the very first page. You won't catch Eliade or Feuerstein doing that!

The Pradipika is, above all, charming. It is, unlike the sutras, a voiced work, with its author a guiding presence in the text. It is also specific. After the sutras and the Gita, delightfully specific. To wit: "The Yogi should practice Hatha Yoga in a small room, situated in a solitary place, being 4 cubits square, and free from stones, fire, water, disturbances of all kinds, and in a country where justice is properly administered, where good people live, and food can be obtained easily and plentifully."

At the time *The Pradipika* was written, there were only eighty-four asanas. The library of asanas grew over time—now the generally agreed-upon count is around a thousand, including variations. The book describes the asanas, all very recognizable as the poses we know now, including lotus, rooster, corpse, bow, and forward bend. There's a lot of description about where feet and hands ought to go, just as in a modern yoga book. But it is rife with charmingly strange non sequiturs (at least they are non sequiturs to the modern reader), including the phrase "Fire, women, travelling, etc., should be avoided." (All misspellings and punctuation eccentricities decidedly belong to *The Pradipika*, which I read in a 1914 translation.)

I felt somewhat vindicated. See! Hatha yoga is an ancient tradition, too! Then I began to read about the dhauti, or the swallowing of a strip of cloth; the basti, which was the practice of sticking a pipe into your anus while squatting in a tub of water and drawing the water into the colon; the neti, which involved drawing a cord through your nostrils and out your mouth. While these weren't poses, they were aspects of physical practice, meant to purify the body from the inside.

The book only got more and more way-out, with instruction for practices involving the smearing of cow dung, the restraint of ejaculation, and a passage that appeared to be about drinking your own pee, though it was either so poorly or so coyly translated that I could not quite tell.

I had read enough to know that these practices were not part of mainstream Hindus' experience of raja yoga. Once again, hatha yoga seemed tied to a tradition that involved all kinds of dubious practices.

I could see that the yoga taught in the sutras was different from the yoga that was taught in *The Pradipika*, which was different from the yoga that I was taught at the studio. But I was a magpie, a bricoleur, a pragmatist: I would take what I needed, and logic be hanged.

11. LORD OF THE DANCE

One night I was out running errands while Bruce was paying the bills. When I came in the door and looked from his stricken face to the pile of bills sitting on the table, I felt as though I'd been out dancing, or smoking crack, or having an affair with a Spaniard. The checkbook dangled from his hand in a gesture that semaphored defeat. I suddenly felt guilty for all those expensive boxes of See's Candies I'd been buying. My husband went to the kitchen. He poured himself the grimmest bowl of cereal ever poured. He hunched over it, his beautiful long spine bent almost to an inverted U, and said, "I just have to say this. Our savings account is almost gone."

I gave him a hug but really didn't know what to say. I was already freelancing as much as I could. I was trying to be frugal. Money was becoming something that sat between us. Though I worked, we were becoming that classic dyad: the man who works, the woman who spends. The cliché of it was as difficult as the reality. How had we fallen into this old, hidebound arrangement when we set out to be a two-earner family? I felt wildly guilty. I started thinking: Trader Joe's, not Whole Foods; consignment shops; no more going out for coffee. Maybe there were some editors left in the United States I had not recently hit up for work. But I knew one thing I would not give up. Yoga.

The next afternoon, a blind woman walked into the studio. She was carrying a cane and holding hands with a friend. I don't know about you, but I personally am plagued by unworthy thoughts. When I saw the blind woman walking into class hand in hand with her solicitous friend, you'd think I might take a moment to reflect on the power of human friendship or the ingenuity of human desire. Instead, my brain unleashed this stream of invective: Oh god, now class is going to be really slow, and we'll spend the whole time trying to be considerate and waiting for her to figure out the poses and why do people have to be so special with their blindness?

Fran chatted with the blind woman and her friend for a minute or two, and class began.

"Drop your hands to the ground on either side of your feet. Step your right foot back four feet. Bend your left knee at a ninety-degree angle, pointing straight ahead. Turn your right heel in forty-five degrees, let your right toes point out at an angle. Bring your hands to your left knee. Rest them there lightly. Make the back of your neck long. Lift your arms over your head. Straight up toward the sky. Palms turned inward. Fingers energetic. Warrior I."

Fran didn't slow down or alter the class; she simply never, ever stopped talking. As she led us through the poses, she articulated every movement of her hand, every adjustment of her head position. I had seen her adapt class for different levels of students, and for different body types, and for pregnant women, and even for the occasional kid who turned up with a mom; now she took the woman's blindness in her stride.

We worked on standing balances, which were a sheer pleasure for me: eagle, with its wrapped limbs; simple tree; wavering half moon; warrior III. They didn't involve any of the dreaded arm strength, and

I found I could muscle my way into them. Somehow, in standing balances, I could will myself to success in a way that I couldn't in other poses.

This was my yoga MO: sheer determination. I would do it. No matter what. I was willing to make a supreme effort. Not all poses lent themselves to effort, but the standing poses did. Somehow I couldn't see the irony of grinding my way toward freedom.

The Hatha Yoga Pradipika had a mysterious passage where it listed the "destroyers" of yoga. The list included no-no's like overeating and talkativeness. It also included exertion. This seemed unfathomable to me. What was yoga if not effort? It would be a long time before I could entertain the notion that maybe my yoga would improve if I didn't try so hard, and a longer time still before I began to question why my yoga needed to improve at all.

Because I could rely on my will and my naturally stubborn nature, I trusted myself in the standing poses. They made me feel strong and wonderful and like I had good hair. We had been devoting ourselves all week to the pose known variously as dancing Shiva, lord of the dance, and king dancer. Most people have done some form of lord of the dance in gym class. In non-yoga circles it's known by the unromantic name of "quad stretch." In yoga, it's done thus: You stand straight up, bend one leg, say your left, reach behind you with your left hand and capture your left foot by the inside arch. Then you begin to kick back with your left foot while simultaneously leaning your torso forward, extending your right hand into the air in front of you, in a position that says: "Onward! Forward! Never stop!" Ultimately, the goal is to bring your foot high enough that you can reach both hands over your head and grasp it.

It was a warm spring day and the front door was wide open. Maybe it's because I was a film critic for a few years and have therefore watched as many scenes of horrific violence as any hardened criminal, but the open door at yoga seemed to me an invitation to gun-wielding predators: Come in! Mow us down! We could not possibly be more harmless! Or more vulnerable! The studio was near Green Lake, and I thought I smelled a lakey breeze.

I wrested my attention away from the gunmen roaming the streets back to the task at hand; I was wavering, which is what happens when you stop paying attention. I gazed forward at my hand, which was shaking. Pretty hard. Visibly. In fact, it suddenly seemed like the most visible thing in the whole room. I glanced around to see if anyone was noticing my insanely vibrating hand. And immediately fell out of the pose.

I picked my foot up and took a deep breath. I tried again, shaking harder than ever. One always wants to say "shaking like a leaf." It's rare that the most common analogy is also the most apt. Usually what we take for analogy is really exaggeration. (For instance, "big as a house.") Shaking like a leaf is, however, not an exaggeration. It even feels right. When you're shaking, you feel insubstantial, papery, leaflike.

I should know. I've had my tremor, which is pretty severe, all my life—it's just one of those weird physical issues people have. When I was six, my hands shook so much at the doctor's office that I spilled a urine sample from its little cup all over my plaid flares. My lucky pants, I might add. Or previously lucky.

My tremor is a window into my ugliest, weakest, most anxious self. I am utterly, completely ashamed of it. It plagues me. For instance, business lunches are an infrequent occasion in my life and ought to be a source of pleasure—I'm eating! Someone else is paying! Instead business lunches become a frenzy of tremor management. Soup, of course, is right out. Salad is awfully forky—that's a lot of jabbing and probably missing. Meat involves cutting, and who needs it? A sandwich is ideal—you just hold on tight with both hands, silently say a Hail Mary, and hope for the best.

My life has involved a lot of tremor management. I have crammed an entire college presentation onto a single sheet of paper so that I would not have to shuffle notes. I have chugged a beer to calm my nerves before a major job interview. (Or maybe that wasn't my tremor. That might've been my drinking problem. Sometimes I get them mixed up.)

The beer-drinking job interview was successful. (Not that I advocate such strategies.) When I got the job—at a local alternative weekly—I had a whole new set of problems. My hands shake a little all the time, but when I'm nervous they go crazy. And I was very nervous about my new job. Try typing with shaking hands sometime. My stories came out looking like ransom notes.

I was nervous around one co-worker in particular. I had read Bruce in the paper for years. Sometimes it seemed like he was the only person there who made any sense at all. His writing was clear and clean and made use of a huge vocabulary. I followed his career in a vague way. When he edited an anthology of Northwest writing, I was irrationally enraged. It was the book I was born to edit, if people can be born to edit things. Never mind that I was, at the time, neither a writer nor an editor. (I was, as discussed, a perennial student who spent most of her time going to rock shows.)

He was so able and so sure that I assumed he was an old or at least middle-aged person. Who could write like that in their twenties?

When I became a staff writer for the same weekly, the courtly publisher led me through the newsroom on my first day. He paused at the pasteup table. (The pasteup table! Yes, I am one thousand years old.) With a flourish of paternal pride, he presented Bruce, the writer and editor whose erudition I had admired for so long. I found myself staring into the face of . . . a boy. This person whose career I cursed and envied was the exact same age as I.

My initial reaction, as anyone's would be, was a strong desire to stab him in the eye.

I watched him in the office, carefully. We were the only two full-time critics on the staff. I was movies and he was books, so he had the moral advantage right from the get-go. He stalked around the office with a fierce look on his face, daring anyone to talk to him. When you cornered him in his cubicle, he turned out to be a chatterbox. I liked the way he wrote, and I liked the way he admitted to wearing clothes his mother picked out for him. He had an air of self-contained riches, like if you stuck a shunt into him, out would pour everything you ever needed. I liked to watch his long wrists and his big spatulate hands as he typed, typed, typed away. He later confessed to long bouts of gazing at the back of my bare neck as I myself typed (shakily) across the hall.

One day we were sitting in the filthy armchairs in the editorial department, having one of those interesting-young-person conversations about what we dreamed of doing with our lives. I was excited, sitting across from this tall, serious person. I wanted very much to impress him. I went on and on about wanting to write an important literary novel. When I was finally done, Bruce said, "I'd love to just make a living as a writer for the rest of my life." I found such pragmatism, in combination with talent, surprising and even enchanting. I didn't see then that money was an underground worry for him, something that bubbled blackly like a tar pit.

I developed a crush on him that I feared was almost visible. Clifford the Big Red Dog had not yet come into my frame of reference, but that was what my crush was like: a huge animal following me around, a flaming mutt that only a complete dimwit could fail to spot.

Bruce was just that dimwit. We stumbled through months of office bonhomie, slipping out for friendly coffees, going for group drinks. Finally we went out for drinks at the Pink Door, a murky, beautiful, cavernous restaurant off an alley in the Pike Place Market. It would be hard to overstate the romance of this place. We drank vodka. We discussed whatever worthy topic we had agreed we were there to discuss. It was very much a *ceci n'est pas une pipe* situation; any fool, except us, could see it was a date. My hand trembled as I lifted the full martini to my lips and we discussed the possibility of a feature about the nascent Bremerton punk scene. It didn't stop shaking for months and months, until finally, literally, Bruce took it between his hands and lifted it to his mouth and kissed it.

There are not many moments in life when you know what to do. When Bruce took my hand, for once I knew: Marry him! Quick! This is it!

We got engaged, and as the wedding neared, tremor management reached its zenith. Just the thought of standing up in front of all those people made me shake. What would happen when I actually had to do it?

I made an appointment with my on-again, off-again therapist.

"Um, so I've decided to have the ceremony outside," I told her as I sat on her striped couch, surrounded by what seemed like a miniature condo of Kleenex boxes.

"You've decided? What about Bruce?" Did I mention she was pretty smart?

"Well, it's just my tremor. If I'm outside, I don't think people will notice it as much."

"When's your wedding?"

"October eighteenth."

"You can't get married outside on October eighteenth! Everyone will freeze!" She was also kind of bossy.

The answer to this seemed perfectly logical: "Well, if I'm shaking, no one will notice my tremor."

"What tremor? What are you talking about?" She peered at me.

"The tremor in my hands! Look at it!" I held my hands out. They were lightly shaking, as usual. "You have to help me! How can I get rid of it before the wedding? All those people will be looking at me. I'm going to have a super-heavy, gigantic bouquet, so the flowers won't tremble." This had happened to me at one of my many, many outings as a bridesmaid. My fellow bridesmaids and I had to carry very pretty, tiny little nosegays of sweet peas. Sweet peas. I ask you! Afterward the ushers teased me mercilessly about my one-woman sweet-pea earthquake.

I went on. "And we'll exchange rings before the ceremony so I don't have to, like, fumble for the ring. And we'll be outside and for some reason I know that will help."

"What exactly are you afraid of?"

"That people will judge me."

"Have you ever judged anyone for shaking, or anything else they've done, at their own wedding?"

"No."

"Lookit," she said. This was another reason I liked her, despite her being my therapist. What adult says "lookit"? "Your tremor shows your weakness. And our weaknesses make us human. Your tremor is just a demonstration of your humanity. Doesn't that seem like a great thing to demonstrate on your wedding day?"

No, it really didn't.

We were married on a gray October day, overlooking Agate Pass; Larry's tugboat lurked around the point, waiting to appear and shoot off fireworks over the becalmed steely water.

Before the wedding, Bruce and I snuck behind the kitchen and, with the sound of dishes clanging, exchanged rings. When we'd made the trade, Bruce gave me a hearty thump on the back. Time to get in the game, kid.

Outside, the rain misted down. The bridesmaids quaked in their sleeveless shifts. My great-aunt looked like she was going to drop dead on the spot. I was being a monster of selfishness—I knew it—but I also felt that if we were to be enclosed within four walls, I would not emerge married. I could've at least told my bridesmaids to bring sweaters. The ring secure on my finger, the heavy burden of bells of Ireland laying in my arms, I marched down the grass.

Finally, years later, after lots of marriage and lots of yoga and a couple of kids and a brush or two with mortality, I realized what I was so afraid of. I was afraid of my all-too-real imperfections.

I was able to sidestep reality at my wedding by the simple device of making two hundred people stand outdoors on a chilly day. That, and the gigantic bouquet, and the secret exchange of rings. Simple! But in reality, I shook. Also, in yoga.

I did yoga because of an idea I had of who I wanted to be: serene, fit, spiritual. I bought a pair of yoga pants and grew my hair longer so it would stay in a ponytail. My ponytail never looked sleek, like those of the real yoga girls, but at least it kept my frizzy hair, with its impenetrable understory, out of my face. My idea of yoga was an idea that had to do with exterior perfection: Others would see me do yoga and would know my superiority. Here is what happened instead: I did yoga, and I was a mess. The yoga was supposed to reveal me as perfect, and instead it did nothing but reveal my deepest weakness.

Fran had begun to teach us about the subtle body, the system of pathways and centers—also known as nadis and chakras—that control the flow of energy, or prana, through the body. The chakras I had heard of, of course—they were familiar from a million send-ups of hippie speak. The nadis, on the other hand, were news to me. Some ayurvedic texts say there are thousands of these pathways. The two major ones are pingala and ida. Pingala is the dominant, right-side, solar, active energetic nadi. Ida has to do with the left side, the moon, and passivity. The sushumna is the central pathway that moves up the spine. These pathways deliver energy around your body; they are similar to the nervous system.

Many years later, I would read a book about yoga that said this: Shaking is a sign that you have awoken the prana body. Meaning, you've unleashed energy that was previously dormant. Shaking is a sign of life. Shaking is a sign of humanity. The energy is flowing like crazy through your nadis, and your subtle body is waking up. Shaking is a sign that you are not quite perfect—and therefore you are not dead yet.

When you do lord of the dance, the first thing is to never, ever think about Michael Flatley or you will certainly fall over. The second thing is this: You must keep your gaze absolutely steady. Even so, there will be movement. Your hand extended in front of you, your leg kicking back, you will waver, and balance, and waver, and balance. All your effort, your anxiety, your imperfection will be on display. In a room together, you will do this pose, and you will all be far from perfect.

Of course, if you could look around, what you would see would be very pretty. All those arms lifting forward and legs kicking back, like a room of bent boughs. The shaking would be visible but repeated by all, and therefore acceptable.

Lord of the dance was a pose that had a beautiful thrill to it. I couldn't yet reach my hands over my head to capture my foot. Maybe I never would. But when I forgot myself and lifted into the pose, there was a kind of ecstasy. I felt expanded, bigger than myself. For work I had been doing some research on the psychology of children's play, and the lord of the dance reminded me of a quote from the Russian developmental psychologist Lev Semenovich Vygotsky: "In play, it is as though he were a foot taller than himself."

The blind woman kept falling out of the pose. Her friend stood by, not really doing anything, just hanging out. The blind woman would fall to the side, and the friend would stand, unmoving, unflinching, a slight smile on her face. You would never have known she was helping out a blind person who was tipping over. Unless you looked at her eyes. Her eyes were constantly scanning her friend, making sure she was OK.

The blind woman seemed untroubled by her falls. She rearranged herself on her mat, stood up tall, visibly took a breath, bent her leg, grasped her foot, and expanded once more into the pose.

Her friend quietly asked her a question, and the blind woman shook her head and laughed and her answer filled the room: "It is what it is."

Sometimes, now, it was hard to remember back to the time when Bruce and I had been so smitten. Lately we had begun to clash, especially about work.

We paid our babysitter well, which created a problem: We could only afford a certain amount of her. Maybe ten or twelve hours a week. These were my work hours. This was what I got. And, in theory, it was what I wanted. Sort of. We had set up our whole lives so that I didn't have to work any more than ten or twelve hours a week. This was the ideal way to take care of children, we had decided. But I could feel my worth as a worker slipping away, month by month and year by year.

I barely had enough time in those ten hours a week to hustle work and organize my thoughts, let alone complete my assignments. I wrote for a strange roster of about twenty venues, everywhere from the Raleigh *News & Observer* (though I'd never set foot in North Carolina) to *San Francisco* magazine. I had even started to write for *Yoga Journal*, where I reviewed earnest books about paths and destinies. I juggled a roster of editors: At *The Nation*, my editor was a cranky brainiac; at *Newsday*, my editors were unpretentious book lovers. I found myself fantasizing about going on picnics with the *Newsday* editors. They seemed like potato-salad kind of people.

My work began to wedge itself into awkward spaces. I found myself scribbling in a notebook next to my bed at one in the morning, conducting a telephone interview during breakfast with Lucy on my knee, typing on Bruce's laptop on a table outside tots ballet class. Always with the desperation of one who is truly not sure that she can make her deadline.

One night, after handing in a book review that had been knitted together out of ten-minute work sessions, I lay on the couch watching a DVD. I couldn't focus. I decided that the situation was intolerable. It pissed me off that I had to ask Bruce for more work time, that the assumption was that he would work full-time, no matter what, and that I would find child care to accommodate my work schedule.

I turned off *Six Feet Under* and went to beard Bruce in the living room, where he was reading a book for review.

"So," I said, "I need more work time."

His eyes clouded over, as though a curtain was coming down between the two of us.

"Well, why don't you go out once a week in the evening and work?"

"Well, why don't you?"

"I am!" He gestured at his book, at the legal pad where he was making notes. He always kept scrupulous notes when he read a book for review. These notes drove me crazy. I myself reviewed books with a strange, complex non-system of dog-eared pages, scribbled margins, and wadded notes-to-self on napkins. His systematic notes marching down the page seemed officious and show-offishly professional.

"I'm too tired to work in the evenings," I said. "Lucy wears me out! It's not easy!"

"I have to keep my contract. I have to support us. Me, by myself. All me."

"So your work is more important than mine because you earn more."

"God, make me say it, why don't you? Yes! It is!"

"Oh, come on! How am I ever supposed to keep my career going without any time to do my work?"

"I don't know, but I do know that I can't take time off from my job so that you can write BOOK REVIEWS for *YOGA JOURNAL*."

I gave him a withering look of the "Oh no you didn't" variety. It is rare in marriage that one feels one has entirely earned a magnificent sweeping from the room with a resounding slam of the door, but this was one of those moments.

I sat on the front porch, then walked around the block. This was easily the most disrespectful thing Bruce had ever said to me. I felt diminished. And lonesome.

The next day Bruce got Lucy up, as he did every day. I got up an hour later, forgetting as I did every day to be grateful for my extra hour of sleep. I read a book to Lucy. I made two cups of coffee at 8:55, so one would be ready for Joelle when she arrived at 9:00. She and I sat together for a few minutes, and then I walked to the café and opened the laptop and tried to remember what I had been going to say about the new Jane Stevenson novel. I thought it was really good, but now I couldn't remember exactly why.

12. CHILD'S POSE 3

By 1977, things had settled down. We lived in our family's sedate house in leafy Laurelhurst during the school year. We went to a fancy prep school and knew nice children from nice families. We shuttled back and forth between my parents, gamely sleeping wherever we were told we were supposed to sleep. And during the summers we lived on a sailboat, or near some hippies in Port Gamble, or in a chicken coop in the San Juan Islands.

My father went to work downtown, in a public relations company which he helped start. (I worked in the office in my teens and early twenties, and I often heard from his employees that he was the best boss ever.) He wore a suit, mostly, and though his sideburns grew longer and his hair more floppy, he essentially stayed a professional man. He was a creature of his time, and of the West. His own father had started with nothing and made a fortune in the fur business; now my father was a professional. This was the way the West was supposed to work.

Now his wife had left him, for a man sixteen years his junior, for a man who was part of something new altogether. My father had to make a new life, strike out on his own. He slowly built his life, a made thing. It had to do with work and being in the mountains and reading books. And us, my brother and me. Part of the time we made this life with him. It seemed like a strange thing to do, grow a new life.

My father lived in little houses on the water, one after the other. When we went to see him, we would spend days outdoors, with the rain falling in almost invisible pinstripes and the good, hard-work smell of creosote in our noses. We played hide-and-seek on the empty beach, where there was nowhere to hide.

Eventually he took up residence in a houseboat on Lake Union, the most urban lake imaginable. The rest of Seattle tricked you into believing in its near-wildness. Where we lived with our mother— where we had once lived with our mother and father—the parks and lawns and shores of Lake Washington were relentlessly pastoral, right down to the otters that built at their shores and up to the winging V's of geese overhead.

Lake Union was another story. Apartment houses climbed away from it; houseboats and shipyards obscured its edges. The freeway curved along its flank to the east; the old highway to the west. Its pollution, its urbanity were incontestable and somehow restful. Despite its general air of shoddiness, dirty gray urban Lake Union somehow had more integrity than Lake Washington. Lake Washington was ringed by trees and green with open space. It pretended it was wild. Lake Union was not wild. It was barely a lake. More like a wet, windy spot between parking lots.

Looking south from my father's houseboat, across the expanse of the lake toward the upright rectangles of downtown, you saw only gray. Maybe you don't need just blue sky to make blue water. Maybe you also need the green of trees. The lake didn't know or care; it just kept being gray. Across the water to the west my dad had an unobstructed view of the old Seattle gasworks, a hulking brown-black structure that looked like the devil built it. The smooth, rolling green lawn surrounding the structure made it all the creepier, like a noose displayed on a cake stand.

On this urban, gray, deeply real lake, my father made his home.

His houseboat was clad in wood shingles on the outside and lined with bookshelves on the inside. With its massing of books and art and music, it might be have been mistaken for bohemia if it hadn't been so relentlessly tidy.

The bookcases were filled with volumes dedicated to my father's various esoteric obsessions: German history, soccer, mountaineering, skiing, hiking, the films of Woody Allen, the poetry of Elizabeth Bishop.

There was a basket of rocks he had collected from all the places he'd hiked. There was a mounted collection of ski-lift tickets dating back to the 1950s. One wall was lined with photos of his parents, his siblings, his children. Everything was clean and tidy and orderly; if Linnaeus had lived on a houseboat, this is what it would've looked like.

A tiny galley kitchen was filled with my father's foods, which were nursery foods, really: Wheat Thins and applesauce and cereal and pasta, which we still called noodles. He always had lots of the thick white pancake-size crackers called pilot bread, which he and my brother adored heaped with jam. Eating at my father's house was a comfortable proposition, with lots of plain starch in the offing.

Everything about the houseboat was chosen by and organized for just one person: my father. It was entirely his realm.

My father was a tall, long-faced man with a nimbus of gray-black hair. What with the height and the nimbus, he had a kind of regal quality, and that was just right, because despite his asceticism, my father possessed the soul of a monarch. His kingdom was one person: himself. He did what he wanted, all the time, and he believed, for the most part, that you should, too. He lived his life with a Gallic shrug: Suit yourself. This was a great way to deal with an ex-wife—or, in his case, a wife who lived across town. How it played with a real wife, I'm not sure.

There was one object in the houseboat that was not of my father's choosing. The previous owner had installed a water bed. A water bed is not an easy thing to install or, eventually, to uninstall from a small houseboat at the end of a narrow wooden dock. There was no extra bedroom for me and my brother; we slept in my father's bed when we came to visit, and he slept on the couch. We bobbed on the lake in his water bed, doubly at sea.

He did not have a girlfriend, never a girlfriend, at least until we were in high school. It was always three of us: him, me, Dave.

Whenever I went to my father's I made sure I had a book. I always had a book, in fact. When I was a kid, and a wish came my way, by means of an early star or a white horse or a ringed rock, I always wished for the same thing. I wished that I might have the power to enter any book I liked and live there.

I think I wanted the rules. Books are enclosed universes. Things happen the same way every time. Characters are dependable, whether they're bad or good. If I stepped into a book, I would be subject to these rules. I would be a character. My own volition would be entirely removed. This is what I wanted: to know what I was supposed to do.

I read on rocks and in rowboats. I carried books in my backpack miles and miles into the wilderness. There's a picture of me, about age twelve, driving a tractor and reading a book at the same time.

Put your book down and look at the view! Don't you want to go explore? I hated it when my parents said these things (separately, at separate times) to me; I didn't want their view. I had come, with my book in my hands. That was as much as I was prepared to do. Didn't I want to see things? they asked. No, thank you. Frankly, I had seen enough.

I had twenty or thirty favorite books, which I read over and over. But my crucial book was *Little Women*. Other books were creeks and freshets and brooks that made small paths through my brain. *Little Women* was the Mississippi. It defined the territory.

I was hardly the first girl to fuse my self-image with the character of Jo March, but I didn't know that. I didn't know that other girls read this character with the relief of recognition.

There was just me and Jo, together. She was bookish and brave. She had long chestnut hair, her one great beauty, her mother said. She wrote stories and munched apples and pretended a tree branch was a horse. She lived with her saintly mother, Marmee; her matronly sister, Meg; her ailing, angelic sister, Beth; and her beautiful, bratty, artistic sister, Amy.

Jo reflected my own shortcomings and quirks back to me, dressed in the flaming garb of courage. Her reading, her writing, her dreaming were all presented as signal qualities of a searching self, a self that was unconstrained by the mores of the day. Jo didn't care about clothes; she skated and ran and climbed trees. These were normal things for a girl of my era to do, but in Jo's time they were considered rebellious. This rebellious image pleased me; I could be my regular, chubby self and a brave hellion at the same time.

Jo was always struggling toward being good and constantly in danger of not arriving. Looking back on my reading of *Little Women*, I think it was this struggle to be good that most attracted me. To me, the concrete nature of goodness in *Little Women* was a relief. Goodness, in *Little Women*, was a very specific quality: You were kind and didn't fight; you included your sisters in your games; you were respectful to your elders; you helped the poor. Jo knew how to act; she just failed sometimes.

I lived the hypervigilant life of the daughter of a single mother; I was attuned to her needs and her desires, so much so that I didn't really know what I wanted myself. (Except to keep reading, keep reading.) On top of that, I existed in a constantly shifting state of circumstances. I was in a family, but not. My parents were divorced, but not. I had a dad, but not. I had a stepdad, but not. Books were there to be the same; to be ordered; to present life as a manageable, dependable proposition. Books were my stable family. The Marches were my sisters, my mother.

My real-life brother was the other constant in my life, shuffling through the changes with me. Dave didn't hide in books. Instead, he mastered every situation that came his way. He wrapped competence around his neck like a superhero's cape and learned how to do everything the men were doing.

He had a special bond with my father, a bond that I was hard-pressed to understand, that involved doing stuff. The two of them skied and hiked and fly-fished. I did those things, too, but as a kind of slipstreamer, along for the ride. Dave mastered them. Eventually he surpassed my dad, at least in terms of technical difficulty, that department which seems so important to men, and he went climbing in Yosemite and Eldorado Canyon and bouldering in Chamonix and skiing in the wild backcountry of the Cascades, of the Wasatch, of the Alps, scaling the hills with skins on his skis and free-heeling his way down the mountain in the beautiful, impossible stance of the telemarker.

I shambled along behind, sloppily doing my best. I had a lumpy shag hairdo and a tummy. A book was a terrific place for me. I went there as often as I could.

In our dad Augusts, we drove and hiked and drove and hiked: Alaska, Vancouver Island, the Oregon coast; eventually, in our teenage years, the White Clouds of Idaho, the Enchantments in the North Cascades. My brother and I fell upon each other's company. We slept together in a heap. We played together. We fought and read and wrestled and drew and ate together. Lying in our slightly sour-smelling tent, in a mossy grove, we read as our father fished at the lake nearby. I was reading *From the Mixed-up Files of Mrs. Basil E. Frankweiler* for the second or third time. If you have read the book, you might remember the letter that opens it from the titular Mrs. to her lawyer, Saxonberg. If you have not read the book, you should stop reading this book right now and go read that one. This fictional letter, to my eight-year-old mind, was a masterpiece. It was written in dry, formal language, laced with wit and sarcasm. These jokes and arch bits were hidden cleverly in the adult language. I loved decoding the secret language of the letter—it looked like a grown-up document, but it was funny, and it was about children. This seemed to me somehow the greatest thing ever. The best way to unearth the humor of this letter was to read it out loud. And so I did, that rainy afternoon, in the damp tent, in a high alpine basin of the Cascades.

"To my lawyer, Saxonberg," I read. When I finished, I said, "Isn't that great?"

"It's pretty funny," said my brother. Then he made a fatal error: "You read it well."

I must have read that letter to him fifteen or twenty or thirty times. After the first few times, he grew mean. Then he pummeled me a bit. Then he ignored me. Then he read it out loud himself a couple of times, just to show me the way the thing really ought to be done.

The thing was, he couldn't leave. We were in a mountain redoubt. It was pouring rain. As anyone who has camped in the Northwest knows, you can never go outside of your tent during a rainstorm because once you get wet, you will never, ever get dry again. We were literally trapped in a wilderness together. Our dad seemed impervious to the weather and was out fishing.

I'm sure it was hell on my brother, but for me that day was like heaven. Trapped with my big brother, with my father nearby, my voice ringing with urbanity and wit to the far reaches of a nylon tent.

My father came whistling back from the lake.

"It stopped raining," he said.

My brother unzipped the tent and peered outside dubiously. He had blond ringlets he wore in a wild Afro and green eyes and was very handsome, even then. Although he was a couple of years older than me, he was still smaller in size. He was neat, and coordinated, and self-contained. He could do any sport. Probably he could do anything at all. Beside him I was a big fat mess.

"I'm going out," said Dave.

That was the end of that. My dad had gutted the fish at the water's edge—that was back before catch and release. Now he showed Dave how to fillet it. He let Dave light the little Coleman stove.

I read for a while longer, hearing my own voice declaiming, and then joined them. My dad, leaning against a log, let me sit between his long legs and lean back against his chest. He had a way of snuggling me without actually touching me. In retrospect, I think this came from a kind of courtesy. He was a solitary person and understood that even in a family, people needed a little room to move.

13. HALF MOON

 "What shall we have for lunch today, my little cherry-blossom mommy?"

I was slumped over the toilet bowl, having just vomited up every bit of my gut, right down to the lemon juice–type stuff you generally want to avoid coming into face-to-face contact with, and my now two-and-a-half-year-old daughter was standing in the bathroom doorway inquiring about lunch, apparently in the persona of a geisha.

It was my second vomit of the day. I was getting pretty cavalier about all this. It had ceased to be an event.

"Noodles," I said. "Apples."

I was pregnant. This had not happened by mistake. It was a bright idea that reached fruition in the backseat of a rental car parked on a dirt road on the west side of Kauai while my parents minded Lucy back at the cottage. The dirt was, famously, red. The moon was a white disk in the sky and a blurry bar on the sea. The car was a huge SUV because the magazine was paying. Bruce was on assignment; he was meant to climb Waialeale and write an article about it. Hard to imagine more fortuitous circumstances for conception.

This time around, the rules of pregnancy were second nature to me. The best possible food—check. No alcohol—check. Copious amounts of water, no soft cheese, no smoked fish—check, check, check. If there were rules, I would follow them. First, because I had almost lost a baby once, and I would appease any god, anywhere, if this baby would only come out OK. Second, because I had grown used to rules. I had grown used to babies being more important than grown-ups. I knew that it was my job to do everything right, not to do what I necessarily wanted.

It was not ever thus. During my first pregnancy, I resented the baby's assaults on my freedoms. I conducted the entire pregnancy in the key of What the Fuck? My body was taken over. There was something in there! I couldn't get over the surprise element.

This feeling of having my body slip away from my own control was strangely doubled by the way the rest of the world treated me. Every day some new incursion was added to the list. A strange man touched my belly. The barista at the café in my office building thought sugary Earl Grey tea might not be my "best choice." As we toasted the birthday girl at a party, a doctor friend gently removed the champagne flute from my hand.

My body had become pure receptacle, not just for the growing baby but for the opinions, analysis, and rules of everyone around me. I found that I did not like this one bit. I was especially startled and dismayed by what I saw as the hypocrisy of the left when it came to pregnancy. Everywhere I looked, I saw lefties explaining how and why I needed to put my baby's health before my own. Deeply embedded in seemingly pro-woman texts like *What to Expect When You're Expecting*, I found a profound ambiguity about women's bodies and who owns them.

I began to read *What to Expect* and its sister volumes the way an atheist reads the Bible or P. J. O'Rourke reads the *Communist Manifesto*. I was looking for weak spots. *What to Expect* and its fellow guidebooks, with their soft pencil illustrations of women dressed in dowdy jumpers made of organic fibers, were the ultimate expression of the liberal birth culture. The message was this: Privilege the baby's needs; suppress your own.

If it gave the pregnant woman pleasure, it was right out. Whenever I cracked a can of Squirt, my husband and I chanted together, "Soft drinks have no regular place in a pregnancy diet." Or we would cite this soul-deadening exercise: "Before you close your mouth on a forkful of food, consider, 'Is this the best bite I can give my baby?'" Even sex was rigorously separated from its glorious dirty self and relegated to the dry and dutiful dustbin of "lovemaking." According to *What to Expect*, sex during pregnancy wasn't about getting off—it was about "strengthening" your relationship and "preparation for labor and delivery." (I guess the idea is that it loosens up your stuff down there?)

It seemed to me that the left, with its constant preoccupation with the baby's well-being, had come dangerously close to the right, as if reproductive politics were shaped like a circle rather than a line. The left, approaching from an entirely different direction, had ended up in the same place: A woman's desires and needs were secondary to the needs of the baby. The baby is always assumed to be a separate, sovereign entity whose needs eclipse the needs of its host.

Slumped on the couch, I used to murmur to my belly: "Mommies are protagonists, too."

After having had a child for a couple of years, none of this shocked me anymore. I was determined to do everything right. And so I turned my attention, intensely, on Lucy. I didn't care to work, didn't want to go out. Even Bruce seemed extraneous to my project, which was growing this baby and grabbing all the time I could with my daughter while she was still an only child. Time spread like batter in a pan, slow and often very sweet.

It was an idyllic and boring summer. These were shapeless days when time became both my material and my burden, like a vast bolt of fabric that just kept unspooling. When things were good, I turned time to my favor, shaping it into tiny rituals: the afternoon "toast party," which was just that—a party with toast. I had also instigated a morning pay-for-play session, when I actually paid myself money to play stuffed animals with my child. For twenty minutes, which was as long as I could endure. At the end of twenty minutes loomed a kind of event horizon of boredom. I would fall off the edge into a black hole.

Because I was home a lot, Lisa took to dropping Sam off so she could go to yoga. She climbed in her van every day and drove to this place, which was in the heart of the neighborhood where we all lived before we had kids. The people who went to this yoga place were not parents. They were young, or our age and childless, which was much like being young, except with jowls and more money. They had lots of time to chant and lots of time to hang out afterward and drink tea or wine and crack one another up.

Lisa started coming home from yoga later and later. She was growing thinner all the time. She didn't eat. Yoga made me want to go get a burger; it turned her into an ascetic. Her arms were awe-inspiring. She seemed to be always in motion, flipping against a wall in a handstand, dropping into a backbend. She had turned into a human parlor trick.

She seemed to grow farther and farther away from Steve. I never saw them together. They exchanged the children and pertinent information, and split up, day after day. If I had been a filmmaker, I would not have shot them in the same frame.

I, meanwhile, kept my focus, zeroing in Lucy, on this tiny world that I was adding to, building, renovating.

During my first pregnancy, we didn't find out what gender the baby was. It seemed to me that suspense might help me soldier through the experience of childbirth. (I was right about this, if nothing else.) I assumed we would do the same thing this time.

However: One summer day, when Lucy was tooling around the patio on her trike, we told her I was having a baby.

"A baby! A baby! I'm so excited!" Lucy had a knack for saying exactly the line the script required. I found it dear, funny, and extremely worrisome.

There was a beat. "It better be a girl!"

And so when it was time for the ultrasound we took Lucy to the building next to the one where she had been born, and she watched while a young woman with eyebrows plucked to oblivion ran the cool wand over my belly and announced, "Look! There's his penis!"

"Oh, well," said Lucy. "Too bad. Oh, well."

I tried pregnancy yoga once. Pregnancy yoga is not yoga. It is nine ladies lying on the floor in a sunny room, farting. I refused to go again. I had my pride.

So I kept going to regular yoga. Yoga as a pregnant lady was funny. People avoided me. Fran was really into partner yoga; she would set us up with partners, and we would yank and pull and adjust each other into position. I was the fat kid in the corner (again!). When it was time to choose a partner, my fellow students stepped around me, their eyes gazing over my shoulder like they were working the room at a cocktail party. Probably they were just anxious about hurting me.

And so I always ended up with the most unusually sized person in the room. There was a guy, Philip, who was scarily tall, taller even than the Norwegian farmer. There was Sabine, a strangely lumpy woman who had dyed-purple hair and an amazing wardrobe of truly ancient NO NUKES T-shirts. There was a nine-year-old who unaccountably showed up every once in a while. These were my partners.

Along with my choice of partners, my repertoire of poses shrunk as well. There were obvious changes. Plank was out of the question, from the strictly mechanical point of view: nowhere to put my belly. Downward dog was grueling and often morphed into a splayed-kneed child's pose. But still I kept going. By October, my practice had narrowed down to a few poses. My favorites were standing balances; adding a large weight to the equation made you realize just what they were talking about when they called them "balance" poses.

Half moon in particular had a hilarious kind of appeal. You stood in triangle, then bent your forward leg, let's say your right leg, and reached in front of it to the ground with your right hand. Right hand and right foot on the floor, you straightened your right leg and extended your left leg behind you into the air. Your torso turned away from the floor, and your left hand rose up in the air. It was an airy pose, a pose that took up as much space as possible, an open pose, a brave pose. When I did it with my huge belly sticking out, it was plain funny. No more coronal plane for me!

In order to sustain half moon, you needed to focus your attention carefully. In order to do this, you chose a spot to gaze at and then you gazed at it as hard as you could. This gaze, directed toward a single spot, was called the drishti. This kind of intense concentration in yoga: dharana.

The fact was that you would not, could not have the expansion, the feeling of flight, the open chest, the spreading arms, the flight of the body, without the drishti. The spot on the wall receiving your gaze allowed you to spread your arms and legs wide. Without it, you'd be lost, a heap on the floor, or at least not a flying thing. Or a thing that felt like it was flying.

When I thought about my baby in the middle of it all, tucked inside my expanded body, protected from a fall by only my gaze, only my fierce concentration, it made me dizzy.

People think yoga is boring. This is one of the big raps against it. And it is, if you're not concentrating. If you fling yourself into the pose, and let your mind wander, and merely tolerate the experience, yoga is, in fact, extremely boring. But if you concentrate hard, boredom opens up and the pose becomes the most interesting thing on earth, in fact the only thing on earth. The more you practice dharana, the simpler the world gets. There's just you and the thing on which you are bending your attention.

This kind of focus on an object has a paradoxical effect; by focusing on one object, you increase your chances of transcending the world of objects. You let the world melt away and move into the next of the eight limbs, that elusive state called dhyana, or true meditation. *The Yoga Sutras* explains it like this:

> Concentration locks consciousness on a single area. In meditative absorption, the entire perceptual flow is aligned with that object. When only the essential nature of the object shines forth, as if formless, integration has arisen. Concentration, absorption, and integration regarding a single object compose the perfect discipline of consciousness. Once the perfect discipline of consciousness is mastered, wisdom dawns.

Concentration, which asana teaches, is something that gives immediate and noticeable benefits. We've all felt it when we're utterly bent on our work: the dropping away of worries, of workaday life, even of time itself. In the Bhagavad Gita, Krishna tells Arjuna, "If thou art unable to rest thy mind on me, then seek to reach me by the practice of Yoga concentration."

Bruce was, as before, a tender character when it came to my pregnancy. He brought me glasses of water in bed. He bought me candy bars at the store. He made huge bland meals. He remembered to tell me that I looked cute.

But when I look back at that time, I can barely remember him being there at all. I just remember Lucy. My concentration was fiercely bent upon her, as if I were banking hours of time alone with her before the new baby came. If I forgot to include Bruce in my circle of concentration, that was OK. It was more important to be a mom than a wife. Wasn't it?

I drove past Lisa's house one afternoon and saw her standing outside, gazing up at the house. In her tight yoga pants and tank top, she looked elegant and plenty pissed off. I got out of the car.

She looked at me, and then raised both hands toward the house in a magnificent double flipping of the bird, and yelled, "Fuck all y'all!"

I guess that was the end of attachment parenting. There was really nothing else to say. She drove off, to go to yoga. I went home, to snuggle Lucy and wait for the inevitable.

14. PRANAYAMA

 Was it just me, or was Fran doing a lot of pranayama lately? Pranayama is the "yoga of breath," as she was constantly reminding us, and it seemed we spent half the class doing breathing exercises.

We did the old standby, alternate-nostril breathing—as pleasing as ever.

We also did a lot of three-part breathing, which, Fran said, toned the sushumna, and who wouldn't want to do that? With three-part breathing, you breathed into your lower gut, and held; then breathed into your solar plexus, and held; then breathed into your chest, and held. And eventually exhaled, *bien sûr*.

Sometimes we did kapalbhati breathing, which was a bellows-like panting. You huffed air out rhythmically and let the inhale sort of happen in between blows. This made me feel dizzy, in a good way, like the acid was starting to kick in.

Whenever Fran led pranayama, I felt that she gazed piercingly at me.

After class one day she said, "Have you noticed all the pranayama we've been doing?"

"Yeah, it's, uh, really great."

"It's for you."

"For me?"

"Yeah, you're going to need it."

"Well, I have to have a C-section. I had one last time, so I'm doing it again."

She looked a bit crestfallen, then brightened quickly. Hers was a basically sunny character. "Oh, well. You might need to do it anyway. You might be surprised."

I was raised with a heightened sense of my own specialness, and if you're my age or younger and privileged and American, you probably were, too. From the get-go we were told how very special we were. We expressed ourselves, our special selves. We made things from felt. We stood on tables at kindergarten and sang out loud. We journaled from the time we could form letters.

Because my mom was a just-slightly-older-than-the-rest hippie, and because I went to a progressive private school, I was on the leading edge of this movement. It was more than a pedagogy, this idea of the specialness of every child. It was a belief system: "Wonderful You," it might have been called.

The modern female's specialness reaches its ne plus ultra in the birth story. Every story is special and horrifying and heroic; somehow it belongs only to her and her alone—not to the baby or, god forbid, to her husband. She is the first woman ever to have a baby, even if it is her third or fourth child. No matter how the details of the birth story go, it always is basically the same narrative: I canNOT believe this happened to ME!

I can't think what the male equivalent of this might be. Probably the experience of balding. No man can actually believe this is happening to HIM! He is the first man ever to go bald. I had a friend who began losing his hair in college. This was back when people used to write letters, and I have a file of letters from him that largely consists of diagrams of hair loss. ("Note sparse growth in figure A.")

Every birth—like every balding—is the most dramatic one ever. You never hear a woman say, "Oh, it was fine. A little heavy breathing and out he came!" (Just like you never hear a man say, "Oh, it's only a little bit of thinning at the front.")

But, reader, my children's births were really beyond the pale. Everyone says so. I don't think I'm living in some special-person la-la land when I say they really, really sucked.

So. We had a few more weeks to go before the baby was due, and I thought I'd throw Bruce a bone. One last bout in the sack before the baby came and my body turned into a milky, ovoid factory. We wrangled for a quick twenty-minute session, called it a success, and went to sleep.

At 3 a.m. something was happening. Some sharp yet muffled pain, like a star exploding very far away. I poked Bruce, and after he shook off sleep we called my mom and Larry, who came right away. They lay down on the two couches, awaiting the moment the next morning when Lucy would awaken. They ought to have been sleeping with their hands crossed over their chests, like noble knights in service of the queen.

Bruce and I were in a room. Hospitals have so many rooms, rooms you never knew about, where all kinds of conversations take place. This was the room where they told you about the cesarean they were about to give you. They told us about it, and then we had to wait until the operating room was available. Or the OR, as they called it. Were doctors scared of words? Why did they always replace them with acronyms?

A cross old Irish nurse came in, looking like she'd stepped out of 1948.

"So, did anything unusual happen this evening?"

How did she know?

As I quickly said, "Nothing," like the guilty teenager I am in my deepest self, Bruce said, "Well, we did have sex."

She pressed her lips together. "Sex?"

Bruce nodded. He was starting to look kind of guilty himself.

"Hm. Well, I think we might need to get this baby out."

And she left us there, inhumanely: no magazines!

We were in this room a long time. Hours. We were in there so long that Mom and Larry showed up with Lucy, looking like visitors from another age and another country.

Only one person was allowed to keep me company in the OR, as I resigned myself to calling it. Bruce walked beside me as they rolled me in. Close on our heels was my mother, who somehow talked her way in.

The anesthesiologist produced a big needle and shot me, or rather my IV, which was now part of me, with a lot of something. An enormous weight began to roll up my body, starting with my toes. Then, like one of those guided meditations we sometimes did at yoga, the weight traveled up my calves, up my thighs, over my waist, pressed its massive hand onto my chest, and then rolled out each arm to my fingertips. It stopped, miraculously and precisely, at my neck and head. I tried with all my might to move my arms, but they might as well have been strapped down. A dark shadow had fallen all over me, except for my head, which remained in light.

A curtain was set up over my waist, so I couldn't see what was happening. The scene was familiar from last time: the bright lamps overhead, the teeming crowd of masked faces, the strangely party-like atmosphere. It was a good thing my mom was there because the minute they started sawing away, Bruce took a quick peek over the curtain and staggered out to the hallway, where, I would learn later, he fainted. Like the Victorian maiden he is. It was a few years before he could bring himself to tell me what he saw, over the curtain, and even then he was terse: "Soup tureen of blood."

Without him there, the room seemed more sterile, more like a place for an operation, less like a place for the birth of a live animal human. This was better, with him gone. My job was to separate myself from my body and my feelings entirely; with Bruce there, it was more difficult.

In my experience, it was not good to treat the OR with anything other than total, freezing-cold seriousness. Its science must not be stained with our human emotion. I could see that this was magical thinking. But even so, I was glad Bruce, and all his feelings, were gone. Now I could start to switch mine off. I did my job (the job of lying there), undistracted by my husband's rosy cheeks and feverish eyes above his square mask.

My mother stepped forward and wielded her motherly genius for being the right thing at the right moment. Now she was cool, like the surgeons, holding my hand in her chilly hand. She knew instantly that she and I had a single job: the job of not freaking out. "Great job," she told me, getting right to the point. She said this a few more times, in an unruffled, calm way. Then she peeked over the curtain. She didn't faint; she bucked like a horse, with the grandmotherly thrill of it all: a new one! And then she produced a camera from under her gown! And clicked away as the baby was pulled from my body! I lay there and watched her and felt fondness for my resourceful mother.

A doctor's voice said, "We've got him!" And the tiny boy was lifted high in the air.

For a few minutes I got to enjoy the fruits of normalcy with my son. I even thought of it that way. These, I thought, are the fruits of normalcy. It's fair to say that by this point I was pretty dissociated from the birth process.

We lay together in the blond-wood-paneled birthing room. The tiny boy nestled next to me; I felt pleasantly like a sow with her piglet. Family members came and went, holding tall cups from Starbucks. Our parents hung about, ready to worship. Bruce carefully lifted Lucy onto the bed and she snuggled me with a terrified look on her face.

And then a nurse came in (a male nurse! later this seemed to add to his culpability), with a gust of inevitability like a cold wind. He took the baby from the unsure arms of my sister-in-law. He frowned at the baby. I knew that frown. Oh, did I ever.

He said, "I'm sure they told you before the cesarean that a baby born a few weeks early might have lung issues."

We said yes, quickly—if we're good children maybe the scary man will go away.

"I'm not liking how this guy is breathing. We need to take him upstairs." That word. He added, unnecessarily, "To the NICU."

There was no longer any need to chat or linger. Bruce and I exchanged looks of extreme exhaustion, and the family faded away.

I was moved summarily from the beautiful birthing suite—*that* went quickly—to the grimmer environs of my recovery room. I lay about recovering for a while, and then I climbed in a wheelchair and Bruce pushed me upstairs. I greeted all the nurses. There was Willie, in his plastic bassinet. He was very beautiful, but that didn't seem important. Small. Not in my arms. These were the salient facts. These facts dwarfed the fact of his beauty.

I couldn't believe this was happening. Again. The nurse came over.

"We've been here before," I said. I told her the story of Lucy.

"Maybe I remember you," she said vaguely. But that was the past. "This one is going to be fine. We'll just keep him here overnight, and that'll give you a chance to rest."

"Are you sure it's nothing serious? Please tell me it's nothing serious," I said.

"Well, he is a little early, but these guys usually do OK. You go rest." All this telling me to go rest made me think she was a witch or a nefarious guardian in a children's book, trying to get me out of the way.

Even so, Bruce and I were Good Sports. "Great!" I said brightly, and Bruce wheeled me away to my room, where I ate my tray of food and fell into a deep sleep.

"Your baby, he had an operation during the night." There was a nurse standing in the half dark of our room, and her English wasn't great and she was saying something that could not be true.

I stirred in my bed and Bruce sat up in his armchair.

"What?"

"Your baby, his name is William, I think? He burst a lung last night. They did just a little operation, just a little one to, you know, reinflate the lung."

She had raced ahead to referring to specific body parts and we weren't even awake yet. We knew what it meant when they referred to body parts like that—"the lung," "the heart"—and it wasn't good.

"What? How did he burst a lung?"

"He was crying and crying. He wouldn't stop. They could not get him to stop. He cried so long he burst a lung."

"But I was right here! Just downstairs. Why didn't they come get me? I could've held him. Maybe I could've nursed him." What I didn't say: Maybe he wanted his goddamn mother!

"The nurses held him. They know what they are doing."

"But I'm his mother!" I couldn't keep it in. I wanted to convince her of this fact. I couldn't quite believe it myself. "I'm his mother! Why didn't they get me?"

I cried and cried. I pulled at my gown. I was, believe it, rending my hair.

Bruce stood by and we were, without talking or even looking at each other, in that strange conjoined state where we lived last time, when Lucy was a hospital baby. He rested a hand on my hip and I began to yell tears, if such a thing is possible.

The nurse advanced through the gray light. "You are going to have to calm down. You have to calm down."

"This isn't the first time!" I cried unintelligibly.

"You don't understand," Bruce tried to explain to the nurse, "what we've been through."

She advanced more closely. The light was dim. "You must calm down, or I am going to have to give you a sedative."

I stood up from the bed and whispered, "Get. Out. Of. Here."

I had not needed to breathe during the birth. Now I tried to remember how. In. Out. In. Out. No biggie. Just keep doing it. Just keep doing it.

On the elevator up to the NICU I muttered, "So much for number three."

"Tell me about it," said Bruce. During the minute or two the Kafka nurse was in my recovery room, we both gave up the idea of ever having another child. We gave it up entirely, simultaneously, and silently.

Upstairs, in the NICU, Bruce and I went into capitulation mode. We didn't yell at the nurses. We didn't even ask them why they didn't come to get us. First of all, we had to keep the nurses on our side. Alienating them would only result in bad things for the baby. Second of all, a kind of fatalism had taken over us. Why bother complaining? It wasn't like we hoped to get better service next time. It wasn't like we were ever, ever, ever going to have another baby.

The news was put to us by a nurse with short blond nurse hair: The baby burst a lung screaming; they quickly ran a tube into his lung cavity to draw off the air that was rushing in. Once a vacuum was established in the cavity, the lung inflated. A success.

"We didn't have time to come and get you. We had to operate immediately," said the nurse.

We didn't ask why they didn't come to get us earlier, when the baby was crying inconsolably. We asked, "What's next?"

She pulled aside the baby's tiny kimono-style hospital-issue onesie to show us the place the tube was inserted. "You can see how tiny the incision is. Look how small it is."

We gazed in the general direction of the incision; we really did not want to look at it.

"See," she said, pointing.

Were we meant to congratulate her on the smallness of the incision? If so, we would do it. We would do anything to make her take especially good care of our baby. We admired the incision: very small.

Then we slipped into the timeless days and weeks of hospital life. This time we had our small anxious person at home to think about as well. Lucy was given to saying things like "We have a baby! How exciting!" and then changing the subject entirely.

Here's something gross about C-sections: When the doctors are done, they staple you shut. Like a manila envelope. Then, oh then, comes the final indignity. You have to have the staples removed. When Lucy was born, I gripped my eyes while they took out the staples, as if I might turn to stone if I caught a glimpse of the proceedings. This time I watched. I lay on my hospital bed and a jolly bearded nurse pulled the staples out with a special little tool. It seemed like the right thing to watch. Watching was the way I said goodbye to my future as a pregnant person and a mother of three. This was the end of my childbearing, and if it was going to be as heartbreaking and revolting as this every time, well, then, good riddance.

Willie was in there a week, and then another week.

I was not at my most together. I ran out of Percocet on Christmas Eve afternoon. Lucy was in the other room getting an *Arthur* fix before we took off for our party marathon. For some reason, I had decided to go ahead with making the krumkake, the Norwegian cookies that were a tradition in Bruce's family. Somehow his mom and sister and cousins, those wily Norwegians, were smart enough to foist the making of the krumkake on me. This involved a special iron, a wooden dowel, and the patience of a saint.

I can't remember why I decided to make them when I had just given birth and had a baby in the hospital. It clearly seems symptomatic in retrospect.

My incision started to ache. Have you ever made krumkake? It's effortful. My incision really hurt.

I checked my Percocet bottle in the medicine chest. Just one left.

I stood in the middle of our living room and screamed at the top of my lungs, "I'm out of Percocet!" I was like Nancy Spungen in a pair of postnatal overalls.

Bruce came running into the room. "It's going to be OK," he said.

"It is *not* going to be OK," I yelled, wild-eyed.

Bruce stared at me. He didn't even bother to argue or laugh. He just stood there. What was that look on his face? Oh. It was fear.

Christmas was its usual gigantic, voracious self, eating time like candy. We squeezed in a visit to Willie in the morning. We drove up and down I-5, grandparent to grandparent. Lucy opened so many gifts that she seemed to have a little mini-storm of wrapping paper whirling around her head at all times, like Pig-Pen's cloud of dust.

After we got Lucy settled into bed I went to the hospital to nurse Willie. One thing about spending time in the NICU: you get to sit in a lot of really nice rocking chairs. This one had gliders, so I moved smoothly back and forth, suspended as if I and the baby in my arms had both moved back into the womb. My breath synched to his nursing, which synched to the glide of the rocker, back and forth, back and forth. This is just pranayama. Just keep breathing, baby.

And then it was over. This is how it works in the NICU. One day they simply dismiss you. The day after Christmas, we brought Willie home.

We lay him on his changing table.

"Look how tiny he is," we said to Lucy. She still had that terrified look on her face. But she came over, interested.

"I think," said Bruce, "I think he might be smaller than my shoe."

He got a New Balance running shoe out of the closet and laid it next to Willie. You couldn't have actually put the baby into the running shoe, but he was certainly smaller than it. Lucy laughed with delight.

Like all C-section babies he had a perfectly formed head. His head was covered with incredibly soft, groovy-looking golden down, like the prettiest Ultrasuede ever. He kicked away on his little mat while I put Lucy down for her nap. He cooed at his black-and-white make-your-baby-smart mobile while she and I played Pretty, Pretty Princess.

I felt like I had to book special dates to admire him. In her novel *The Last September*, about life at a provincial Irish country house, Elizabeth Bowen describes her heroine's youth as "a fire burning in an empty room." I took to paraphrasing the line when I lamented how little time I had to sit around doting on Willie: "His cuteness is a fire burning in an empty room."

When the neighbors came to visit, Lucy introduced them to her new brother: "This is Willie, my brother. He is a genius and a beauty."

15. WARRIOR II

Willie was a sensation. He quickly mastered a huge grin and grew a headful of yellow curls. He had eyes that did tricks: They went from being gigantic blue poker chips to squinty half moons of pure pleasure. More than that, he was possessed of a babyish insouciance; he moved (or, rather, was carried) through the world entirely untroubled. If something bothered him, he yelled and was done with it.

When he was released from the hospital, he was not on an oxygen tank, as Lucy had been. He was not in quarantine. He was entirely portable, which I found novel and exciting. I took him everywhere with me. I took him by the yoga studio, where Fran congratulated me as a coach congratulates an athlete, with some pride.

Wherever he went, he drew an adoring crowd. Hauling him along for a business lunch with an editor, I dandled him on my knee at Le Pichet, a chic, pared-down French bistro near the Pike Place Market. A fierce man dressed in a beautiful suit strode over, his eyebrows beetling. Uh-oh. Many people didn't like babies in restaurants. This one stood in front of us, pointed his finger right at Willie in a classic "J'accuse!" gesture, and announced loudly: "THAT is the cutest baby I have EVER seen in my LIFE!" Then he turned on his heel and walked out the door.

I am embarrassed to admit that this encounter kept me going for the next few months, when Willie wouldn't sleep at all, when Bruce worked evenings as well as days, when our beloved babysitter quit, when Lucy turned from being a lovely little lump of butterscotch into a three-and-a-half-year-old. Being with a three-year-old is like constantly being in the middle of very bad breakup. Irrational tirades and operatic flights of rage are tempered with appeasing manipulation.

"Who are you?" I asked her as she flung her noodles onto the floor. They were too hot, apparently. "And what have you done with Lucy Barcott?"

She climbed off her chair and wrapped her arms around my neck. "I love you so much," she whispered. I was grovelingly happy to receive her hug. Was I developing Stockholm syndrome? Meanwhile, Willie was in the other room, seeking dust balls under the changing table, which he planned to stuff in his mouth. He was successful. I found him with gray stuff hanging from his mouth. What are dust balls made of, actually? I mean, besides dust. What's that stuff that kind of strings together? Is it old hair? Ew. I inserted a finger into his mouth and swept it clean as best I could. I dreamed of a day when my job would not involve putting my fingers into someone else's mouth and seeing what I found there.

I lay down on the couch with Willie. Lucy came in.

"Hi, angel baby."

"Hi, angel mommy. Can we draw?"

"Sure. Just mind your brother for a minute, sweetheart." I was using the overbright voice I used with Lucy when I was very tired. It was, even to my own ears, sickeningly sweet. But it was better than yelling, wasn't it?

I got the crayons and paper, which were not kept neatly in a drawer as they were at other people's houses. They lived in a messy plastic box in a cupboard at the bottom of the china cabinet. Or, rather, they lived near a messy plastic box. They mostly seemed to roam loose through the cupboard. Systems eluded me.

I spread the art stuff on a low table and Lucy and I began to draw. I drew her and she drew me. Then we drew hats on our portraits. Willie lay on his back, kicking his beautiful legs.

Bruce came in from the office for more coffee and found me cooing at Willie.

"Hey, guys."

"Hi," I said flatly.

"We're drawing," said Lucy.

"What are you drawing?"

Lucy showed him and I leaned back for a moment against the couch and shut my eyes.

"Claire, would you edit a draft of my story before dinner? Then I could maybe send it tonight." He was working on an article about environmentalist Christians.

"I guess. I'm kind of busy with the kids."

"I can watch the kids."

"Yeah, so I can work on your article. Not that I have any of my own to work on." Which I didn't. Freelance work was picking up slowly for me. We had decided that for a while I would work as little as possible, to keep child-care costs down. Though I had signed off on this plan, every time I saw Bruce head out the back door to the office, I wanted to throttle him.

"Oh, never mind."

"No, I'll do it," I said in a grudging tone.

"Really. Don't worry about it," he said, and headed out the back door. Before it was even shut, I was already giggling with Lucy over the funny hat she had drawn, while Willie sat snuggled on my lap, pulling my hair.

"Ouch," I said, in the nicest voice in the world.

I waited six weeks after my staples were taken out. Not to have sex; it was very likely I would wait six years before I did that. To go to yoga.

I took my seat in the studio and folded my legs into half lotus. Well, not quite. My ankle kept slipping from my thigh, slumping down to the floor like a drunk man off a bar stool. Things were clearly not quite as they had been. I crossed my ankles instead. Fran slipped into the classroom and beamed at me where I sat in the back row. I had relinquished my front-row status.

She certainly didn't slow anything down on account of me. We moved quickly into the familiar poses. I felt constricted all over; there was a something like a busy street between my expectations of myself and what I was actually able to do. I could see myself over there, on the other side of the street, but couldn't get there.

We did a few sun salutations and moved into warrior II. I stood with my feet about three or four feet apart. My front foot pointed straight ahead, toward the front of my mat. My back foot was turned at an angle. My front leg was bent deeply; I was trying for ninety degrees. My back leg was straight; I was trying for straight. My arms winged out from my shoulder. I gazed over my front arm. I was back, baby!

"Can you feel your core in this pose?"

"Core" was the yoga way of saying "stomach muscles." This locution came, I believe, from Pilates. It sounded good, much more yogic than "abs."

In answer to Fran's question, there was a silence in the room. I for one could not feel my core in this pose. In fact, throughout my experience of yoga I had tried not to feel my core or indeed to think about it at all. Whenever a teacher would mention the core, my brain would shut off, the way a teenager's brain shuts off when you mention car insurance or laundry. I didn't want to deal with my core.

I had never had a strong midsection, and when I started yoga I'd just recovered from my first cesarean. My core seemed a faraway thing, possibly mythical. It was a "How Are Things in Glocca Morra?" type situation.

But it could not be denied: As I did warrior II, I felt a kind of collapsing through my midsection. It didn't hurt. I wasn't in pain. Nothing as interesting as that. It just felt sloppy. My lower gut had been sliced twice now and was staging a walkout. I looked in the mirror and something didn't look quite right. My back was arched in the pose, my butt sticking out.

"Remember: This pose is named warrior II. It's a pose of power. It's not a pose that's about flexibility. It's a pose you've done since you started your practice, but there's a lot of complexity in it that beginners can miss. You guys should be able to find your core in this pose. Really engaging in warrior II is a kind of art."

Fran was like a public radio host at pledge time. She could flatter us into doing the right thing.

"Let's stop and review the bandhas," she said.

Bandhas are locks, or bindings. There are lots of different kinds of binds in yoga, including hand binds. But Fran was talking about energy locks. There are three of them. Starting at the bottom, literally, is mula bandha. You have already practiced mula bandha, whether you know it or not. It's the feeling you get when you try to stop yourself from peeing. You tighten the pelvic floor, including the anus and the perineum. That's right! I said it! You tighten the anus!

Moving upward, you come to uddiyana bandha, which is a constriction of the upper abdominal area. Basically, you suck in the belly button and try to lift it. If you've ever seen one of those photos of a wizened old yoga master whose stomach appears entirely concave, he's likely doing uddiyana bandha.

Jalandhara bandha is the throat lock. You take in a breath, drop the chin toward the chest, and then draw it back, keeping the back of the neck long. Eventually you release the lock and then the breath.

In traya bandha, you do all three locks at the same time. First the mula bandha, then uddiyana bandha, then jalandhara bandha. The air is retained in the lungs, the locks are set, and you hold for as long as you can. Or for as long as the nice lady says you have to.

Fran had us sit on the floor and practice the three bandhas. As we locked up all the available energy in the room, she talked.

"The tightening of the core in mula bandha and uddiyana bandha brings enormous energy to our poses. The bandhas are subtle movements, but they're important to access if we want to challenge ourselves with difficult poses and find energy in uncomfortable situations."

There is, in fact, a photo of B.K.S. Iyengar practicing all three bandhas at once, though of course you can't see if he is truly engaging mula bandha. Thank goodness. He looks like an idol, a statue, something not quite human. And that's how it feels to do traya bandha. Bizarrely powerful, like you could take over for Dr. Evil if he had a sick day.

Then we got up again and arranged ourselves in warrior II.

"Now," said Fran, "we're going to try doing mula bandha and uddiyana bandha while we're in this pose. We'll skip jalandhara."

Following Fran's direction, I did the pose in a new way. I drew my tailbone underneath me, so my back wasn't sway and my butt wasn't protruding. I locked the old mula, as I liked to think of it, and then did uddiyana bandha. I hated to admit it, but my core—I could almost feel it! I gazed out over my front hand. The whole class was lunging forward, looking over their outstretched hands at the mirror. No one was smiling or looking tentative. They looked fierce. Holy crap, they looked like warriors! Thanks, energy lock!

We stood there, our cores locked into place, arrayed like an army with our standards flying. Warrior II felt great. I knew that if I asked Fran, she would say that the warrior in this pose is meant to be a spiritual warrior. But I felt tough, like a real warrior. I hadn't realized it, but I was spoiling for a fight.

A year had passed, a year of Willie's glorious babyhood. It was Christmastime.

"Hi, honey."

"Hi, Mom."

"Lucy told me she wants the Bitty Twin dolls from American Girl for Christmas."

"Weeelll, we haven't decided what to get her yet."

"I thought I would get them for her."

"It's a big gift. Maybe if that's the only thing you get her."

"Oh."

"What?

"Well, there's a stroller, too. It's really cute. It would be much more fun to give her the dolls in the stroller."

"I'll think about it."

"Let me know soon because they might run out."

"Hi, honey."

"Oh, hi."

"Did you decide about the Bitty Twins?"

"It's OK, I guess."

"What about the stroller?"

"Ugh. OK."

"Are you upset?"

"No, it's fine. Just don't get her anything else."

"Well, I need to get her stocking stuffers. And just a little something else to unwrap."

"I have to go to work now."

"Hi, honey."

"Oh, hi."

"I'm trying to figure out what to get Willie. I want to get him something equal to what I got Lucy."

"Mom, he's not gonna know. He's one."

"I know, but I want to thrill him."

"It'll be Christmas. He'll be thrilled no matter what."

"I was thinking a golf set."

"Hi, honey. I'm at the mall. They have those cute cloth dolls at Pottery Barn Kids. I thought I'd get Lucy one."

"Mom, you already got her the Bitty Twins!"

"This is just a little something to open. And they have these adorable dresses, I thought I'd get a couple of those as well."

"Mom!"

"Honey, it's just a little something. What about one of those plastic basketball hoops for Willie? And Larry saw a John Deere tractor he wants to get."

"Will he get a crop to sow as well?"

"Ha! We saw it at Costco. It's really cute. The perfect size."

"Mom, remember they're getting gifts from us, too. And Bruce's parents. And Dad."

"Oh . . . They're going to run out of tractors at Costco soon, can you let me know today?"

"Hi, honey."

"No!"

"No what?"

"No more gifts."

"Well, if that's the way you feel."

"Mom, it's too much."

"I'm just picking up stocking stuffers."

"Last year the stuffers didn't even fit in the stockings. They were all piled on the ground. They're not stuffers, they're pilers!"

"It's Christmas. I saw these cute finger puppets at the University Bookstore. Don't you think Lucy would love them?"

"Finger puppets sound good."

"And then they have this adorable puppet theater, too."

Christmas came and went. I spent two weeks loading and unloading gifts thanks to the generosity of our families. Soon enough, it was my birthday, which falls like a hangover a few days after New Year's. My mom and Larry were babysitting so Bruce and I could go out to dinner. We ate cake before we left, and the kids sang "Happy Birthday." After we finished cake, Larry and Bruce watched basketball while I bustled around getting ready and my mom entertained the kids.

Lucy was amazed that Bruce and I had eaten dessert before we went out to dinner. "Dessert before dinner," said Lucy. "Now that's something you don't see every day."

"Your mother is a woman with opinions," said my mom. "I hope she has room left for dinner at that fancy French restaurant. One day I'll take you out for French food. We'll eat snails and frogs' legs."

"Gigi!" said Lucy in a shocked voice. "How will we get the legs off the frogs? Anyway, I'm not eating them."

"You'll like them when you're a grown-up," said my mom. "For now, we'll eat crepes."

"Those, like, little pancakes?"

"Yes, those ones."

"Oh, good."

"And boeuf bourguignon," said my mom. "And cassoulet. And pommes frites! Do you know what those are?"

"No," said Lucy, rapt.

"Pommes frites are french fries," said my mom in the voice of one beginning a fairy tale.

"OK, let's go," I said.

"Have a good time," said my mother. "Have the roasted chicken, I hear it's fabulous."

Bruce kissed the kids and stared at the ground as we headed toward the door.

"She said the chicken is good, Bruce!" I said, trying to cover up for his quietude, which I read as rudeness. This was more and more the case of late. Bruce was retreating into himself, which made my mother sort of come after him, with a frightening jollity.

"OK," said Bruce in bleak tones.

Dinner out was not entirely successful. We were exhausted and on deadline. We had colds, or maybe the flu. We were not in the mood for a night out, but there we were, huddled over a table at Café Campagne, celebrating that vaunted American custom, date night. When you are married, date night buzzes irritatingly on the periphery of your consciousness, the way New Year's Eve does for single people.

Everyone else had fun on date night, just the way everyone else is always having fun on New Year's Eve. "Date night!" chimed those well-suited, highly educated, happy couples, like it was the biggest pleasure they could possibly think of. "We were having a really hard time," these couples would confess. "We just couldn't get along. But we made ourselves stick to having date night once a week, and now we're doing great!"

Date night, like any kind of enforced fun, bore little resemblance to actual fun. Our best date nights came when we resisted the orbital pull of the restaurant dinner. At one point, though neither of us golfed—in fact both of us sort of loathed golf—we took up visiting the driving range. At least whacking a bucket of balls under flood-lights didn't have any of the dreary, conversation-making, forced gai-ety of a true date night.

The thing of it was, as a Norwegian farmer, Bruce hated restau-rants. It was a matter of principle, or possibly of genetics. I, not a Norwegian farmer, loved restaurants. I'm using the word "love" in its peculiarly American vernacular, meaning "thought I was supposed to like." I thought I was supposed to like restaurants. And restaurants were supposed to mean romance. The whole thing was like a strange Ponzi scheme of obligation.

Bruce looked like he was going to fall off the banquette, so I told him some jokes about editors of his I had met. I compared them to various animals: weasel, rat, ferret. It wasn't very clever, but it animated him out of his restaurant torpor, which was even worse than usual.

"Maybe you should bring him bits of cheese!" I concluded. "He would dart back to his hole with his bit of cheese. And then he'd fire off an irate e-mail." I smiled. I felt cheap for pandering to Bruce's more base conversational tendencies.

"Maybe," he said, but he didn't jump on the image and develop it, the way he would have if we had been eating bowls of cereal at home. Restaurants, I believe, somehow literally removed his ability to speak.

I think it didn't used to be like this. He used to be my secret chatterbox. But now he had stopped.

I appeared to be placidly cutting my chicken and drinking my wine, but in reality rebellion was fomenting over on my side of the table. I wanted him to desire me ardently and hopelessly. This was of course impossible. I was married, and therefore known. I wanted to be perfect and adored for it, but any fool knows that you cannot be known and perfect at the same time. I glared briefly at my husband.

"What?" he said. This may be the most ominous syllable in the lexicon of marriage. And of course there was only one answer for me to give, and I think any married person knows what that answer was:

"Nothing," I said.

He set his fork down with a minuscule, almost inaudible clank, a tiny little sound that was marital shorthand for "This dinner is pretty expensive. Do we have to ruin it with whatever is about to happen?" There was a little bit of "Go fuck yourself" thrown in for good measure.

"What?" he said.

"Nothing," I said. Really, this two-word exchange could make up an entire play about marriage.

Then I steeled myself and said it: "I've told you I want more romance. It's embarrassing to keep asking."

The Norwegian farmer looked around elaborately, his gaze taking in the candles, the delicious food, the absence of puling children. The Norwegian farmer was good at this kind of look. "I thought we were having a romantic dinner," he said. "We came all the way downtown just to have some romance!"

I wasn't falling for that. "Sometimes I feel like you don't even notice that I'm here," I said.

"How much more can I notice you?" he asked. "Who else am I noticing? I don't even understand what you're talking about."

"It's just how I feel!" I say. "Isn't that important? How I feel?"

"Claire," he said, frowning at my drained glass of red, "I don't know what you want from me. I feel like I do things for you, and you don't even see them. I do chores and I bring you candy bars from the store. I quit work early so you can go to yoga or go out with your friends. I let you sleep in this morning. I even brought you breakfast in bed."

I didn't know how to say it to him, but I could feel something going off the rails between us. It used to be that there were two of him: Norwegian farmer and Croat fisherman. He was the silent Norwegian in company, and the voluble, passionately emotional Croat when alone with me. I had joked about this, about how he was my closet chatterbox. But now he seemed to be internal, and silent, even when we were by ourselves. I missed my chatty old demanding Croat.

In *Light on Yoga*, Iyengar is forever implying that the forces of prana that move through us are more powerful than we can imagine. The kundalini that rises from the base of the spine to the crown of the head is a dangerous force, so dangerous that teachers believe that, wrongly used, it can destroy you. And yet the very purpose of yoga is to harness and use this energy. Iyengar writes: "Without the bandhas, prana is lethal." I love this line; it has a certain big-haired hard-rock sound to it. It could be a line from a Bon Jovi song.

The bandhas: They were saving my sorry ass. After two cesareans, my stomach muscles were fatally compromised. The bandhas gave me the strength I needed. I could still be strong and not notice that my stomach muscles were basically not working. Structurally, I was kind of a mess. But I could compensate by going into lock-down mode and find a way to hold a pose as long as I liked.

Just as I was regulating the mood in my home. I was pretending that things were not getting dark; that Bruce was not retreating from me. I used a cheerful strength to do this, a strength I had been developing for years. A strength that wouldn't admit that anything was wrong. Because if something was wrong, maybe it would all unravel.

I needed my strength because I didn't have the grace or courage to acknowledge what was happening: My husband was shutting down.

I couldn't even admit to myself that it was happening. And I certainly couldn't admit it to anyone else. I felt a shame when I noticed how sad he was, and how sad it was making me. His beautiful long spine bent all the time, like a weighted drooping flower. The saddest flower ever.

I felt contaminated by Bruce's sadness, as though it reflected badly on me. As though I had bought a lemon. I had been married to him for years and I was still kicking the tires, wondering if I'd made the right choice. I think this constant assessing and reflecting on our spouses is one of the actual legacies of divorce—do I still want this thing?

I was so ashamed that there was a problem that I never asked him: What's the matter? Sometimes we chatted as in days of yore, but I always stepped delicately around the question I wasn't asking: What is wrong?

I withdrew into the children. It was like I could smell something on him: some failure, some darkness. I didn't know what to do with that darkness. I didn't want to admit that it might exist (though it had always been there, lurking in his long silences, his workaholism, even in his black eyebrows). I pretended his darkness wasn't happening. I was strong and cheerful; until I wasn't. I saved my weakness and cheerlessness for when Bruce and I were alone together. For everyone else I was a model of happy motherdom.

When I was a little kid, my mom had a way of answering the phone that drove me nuts. We could be in the middle of a pitched battle. She might be screaming at me. And then the phone would ring, and she would answer it in the sweetest, most trilling voice in the world: "Hellooo!" The outside world must never know.

16. CHILD'S POSE 4

1977

We arrived, of course, by sailboat. It was an island that could not be reached by ferry. The hundred or so people who lived on or spent their summers on Stuart Island had to get there under their own steam. We set anchor in a small cove and the four of us—Mom, Larry, Dave, and I—rowed in to a tiny beach of gray wet pebbles. Blond hills stretched above us. I felt like I was at one of the *Dawn Treader*'s destinations.

Larry and I hauled the little skiff to shore. He led us up a steep path. There was no birdsong except the sharp, weirdly comic calls of seagulls. A couple of hawks wheeled silently overhead. The smell was salt and grass. The air was still and yet not quite soft. The hillside was yellow with dead grass and lumped with bare gray boulders. Twisting between them grew madrona trees, with their pistachio bark, dark orange peeling away to reveal lime green.

The path opened into a clearing. The clearing was so quiet that it was impossible to imagine the trees growing—too noisy. To the left, woods. To the right, nothing. Just water, a hundred yards below, crenellated by waves.

"The property goes that way." Larry waved his hand away from the water. "You can follow it across the island, and it comes out on the other side, on Johns Pass."

We walked into the woods, down a path that ran into a narrow dirt road. The air smelled of old mold, as organic as a library. We turned off the road onto a path that was wide enough for a cart or a wheelbarrow but not quite wide enough for a car. It had been worn utterly smooth. The ribbon of satiny dirt glided sinuously over roots, around trees, up and down gentle grades, a story written by feet and wheels. Onto a small dirt road, and then off onto yet another smooth, functional path.

Then, suddenly, you were coming steeply out of the woods, the gray-green, fast-moving water of Johns Pass below you. The woods began to straggle, an occasional madrona here or there, standing twisted and alone in the shaggy grass. Then there was no path, just a wide grassy place sloping all the way to the rocky beach and the water. We had walked from one side of the island to the other, from beach to beach, all on our own property. In between we had seen woods and gigantic erratic rocks and old fruit trees. We had seen narrow deer paths reaching between mossy rocks. We had seen tiny meadows, with boulders like furniture in them. I was ten. I felt like I had come home.

Mom and Larry and Dave headed back toward the other side of the island.

"Can I walk back by myself?" I asked.

"Oh, honey, you'll get lost," said my mother.

"So what?" said Larry. "It's an island. She'll find her way back. She just has to keep walking till she sees water."

They left, chatting about where we might build a house and when we might start to build. I sat on the beach. It wasn't mine, exactly. It was Larry's. But I felt like a king. Not a queen, with her mediated, sometime power. A king, a sovereign.

I walked through the woods. I saw a tiny deer path heading through the trees. With branches grabbing my hair, I followed the path. It led from one meadow to another. Each one seemed perfectly sized for something not quite human, something more, to occur. I wandered from meadow to meadow, as one drugged. I was lost but not panicked. I felt I was somewhere eternal, where panic never occurred. The mysterious rhythm of the fields compelled me deeply. Forest, field, forest, field. I thought I might go on forever. Alone and roaming.

I came out above the harbor and could see our boat far below. All I had to do was follow the cliff and I would find the beach where we had landed. I weaved along, climbing boulders and legging over fallen trees, until finally I climbed down to the pebbly beach. The skiff was gone. I yelled to the boat and Larry rowed in to get me. We rowed back to the boat, I remember, in perfect silent accord.

We moved into an abandoned chicken coop on the edge of our new property. Mom and Larry got the mice-infested bed in the corner. Dave and I had a big canvas tent outside, where we lolled in our sleeping bags, reading the mornings away, the light olive-green and submarine even on the sunniest days.

The next couple of years were busy. Larry started a tugboat company. He built a house. In the middle of the night one night, at the highest tide, we floated the lumber for the house from the tugboat's barge to the shore; of course there was no mill, no lumberyard, on that faraway island. There were just houses and a little school, where Louise Bryant, girlfriend of the Communist activist John Reed, taught in her prerevolutionary days. She was the one played by Diane Keaton in *Reds*.

I stood in the freezing Puget Sound water, waist-deep, and guided enormous twelve-by-twelves to shore. Standing in the water, doing my job, I felt wild, brave, exceptional. Larry had told us it would be fun, and it was.

We were absorbed into the life of the island. We hadn't been there long when Stan and Mimi decided to move up there, with their baby, who was by now a beautiful, solemn toddler. They borrowed a piece of beach from us and built themselves a Visqueen tepee. The whole island was a like a showroom for the contingent structures favored by hippies: tepee, coop, tower, shack, beached boat, A-frame, tent platform.

The island was constellated with couples just like Stan and Mimi. Of course, no one could be just like Stan and Mimi, and that was the point; the couples were weird, unique; each had their own eccentricities, their own gimmicks. They were, to me, like collectible dolls. I delighted in them. There were Sally and Billy, who were clever with their hands and made everything beautiful. Sally planted thyme between the cracks in her front walkway and knitted sweaters that made you dizzy with their patterns. Mark and Jan were mean and you could tell they took drugs. Eric and Annika were soft and upright, like Quakers, but they lived on the far side of the island and so were mysterious. Connie and Jim were decent, normal people—how'd they end up here? Adam and Gus each lived alone, womanless, deep in the woods, and seemed to match each other in sadness: Adam's was kind and Gus's was sharp.

Presiding over them all were Toots and Norm, a tough old couple with the most beautiful spread of land, everyone said, in all the San Juan Islands, a jutting point that was part meadow, part sheep pasture, part forest, part beach. Everything was just so on Toots and Norm's property. Toots was one of the famous half-Indian Chevalier girls from Spieden Island, and Norm always treated her like she was his new bride. I am sure they were not perfectly happy people, but that is how they always seemed to me. They could remember the days, early in the twentieth century, when the Haida would still paddle down from Canada and camp in the San Juans.

I spent my days visiting, never giving a thought to whether or not I was welcome. I would walk from little house to little house. The mothers were younger than my mother—Larry's age. They were pretty and they baked. Their babies crawled into my lap as the smell of food filled the house. These tiny families were my refuge. I was in love with them, each and every one. Family life in the woods, on the beach: It seemed exotic and beautiful to me.

There was no running water on the island. We went by boat once a week to take a coin-operated shower at the marina in Friday Harbor, the nearest town. I grew to know by heart the catechism of unwashed hippie smells. I knew patchouli, I knew brewer's yeast. I knew marijuana smoke that had lived for a few days in long, tangled hair. I knew all the different kinds of sweat: sweat mixed with diesel, anxiety sweat, carpenter sweat, alcoholic sweat.

Our own house was sunny and open. We slept in little lofts. Those twelve-by-twelves studded the walls, but despite the weight of the materials, the house was a light place, with rows of windows and unstained wood everywhere. We had a woodstove and curtains for cupboard doors. Here were some of the books on our shelves:

The Forsyte Saga
Chainsaw Savvy
Peril at Sea
Indian Affairs
Shogun
Diet for a Small Planet
The Survival of the Bark Canoe
The Professor of Desire
a Scrabble dictionary
a 1975 almanac
Elmer Gantry

One Sunday night Stan and Mimi hosted a party, and as we sat around the fire waiting for the guests to arrive (I considered myself part of the family, probably tiresomely so), Stan decided to explain to me why he no longer did drugs. He stretched his long legs out toward the fire, shook his huge mane of hair back from his face in a characteristic gesture, and rested his hands peacefully on his small paunch, which was hardly noticeable on such a tall man. Larry sat next to me, silently drinking a beer.

"One day we were doing Lucky Strike. You don't know what

Lucky Strike is, and you don't need to know, girl. Unreal. That shit was unreal."

Stan combed his fingers through his hair and looked into the distance that the fire held. He only drank beer now and then, and Mimi wouldn't even drink coffee, she was so alarmed by her experiences with narcotics. Cookies, she said, it was cookies for her from here on out.

"I started to feel, well, red. And bumpy. I realized I was a strawberry. I needed to be cold. I required refrigeration. So I opened up the fridge, and took out all the shelves, and climbed in. Somehow I got the door closed and promptly passed out in there."

Larry laughed, but I was caught up in the story.

The sun had slipped down in the sky, and now the fire took on a more definite form against the late-afternoon trees.

"Mimi got me out just before I went hypothermic. That was the last time I ever did drugs."

Drugs were everywhere. Usually it was a little pot, treated as an innocent, private, and almost entirely universal pleasure among the adults. The smell was omnipresent—to this day the thick herbaceous fug of burning marijuana is evocative of childhood for me. A deckhand of Larry's smoked a huge amount of pot, lost a hundred-thousand-dollar crane over the side of the barge, and tried to climb into my sleeping bag with me when I was twelve. Mark and Jan, who lived across Reid Harbor in the informal commune there, were constantly leaving the island under shady pretenses. And then there was Flagler, an old friend of Stan's who was at the party. Maybe it was Flagler who put Stan in mind of his drug days. It was funny to have Flagler at a dinner party because Flagler didn't eat. At mealtime, he laid out a series of pills on his plate and tossed them back as everyone else ate. There was plenty of food: salmon, zucchini bread, blackberry pie, corn on the cob, and boat dish, which was a casserole of corn and ground beef that some marina friends of ours had invented when they were living on their sailboat.

A *baa* was heard. Stan and Mimi's goat, Nudge, was rummaging in the blackberry bushes. Flagler, half naked and bearded and balding, went over to commune with her. He looked remarkably like a goat himself as he approached her. My mother and I caught each other's eye. We started cracking up. Our contentment seemed perfect.

When I went east to college, a classmate wrote a song about me: "I don't believe you exist" ran the chorus. It wasn't my rare beauty that inspired her, or my fierce intelligence. It was the bare facts of my life, which looked weird when observed from a vantage outside the Northwest. (I went to college back in the 1980s, when people knew nothing, and I mean nothing, about Seattle. In the summer between freshman and sophomore year of college, I got mail addressed to me in "Seattle, Oregon" from a New York friend.)

Specifically, my classmate was enchanted by my summer job: tugboat deckhand. Larry had bought the *Cotton No. 6*, a small wooden tug built in 1916, and constructed a wooden barge that he named *Donna May*, after my mother. He motored around the San Juans, hauling building supplies to islands that had no ferry service.

As a deckhand, I wasn't really much use. I couldn't work on the engine; I never polished the brass fixtures; I wasn't great with a chart. I could cast off, drive the tug, tie up at docks, and manage the lines between the tug and barge. I wasn't very good at it, but Larry never seemed bothered by having a spaced-out, boy-crazy eighth-grade girl in braids driving his boat straight into a dock while all the manly types at the dock looked on and laughed. I never fell in, I never got crushed between the boat and barge, and I never lost any cargo.

Tugboating, it turned out, involved a lot of heading out across the sound at strange times of day. Partly this was because of the tides. Partly it was because, aside from finding work through the more usual routes, Larry had become a kind of maritime ambulance chaser. He had hooked up a ship-to-shore radio in our living room, and as we played Scrabble or just sat around reading in the evening, he'd keep it on low and listen for folks in distress. If someone ran aground, we'd head out in the tug to pull them off the shoals.

At, say, five o'clock or so on a July evening we'd find ourselves motoring out of Reid Harbor, the sun glancing into our eyes. Larry was good-natured at all times, but on the tugboat, he was quiet and short on words, with no nonsense about him. We'd have almost four long clear-lit hours ahead of us before the sun disappeared entirely. The water in Puget Sound is never perfectly still, and now it was peaked with tiny waves, black on one side; the other side of each wavelet shifted lavender to gray to algae-green. The smell of diesel, which was and is to me the smell of maleness, was everywhere. I was in the pilothouse, at the wheel, grasping its rounded wooden spokes. The radio was on and Larry was swinging around the boat like a higher order of monkey, checking lines and bilge and engine. He was nimble in his body and his mind as I would never be.

He came into the pilothouse and sat a little behind me on a stool, one Levi'd leg slung over the other. His feet were in the leather slippers that on the Olympic Peninsula they called "Romeos." Unlike effete Top-Siders (common at my prep school), Romeos were and are what workboat people wear. He studied a chart and every once in a while directed me more perfectly to where we were headed: a stranded boat on the west side of Waldron Island.

Van Morrison came on the radio, singing his poetry, by turns strangulated and open-voiced. I was steering us past Spieden Island. I turned up the radio a little and we smiled at each other and rode in silence. The wild, cold waters lapped all around us. The sun was still hot through the front windows, but the raw breeze that came through the open pilothouse door reminded you that you were in a northern place. I hadn't lived anywhere else; I just thought it was normal, the way air was supposed to feel, hot and cold at the same time. I knew enough, though, to feel lucky. It was lucky to be a girl in a wheel-house, with the islands all around, their bleached-grass hillsides a pure straw color, like the hair of a girl in a Beach Boys song. It was lucky to be driving a tugboat. It was lucky to be riding in this pilothouse made of sixty-year-old wood with this diesel-smelling person who was older than a brother and younger than a dad, who loved me so much and would never, ever say it.

He leaped up and sighted our destination.

"Go for that point there," he said.

"Is that Waldron?"

"Yup."

"Are we gonna turn in before the point or after it?"

"We're gonna turn in right after that point. There's a big rock just off the point, so swing wide and then slow way down."

I brought the boat wide around the point while Larry hung out of the wheelhouse scanning for the party in distress. Once we rounded the point all the way, it wasn't hard to see: a sailboat that had wedged onto a rock. The tide was coming in, and the boat was beached like a whale.

"Bring it into the harbor," said Larry, passing his hand like a squeegee over his beard. "Slow it down. Way down. Reverse now."

I threw the boat in reverse and the water around us churned up into a white roil.

"Yeah," barked Larry. "Now hold it steady."

I held the boat in place while he stood looking at the sailboat. You could tell he was thinking because he was holding still; once he was done he would be in motion.

And then he had a plan. We would hold off till the tide was all the way in; we would pull the sailboat off the rocks, as gently as possible, we would tow it to the nearest marina in case it had a break in the hull.

It all went tickety-boo. We had the sailboat off the rocks in an hour and over to the marina at Eastsound before nightfall. The Roche Harbor marina was closer but for some reason the guy wanted to go to Eastsound. This was good; more money. Then we made our way home in the dark. Larry didn't give me any compliments or tell me what a good job I'd done. He bought me a Coke from the machine at the marina and let me choose the radio station. He laughed at a lame, snotty joke I made about one of the swollen, perfectly white yachts we saw at anchor near the marina. "They're probably watching TV," I said. His laugh made me feel entirely included: happy and cool at the same time. Those were two things that didn't always go together. We motored into the darkness and finally made it home after midnight.

We climbed into our separate lofts. I felt an exquisite sense of belonging. Like every kid, I craved that feeling.

We had developed a precarious balance, Mom and Larry and Dad and Dave and I. We had figured out a way to move through the world together, as this strange attenuated family. Larry and I had even found a way to be related to each other, in a quiet, joking way. This family, this strangely made thing, this delicately balanced contraption, felt like eternity to me at the time. I thought it would go on forever. But now I see that it was contingent, like the frying pan on top of the filing cabinet. And I was the one to upset it. And I did that by becoming an adolescent.

17. VINYASA

All this reminiscing about the past was done on the night shift, of course. Between, say, two and three in the morning. Because during the day there was no time for such a thing. Everything seemed to get busier and busier. Even yoga was about to get busier.

I noticed a new offering on the menu: vinyasa. This was the yoga I had done at Lisa's studio, the fast stuff. I thought I might try it again. I did my usual yoga for a few more weeks until I didn't feel like my scar was going to burst open every time I did forward bends, and I went to vinyasa. I was hoping to address my belly, the way a golfer addresses the ball.

It was funny to walk into the same studio, the same room, where I had learned so much and been so comfortable, where I had felt at home. The same studio, but laced with a kind of menace, or threat. Amazing how a new group of people can make a space feel entirely different. My regular group, from Fran's class, was comprised of men, older women, athletes, a few hippie couples, and the small coterie of former gymnasts whom Fran attracted.

But this was the kind of group that scared me before I started doing yoga—a room full of young, beautiful, slender women. When non-yoga-doers imagine the horrors of doing yoga, this is what they imagine: all this dewy, taut skin.

The women were already moving around the mats, demonstrating their flexibility before class even started. They were stretched over their legs in seated forward bends, or splaying their legs in cobbler's pose. Some were sitting perfectly still with their eyes closed.

The teacher—also young, beautiful, and female—came in. She was possessed of a walk that appeared to be totally silent. I mean, all walking is silent when you're barefoot, but her walk was visibly silent. It was quietude on the hoof.

She took a seat by a little shrine that, presumably, she had set up earlier: a miniature brass Buddha, a singing bowl.

"I am Mindy," she said, as if her name were an honorific. Her hair was drawn into a proud puff on top of her head; she was infused with her own intrinsic royalty, was Mindy. "We ask that you honor your own ability, where you are on this day, not yesterday and not tomorrow. Take a moment to set an intention for your practice. Hold space for that intention throughout practice."

And we were off. Once we had dispensed with the usual class-openers—seated stretching, om, more seated stretching—Mindy stepped to the front of her mat, and the weirdness began. We progressed through a regular sun salutation, but suddenly it started moving very quickly. Mindy was walking among us, not demonstrating the poses but announcing them. And instead of announcing them by their English names, she was calling them out in their Sanskrit names: "Samasthiti! Urdhva virasana! Uttanasana! Ardha uttanasana! Chaturanga dandasana! Urdhva mukha svanasana! Adho mukha svanasana! Ardha uttanasana! Uttanasana! Urdhva virasana! Samasthiti!" "Move through vinyasa," Mindy would say, with her special intonation: "Moooove through vinyaaahsa." It took a while for the penny to drop. Moooving through vinyasa simply meant moving quickly through a few of the movements of sun salutation (or as it was known here, of course, surya namaskara A), with a single inhale or exhale devoted to each movement.

Of course we had connected our breath to our movements in Fran's class, but not with this kind of rigor, where the breath was so firmly connected to the movement that you would never even think of breathing out during upward dog. Likewise, I knew all the Sanskrit names for the poses, but had not encountered them so nakedly unaccompanied by their English partners, and coming so quickly.

After a few passes through vinyasa, I caught the rhythm of it:

Urdhva virasana. Inhale. Hands over the head. Elbows next to the ears. Lift your chest but keep your ribs tucked in. Shoulders down. Engage your core. This is a moment of readiness. Anything is possible, for at least next three seconds.

Uttanasana, also known as good old forward bend. Exhale. You're only here for a moment, so enjoy it. Well, I suppose that's true of every pose in the vinyasa sequence. I suppose some yoga type would say that it's also true of every moment in life. You could think about that, except it's time to move on.

Ardha uttanasana. Inhale. You lift halfway out of forward bend— here known, of course, as uttanasana—with your back straight and your fingertips resting on the floor or your shin. Ardha uttanasana is where the loop between perception and reality starts to break down. Your back might or might not be straight. Will you ever know? No, because when you do vinyasa, you're not really doing poses. You're moving through poses so quickly that you never quite know if you're pulling them off.

Chaturanga dandasana. Exhale. Leap back into plank, also known as push-up position; from plank, keeping your body perfectly straight and your elbows right next to your body, drop to the floor. If you are someone not me, someone I envy and perhaps even hate, hover with your body in a straight plane an inch above the floor. Chaturanga is the fulcrum of vinyasa. It's the most difficult part, and the part that haunts you when you fall asleep at night.

Urdhva mukha svanasana, or upward dog. Inhale. From chatu-ranga, with the tops of your feet on the floor but your knees drawn up off the floor, pull your torso forward between your arms. Arch your back like a seal.

Adho mukha svanasana, or downward dog. Exhale. Pull your seat back; roll over the tops of your toes with your legs straight, and there you are in downward dog. It feels like coming home, every time. Downward dog was so named, we're told, because it looks like a dog stretching its back. But it's well named for another reason. Downward dog is man's best friend. When you return there in the flow of vinyasa, everything feels like it's just where it belongs. Vinyasa, if it does noth-ing else, will improve your downward dog, because your arms will be so tired that you will draw your weight back toward your feet. Weight toward the feet; weight toward the feet; weight toward the feet. This is your new mantra. You've heard your teachers saying it over and over, maybe since the very first time you did downward dog, but now you really get it. Weight toward the feet. Until it's time to leap toward for-ward bend. Ardha uttanasana, again. Inhale. Your feet have landed by your hands, god willing. Rise up halfway.

Uttanasana, again. Exhale. You're almost there, except, as Gertrude Stein said of Oakland, there is no there there. There is just this, over and over and over.

Urdhva virasana, again. Inhale. Head rush.

Samasthiti. Exhale. Wonder why your teacher always pronounces this word samasthiti-heee, with a long, almost whistling exhale at the end.

This series of movements linked other poses together as we went through class. So after triangle, you dropped into plank, through cha-turanga, into upward dog, and back into downward dog. Then you got ready to do the whole thing again, starting with triangle on the other side.

In a usual class, this series of poses could take up many minutes of time; maybe even a whole class full of time. Now it was done in sec-onds, and then done again, and again, and again, until you were like a windmill rotating through space.

I remembered Jonathan telling us in one of my beginning classes that downward dog is actually a resting pose. At the time I suspected him of some kind of bizarrely motivated Machiavellian manipulation, but now I got it.

"Take child's pose if you need to," said Mindy. "Honor your own practice."

There was no way, no way, that I was going to honor my own practice. I caught a glimpse of myself in the mirror. My face wasn't just red. It was maroon, burgundy, almost purple. I looked like an old German man having a heart attack.

Fran's class was like algebra. It had a logic to it. It moved forward, one thing leading to another. You stretched an area, then you put it to work, then you stretched it again. You spent an hour on your hips, then you did side crow. You worked on your hamstrings, and then you gave splits a try. Algebra.

Vinyasa, on the other hand, required calculus's leap of faith. Where am I going? I have no idea. I'm going to keep going, and maybe I'll get there. Or it was a Beckett play: I can't go on, I'll go on.

This leap of faith was also a literal leap. You sprang from forward bend back to plank. You were meant to land like a bouncy stick, with buoyancy and strength. And you sprang from downward dog to forward bend. Here you were meant to land silently. "Float through the air," said Mindy. "If I can hear you, that means you're not using your core."

This seemed to me anathema to everything I had learned about yoga, which was all careful easing and sustained pose-holding.

Even so, I went back the next day, and again and again. Eventually vinyasa revealed its patterns, and I got the hang of it. Over the next couple of years it took hold of me. Its rhythms, the speed of it, matched my mood exactly. I did not want to slow down, to appreciate things as they were. I wanted to improve!

And vinyasa, which never slowed down, which demanded nothing short of everything from me, suited me down to the ground.

———

Our house began to fill up with travel guides with cover photos of palmy beaches and aquamarine water. These books were everywhere: on the back of the toilet, in the office, on the kitchen table. You never knew when you were going to trip over one. They fell out of the cupboards and bonked me on the head; they sprouted in the garden. At least that was how it seemed to me, the person not going to Belize.

The magazine Bruce wrote for was sending him. This was the culmination of a series of dream assignments: kayaking in the Sea of Cortés; skiing with the U.S. Ski Team in Austria; and now a jungle expedition in Belize. Belize! It was my policy to encourage Bruce to go. Sometimes I grumbled when he came back, but I never discouraged him from going, and I tried not to get too envious of his good luck.

Our life was much as it was before Willie came, only faster. I was getting more work, Bruce was getting more work. I was getting less sleep, Bruce was getting less sleep. Bruce was also traveling for work all the time. The Belize trip was a big one. It would be a major feature about some woman who ran a zoo down there. Apparently she was battling a multinational company that wanted to build a dam right smack-dab in the middle of the country's most pristine jungle. Bruce would be going on an expedition to the dam site with her and a group of photographers and scientists. I wasn't invited, natch.

Bruce's trip to Belize went well.

He told me all about it when he got back. He flew down on TACA, an airline based in El Salvador. He told me about the feeling that he had left America as soon as he stepped on the airplane. He told me about the mustachioed Salvadoran men, striding down the aisles looking for drinks, cowboy hats high on their foreheads and proud paunches hanging over their belt buckles; and about the Carib businessmen in guayaberas and slacks, shuffling their paperwork.

He told me about Belize City, a place that seemed put together without rhyme or reason. It had all the visual cues of the tropics: the sea, the blue sky, the palm trees, the colonial buildings. But, he said, it was as if someone had gathered these symbols and flung them in the air and they had landed willy-nilly. The Caribbean lapped high and muddy against the bulkhead at the end of town. No beach, no promenade: the entire massive ready-to-hurricane sea was sloshing at the curb.

He told me about climbing in his rental car and heading away from the city and the water, through the green valleys of the Belizean Bible Belt, and on into the jungle, where he met up with his expedition and saw all manner of astounding things. Macaws flashed through the trees; blue morpho butterflies hung pendulous from branches; howler monkeys called from the darkness. There were campfires at night, and machetes, and crocodiles in the river. His face was animated as he talked. He looked . . . happy. It occurred to me I had not seem him look so happy in a long time.

He decided he wanted to write a book. A book about Belize. That is, a nonfiction book set in Belize. Bruce was a man in love with a country. My husband's gloom had lifted a bit, and it happened because he had found a new, fascinating place. A faraway and strange place. It seemed lonesome, for the both of us.

When we forgot to breathe, Mindy was right there to remind us. "Exhale," she said as we hoisted backward into downward dog, leading with our rumps. Except here's how she said it: "Exheel." And also: "Inheel." As we thrust ourselves chest-first into upward dog, she urged us: "Inheel."

Mindy traveled in a pack. There were three or four of them, serious, intense young women with arms like Angela Bassett. They taught vinyasa all over town. Sometimes they were so serious and intense that they seemed almost feral. A few years later, vinyasa would become the most popular and widespread kind of yoga, especially at the gym: so aerobic! But during this period, a much smaller population practiced it.

It was almost all women who practiced it, and one of the reasons they were so devoted to vinyasa was that it worked. Worked in the very specific sense of making you thin. I felt I needed vinyasa's help with this. Frankly, I was getting chubby. We have not talked very much about my body in this book. My body is pretty average. I'm somewhat rangy and can hide a spare five or ten pounds if I dress carefully. I have hips, and thanks to two C-sections, a soft, spongy belly that will never be hard again, no matter what.

I can remember everything bad about my body that has ever been said to me.

"Claire is fat because she eats the fat." Said by my brother at the dinner table over a plate of ham in about 1976.

"It doesn't matter. Really." Said by a boyfriend, right after he pinched the roll of fat around my stomach as we kissed in 1985.

"You have, uh, Slavic limbs." Said by a co-worker at a restaurant in San Francisco in 1990, just days before the big earthquake. Not a compliment, FYI.

"Your ankles look like forty-ouncers." Different boyfriend this time, 1993. At least he got right to the point.

There are more. Obviously. I could go on and on. I am guessing everyone has a list like this in their head—or every woman does. These statements brought out a funny feeling (ha ha!) in me: guilt. Being fat, even a little bit fat, makes me feel guilty. My parents and brother are all very thin and so this is how I thought I ought to be.

I was chubby as a child. This is not just a perception. I look at old pictures, and there are my cheeks under my curling shag hairdo, and there is my stomach under a yellow T-shirt. Meanwhile, there's my mom, a hippie Twiggy, all teeth and aviator glasses and hair. No body to speak of.

I tried, just once, to claim my fat as a source of pride. I was about eight years old. Bridget and Marie and I were playing in the attic of their house. They were as thin as my family, spindly and straight. One of them had just poked the globe of my gut.

"If I were thin, I wouldn't be myself!" I said.

"Sure, you would," said Bridget.

"You'd be yourself, only thin. You'd be you, but better," said Marie, who was the boss.

This was a strictly theoretical talk, however, because it would be many years before I lost the baby fat. In eighth grade I seemed to grow about five inches in a single year, and after that, I stayed pretty thin. That is except for the soft stomach and the forty-ouncers.

I have that former-fat-kid thing of always waiting for the fat to come back and claim me. And this, of course, was one of the reasons I went to yoga. To barricade myself against the return of the fat. No one likes to talk about this aspect of yoga: It makes you thin. We were all supposed to be focused on breathing and being in the moment. How many thousands of times did I instead focus on envying Fran's toned arms and narrow legs? Yoga is supposed to be above all that, somehow.

Vinyasa was unbelievably effective at making you thin. Its teachers were inspirations, both in word and in body. They shared a kind of cult status; their students followed them from studio to studio.

All of these women spoke with the same accent: "Exheel." "Inheel." Where did it come from? Why did they do it? This strange pronunciation was paired with an odd grammar. Definite articles were shunned. We were urged to "Mooove through vinyasa." We were also told to "Breathe into sensation." And finally: "Remember intention."

Was it just me, or was there something almost offensive about these pronunciations? Didn't these pretty white girls sound a little like Peter Sellers playing Mr. Lalkaka on *The Goon Show*?

In fact, I started to notice this in a lot of yoga teachers. There was this weird adoption of Indian patterns of speech. Some of them took class time to tell humble little fables about monkeys and lions and tigers, as though we all shared subcontinental Asian animals as our cultural touchstones, rather than *Survivor* and M&M's and the Rolling Stones. Some of them wore bindis. Some of them actually seemed to worship Vishnu and Krishna and Kali rather than thinking of them as neat stories. They were trying to integrate the spiritual aspect of yoga into their physical practice; this process was ungainly and sat strangely in the yoga studio, which was, when you got down to brass tacks, a place for exercise.

Meanwhile, Bruce and I were being inducted into another strange culture. It was time to find a grade school for Lucy. We arrived at our choice after a laborious process that involved looking at, I estimate, oh, say, every school in the entire city. This was a process fraught with worry and class anxiety. We started when Lucy was just four, and we started—where else?—with the school where Bill Gates sent his kids. We were like nervous schoolgirls as we loaded ourselves in the car. Would they sneer at us? Were we wearing the right sweaters? Were sweaters even the done thing? Here we were, writers, bohemians if you squinted a bit, presuming to storm the palace gates.

We pulled up to the school and looked around anxiously for our snacks. Now I am going to tell you the secret to a lasting marriage: Choose a spouse who needs to eat as often as you do. Bruce and I are like toddlers on a big day out. We need a snack, no matter where we are going or how long we are going to be gone. If we are headed out for dinner, we bring a Baggie of cut-up cheese for the car ride to the restaurant. It's a good thing we never became stoners because the grocery bills alone would've killed us.

So on the day we visited the school where Bill Gates sent his kids, we brought along an apple (me) and a banana (Bruce). We got out of the car, already giggling with nerves, bit into our fruit as we walked along the sidewalk, and said at the exact same moment: "I hope they don't think we're fruitarians!"

We were, on that first day, indoctrinated in the Rite of the School Visit:

- The civil, rushed greeting by the nice lady, who might be an admissions person, or a volunteer, or the head of the school. But it was always a nice lady.
- The greeting of the other parents, the majority of whom were always Microsoft people in expensive, over-soft leather jackets. Unless it was a public school. Usually you ran into someone you knew and expressed mutual disbelief that your child was almost old enough for kindergarten. Incredible!
- The tour through the rooms, in and out of the various chambers of the school, as though we were a group of history buffs visiting an ancient castle. The third grade, the lunchroom. This being Seattle, a well-equipped computer lab always elicited an almost

pornographic gasp of appreciation. Bruce and I were always on the lookout for a dress-up box. We were in favor of play.

- The Q&A session. This was where you asked the nice lady, or her higher-up, questions about the school. These questions were always hilariously transparent. "How do you handle highly capable children?" meant: My child is a genius! Know it! "What conflict-resolution techniques do you use?" meant: If my child gets beat up, I am going to sue you.
- The ride home, which for us was always the same. I was always sure that whatever school we had just visited was The. Greatest. School. Ever. Bruce was always skeptical, as if the whole concept—this thing we call "school"—was suspect.

There was no dress-up box at the Bill Gates school (probably not a problem for BillG), so we nixed it from our list. We had standards! A kindergarten without a dress-up box was not a kindergarten we cared to spend time with.

I learned a lot of things over the next year: I learned what "The Pink Tower" is. (A wooden block puzzle used in Montessori classrooms.) I learned about those crazy/awesome Waldorf lunch baskets. (Waldorf students are not allowed to bring plastic materials into school; they use wicker baskets and waxed paper.) I learned that numbers don't have fixed values. (Twenty is an enormous class in private school and a tiny class in public school.) I learned that looking for a school for your child can be a shopping trip to rival home buying. I got the same dizzy thrills, felt the same cutthroat competition. It was the ultimate bauble, and it was even more desirable because you couldn't control the outcome with money.

Hence the new status symbol: the gifted child. Money wasn't enough to get you into one of these mini-campuses, but there was something else that would do the trick, and that was a good score from the special giftedness testing center at the University of Washington. Here's the funny thing. I never met a kid who got under 98 percent—meaning that every kid in North Seattle is smarter than 98 percent of the entire American population. Can this really be true?

One by one, my friends and acquaintances came through my kitchen and said, in hushed tones, "Claire, it turns out that Dylan/Sophie/Jackson/Camille is very gifted." And then, whether you asked or not, they'd tell you "The Number," which vacillated wildly between the polar extremes of 98 and 99.

The class ascension and social climbing that was part of signing on for private school did not fit the North Seattle parent's idea of him or herself. And so, the gifted child was invented. The gifted child freed these parents from guilt. They had no choice, these parents. They had to send their kid to private school. They had to nurture these very gifted children.

We were caught up in a kind of striving that felt bigger than us. Well, honestly, bigger than me. Bruce would've been happy sending Lucy to the local public school.

But I had become a striver. Looking back, I can see that I was in the grip of an unsustainable cultural obsession with having the best. Strictly on a financial level, I looked around me and many of my peers had become very wealthy. Their children had European clothes and wooden European furniture and European strollers. They were sending their children to expensive private schools; in fact, to the very schools where I myself had gone. I felt an irrational anger when I thought about these things. Just because they had more money, they were not more deserving. And I decided that my children should have everything these wealthy families had. I didn't admit to the x factor in the discussion: These parents all had jobs. Bruce and I had chosen our more contingent, artsy, writerly path. So I decided that somehow I deserved a great education for my children, on a writer's budget. I locked onto this idea and dismissed public school as a possibility.

It's no excuse, but I was not alone in this striving. This was, of course, the era of people spending above their station. And the school enrollment in Seattle proved it. In North Seattle, at that time, at least half of all kids went to private school.

I was impelled toward private school beyond the capability for discussion. Maybe Bruce sensed this and was a realist. Maybe he thought this was my department, and he would do whatever, as long as it wasn't it too expensive. Either way, it was certainly my project. The whole city seemed to be made up of five-year-olds and their parents, knocking on the doors of private schools like we were seeking admittance at the giant gates to Oz.

This striving was entirely reflected in my yoga. I had left Fran and her quiet ways behind. Where I had once sought silence and quietude in my yoga, vinyasa seemed to ask for a blind devotion to speed, to action. Even to noise; in vinyasa classes, music played. Sometimes it was recorded chanting, sometimes a New Age chanteuse like Deva Premal, sometimes it was flat-out dance music, and I wondered how close we had veered toward exercise class.

And yet, as if to deny that this was an exercise class, vinyasa determinedly included a lot more spiritual stuff than I was used to. Mindy always set up her little shrine for class. A couple of small bronze statues; maybe an embroidered cloth. We chanted before and after class, reading from little slips of paper that Mindy brought with her. A student passed these out for her and picked them up when we were done, with a humble, I'm-an-acolyte look on his or her face.

The chant was transcribed, but not translated, and so I found myself saying these words

Om
Swasthi praja bhya pari pala yantam
Nya yena margena mahi mahishaha
Go brahmanebhyaha shubhamastu nityam
Lokaa samastha sukhino bhavanthu
Om

without understanding them even a little bit. Even so, I kept saying them. It wasn't that I had faith that chanting would be effective. It was that the teacher, and her students, presented such a seamless, fluid image. This perfection extended from their bodies to something invisible, something inside.

Ruthie's little boy was going to a cooperative elementary school. Ruthie loved it, and so did her son. I decided to check it out.

When we went to visit the co-op, Lucy came along. We walked in the door and were confronted with a hallway that was kinetic with action: Grown-ups clustered and laughed; children yelled and threw things; balls rolled; someone sang; even the art seemed to be flapping on the walls.

Without a moment's hesitation, Lucy ran forward and disappeared in the throng. After all that research, the thing was pretty much decided for us in a flash of thrilled little girl.

The school made me cry, literally. It fit every (admittedly not-very-well-developed) notion I had about how kids ought to spend their days: making art, running around like wild creatures, picking up the occasional math fact. There was a gigantic, wobbly, cardboard jungle, obviously made by the children, filling the library area. There was a handmade sign over the door reading CHILDHOOD IS A JOURNEY, NOT A RACE. There wasn't just a dress-up box. There was a whole dress-up wing. We signed her up on the spot.

To be honest, I was happy to be at a co-op, as we had been when Lucy was a baby. At a co-op, you literally got to go to school with your kid, albeit only once a week. For the intense kind of mother I had become, this was ideal. I could hover over her as she molded clay, resolved conflicts, and acquired pencil skills! Yes!

The school had about twelve kids in each grade. It was a true co-op. There were four teachers and a couple of specialists, and every-thing else at the school was done by parents. Janitorial work, assistant teaching, fund-raising, building, answering the phones, procuring curriculum materials, hauling lumber, cooking. This made the school less expensive, which was welcome.

Everything we did, we did by hand: We felted purses and sewed quilts and baked empanadas. It was like Colonial freaking Williams-burg in that place. Let me put it this way: When I tell you that, for a unit on Pacific Northwest Native Americans, we tanned hides, I don't mean we gave the kids spankings. Meetings were epidemic, as anyone who has ever been involved in a cooperative anything will know. Meetings involved arguments and singing. At first I loved the arguments and hated the singing. It was fun to go to a school with a plot! But very soon I grew to hate the arguments and grudgingly enjoy the singing. There were just so many arguments; they lost their novelty value.

I learned the non-arguer's all-purpose phrase to deal with these fractious yet touchy-feely encounters: "Thank you for sharing." It's true. It made me feel like I was in an Edward Koren cartoon, but it worked like a charm. I used it all the time, spent it like it was change for the parking meter.

There were arguments about curriculum and arguments about recess. There were arguments about Spanish and arguments about the school camping trip. There were many arguments about how to argue. But above all, there were arguments about food.

It only stands to reason that certain people with issues about food would seek a cooperative elementary school. Because many people who chose the co-op chose it for the same reason I did: fear. Everyone seemed driven by this big, wobbly, jellylike terror that something was going to hurt their kids. Social anthropologists have theorized that this worry stems from the small size of the modern family; we have more invested in each kid and don't have extras to spare. At any rate, this endemic fear has other names, like love and concern. And these people's concerns for their children centered around food.

For some kids, this was a very clear-cut deal: They had bad allergies or serious health issues. Lucas had severe celiac disease and truly could not ingest any wheat. Kendra was fatally allergic to peanuts.

Then there were the nonmedical cases that were still at least rational: Serena and Porter came from a vegetarian family and needed help learning how to identify and pass up dishes with meat in them.

Then things started to slide down a slope that was as slick as soy yogurt on a banana. There were parents who were against sugar. Parents who were against trading lunches. Parents who were against "kid food." Parents who disliked food as a reward. Parents who shunned food with "chemicals" in it. All these things needed to be discussed.

From there, it got even more confusing. Many of these preferences were expressed as medical necessity. Parent A's decision to limit the dairy products in their household became her child's "dairy allergy." Parent B insisted that Grayson was allergic to wheat; why then did we sometimes see Ritz crackers packed in Grayson's lunch box? The mom who hated chemicals smoked cigarettes and included candy in her kid's lunch.

How did I know this? We were all there. We saw everything. That was why we had chosen to send our kids to a co-op. We were the kind of good parents who didn't want to miss a minute of anything. Wheat and lunch trading and dairy allergies: These were the topics of the day.

School brought new structure to our lives. Each night Bruce and I went gamely through the ritual/prison sentence of dinner, bath, reading, bed. This was the hour of little ease. It wasn't that I minded the various tasks; they were fine, unto themselves, as tasks. They contained small, gentle ecstasies that somehow never failed to surprise, even though such moments were daily occurrences: a child reading a word aloud, a burrowing snuggle, a bubble-bath beard. But somehow these moments seemed less important than the vista. The problem was the vista. It was like looking out over a plain, with these monoliths standing there, things I had to get past. It was the world's slowest obstacle race.

We constantly tried to make time work in our favor. We became famous for arriving at dinner parties in separate vehicles. That way, one person could keep working after the other left for the party. And one person could leave early so that we could get the kids to bed on time. This often involved complicated timing maneuvers and planning down to the second; we got so good at it that we should've considered taking up heisting.

This was very important to us, this idea of putting the kids to bed on time. We thought that because we worked at home, we were free of the clock. We thought we had an advantage over those people who had to be at an office at a certain time. We could not see that our time had become occupied space. We never let time simply occur; it was as if there was something about the unmarked passage of time that was upsetting to us. Time had once been a vacant lot. Now it was as crowded and absent of surprises as a subdivision.

Chaturanga was a kind of nexus; it was here that you encountered the impossible, over and over, each time you moved through vinyasa. Everyone has poses they decide they can't do. I mean, probably not everyone. OK, maybe nobody else has them. But I did. The pose I had made up my mind that I couldn't do was chaturanga. By this time I could do all kinds of more difficult things. I could do scorpion— a kind of arching headstand where you balanced on your forearms. I could occasionally do side crow if I could just stop myself from thinking for one goddamn second. I could do full splits and I could back-bend from pigeon and almost, almost catch my foot from over my head. I could lift into wheel and though I couldn't raise one leg straight up to the sky, at least I could raise one foot off the ground. I could do stuff.

But I was convinced I couldn't do chaturanga. Ever since I first laid eyes on it, it seemed something beyond me. It was OK to not be able to do chaturanga when I was doing regular yoga—after all, it was a tiny fraction of my practice. But once I started vinyasa, chaturanga became a big part of my life. The modified way to do chaturanga is to keep your knees on the ground, and your body stiff and strong from knees to shoulder, and lower yourself toward the ground. This I did every day. And every day I told myself that I could not lift my knees off the ground, that I could not perform the full version of the pose, body dropping to the ground in one long straight strong line from toes to head.

I can't, I can't, I can't, I told myself. What happens when you tell yourself that you can't do something that you are asked to do over and over every day?

The fact was, after all those down-on-my-knees chaturangas, my triceps were actually hard. The fact was, I was strong. But it happens all the time: We make decisions about ourselves and our lives that are not based on fact.

So it was with my marriage. On some basic level, I believed in its fragility. I believed that it was too fragile to hold up to the rigors of truth—the truth about Bruce's depression, the truth about my perfectionism, my self-doubt. I went through my marriage every day, devoting myself to it, yet believing in its essential weakness.

I lay on the couch at Steve and Lisa's house, playing with some paper dolls that Lisa's daughter, Sarah, had left lying there. Steve lay near me on the floor, playing, over and over, the Thin Lizzy song "Jailbreak." Which was turning out to be a really great song, the more we drank. The music was loud, which meant there was no need to talk to each other. (Maybe this is why god invented Thin Lizzy?)

We'd already cycled through the first part of the party. Bruce had dutifully attended, chatting with Lisa and Isabel and Ruthie until it was time for the babysitter to go home. Now he was home in bed while I stayed. Why, I'm not sure. Part of me wanted to be home in bed as well. Another part of me believed that a couple of drinks was a question, and the only possible answer was: more drinks. This part was Irish.

So: more drinks. Everyone at this party had a big mouth. There was yelling, and the room had that hard edge that develops when there's real drinking going on, the kind of drinking we used to do before we became parents. A few people clustered over the hot metal knot of a pot pipe. People tried to dance to Thin Lizzy. People threw food at each other. It was, in fact, the kind of party I remembered from my childhood. My parents had wild parties because they were so young. People sang and yelled and kissed against the fridge. Adult life was not so cushiony, so blameless then. There was still the ability to sin, and the capacity for regret.

I didn't know a lot of the people at the party; they were friends of Lisa and Steve's from their kids' school, or friends of friends. Our old friends were dotted among the crowd like raisins in oatmeal, but the rest of the crowd seemed like a great mush of humanity.

A big blond-haired man named Charlie, who was ostentatiously of Scottish extraction, sat down next to me and leaned in close. "What are you reading these days?" I often saw him at parties and he always, always, always asked me this. He obviously had me pegged as the Smart One, like a bespectacled character in a teen girl's novel waiting to be seduced gently from her shell. It made me want to smack him, so I said, obnoxiously and entirely untruthfully, "Um, actually I'm rereading Borges these days." Actually, I was not rereading Borges. Actually, I was burning my way through the entire Nancy Mitford oeuvre. Again.

"Oh, I love *Labyrinths*," said Charlie. "One of my favorites."

Fuck.

"Does Janie read much?" I asked.

"Janie reads magazines." He leaned in a little closer.

"Which ones?"

"What?" All of a sudden we were in the middle of the scorching guitar solo that came halfway through "Jailbreak." I lost the conversational thread while I listened to the way it chunked time into gorgeous little blocks.

"What were we talking about? Oh, which magazines does she read? Does she read *O*? Does she read *Real Simple*?" I asked.

"Shut up," he said. He thought I was mocking Janie, but really I just loved magazines. I didn't care which ones she read. He probably thought that as the Party Egghead, I only read *The New Yorker* and such. He probably didn't know how much of my life was spent thinking about how much better I would be than the usual lame-ass "Fashion Police" lineup.

"Jeez," I said unhappily. "I was just making conversation."

"You don't seem very happy to see me," he said. "You never seem very happy to see me."

I looked at him and the mood of the party caught me for a moment. I leaned toward Charlie and licked the side of his face. His skin felt stubbly under my tongue and smelled like grapefruit. "There," I said. "I'm happy to see you. Now run along."

And amazingly he did. Steve laughed but didn't seem disturbed by the scene. In our pre-children days we were much given to bad behavior at parties.

"Hey!" I said. "At least I got him to go away."

Steve lay there and looked at me balefully. I kicked him, 'cause why not?

"Go home to Mr. B," he said, which was how he always referred to Bruce.

"Bleh. I don't want to go home. And I don't want to go out. I don't know what I want to do."

"Did you read *Atonement*? By Ian McEwan? There's that awesome line where the girl says she doesn't want to be inside and she doesn't want to be outside and she wishes there was somewhere else to go." Steve was given to unearthing these kinds of nuggets.

"How perfect," I said. Steve moved the needle back to the beginning of the song—he was a vinyl kind of person—and we settled in companionably to listen again. Everyone else was avoiding us. After a while he gazed down at his outfit: butter-yellow T-shirt and light green shorts.

"I came as a website," he said. We cracked up.

"No, no, you came as Martha Stewart's towels."

Ruthie came over to check on us. She, too, kicked Steve as she passed him, collapsed next to me, and took the paper dolls away. "Let me do that awhile," she said. "These people exhaust me. What's up with *that* one?" She pointed at a totally harmless-looking woman with curly red hair and a flowered dress.

"What's wrong with her?" I asked.

"She keeps asking me how long I'm going to breast-feed my kid.

I've never even met her before!" Ruthie had given birth to a second son and was not planning on weaning him any time soon. She was souvenir nursing.

"Lisa must've told her."

"Whatever."

Steve went over to change the record and Ruthie leaned into me and whispered, "Go look in the kitchen. And come right back."

I went in the kitchen. Lisa was sitting on a chair laughing and pulling her shirt up to show her beautiful breasts, which were housed in some kind of structure built of lavender lace. This had been a thing of hers back in the olden days before children, kind of a party trick. Why was she doing it now? What did it mean? Was it some kind of regression to an earlier self, as my face-licking had been? I had to say, this seemed more extreme.

People were not wondering these things. People were looking, and there was plenty to see. I looked. It was an astonishing body, long-limbed and made sinewy by her yoga addiction. The arms alone were worth a look, and the breasts were clearly crowd-pleasers, but her face was the thing.

Her face was laughing but curiously closed. She was intent on this action, her eyes almost squeezed shut—with joy? Certainly she was transported, and as with all people who are transported, we could not follow her. She was neither in the house nor out of the house. She was somewhere else. Jesus, she really did have a nice rack.

I stood and watched for a while. Everyone was laughing, but it wasn't really funny. It wasn't sad, either. It was more . . . large. It seemed like a large adieu to all this. All this was clearly about to change, if you were going to go around pulling up your shirt.

I went back to the living room, where Ruthie was fiddling with the paper dolls and Steve was gazing at the stereo, which had softened into some permutation of the Palace Brothers, which always makes everyone immediately want to smoke heroin. I knew where this was headed, musically if in no other way. Soon we would be on to Cat Power, and then off to the bathtub to slit our wrists. I bugged my eyes out at Ruthie: What the hell is going on? She bugged hers back at me and held up her hands.

We met in the bathroom. "Well?" I asked, peeing.

"Well, nothing. It's historically accurate, at least. I mean it's not like we've never seen it before. Not like we've never seen them before!"

"Do you think we ought to tell Steve?"

Ruthie looked at me like I was crazy. "Ah, no."

"It seems weird to just leave him sitting in the living room, not knowing what's going on."

"You think that's what seems weird about this situation?"

I washed my hands and we went back into the kitchen, where all shirts were approximately where they belonged.

I said to Lisa, "Aw, man, I gotta get up with the kids tomorrow while Bruce works."

Ruthie said, "I gotta go, too. I'll walk you out."

"Hags!" said Lisa. "Loser hags."

Only the truth, we shrugged. Not only had we lost our energy and our looks and our sex drives, we'd lost our curiosity. We were, in fact, anti-curious. We spurred each other out the door. We truly didn't want to know what was going to happen next.

And a good thing, too.

Imagine this:

You've had a baby crawling up your body for, oh, the last ten years. First one, then another, then another. You gave these babies every bit of yourself. You nursed them with your perfect breasts and slept with them every night and quit your job. You made them beautiful meals and when they were old enough taught them to love salad and sushi and avgolemono.

There's a line from the Lou Reed song "Street Hassle": "So the first thing that they see / That allows them the right to be / Why they follow it, you know, it's called bad luck."

OK, so it's true that Lou Reed wrote that line for an absolutely filthy, completely depressing song about junkies and whores. But let's push it to include housewives. Lisa followed the first thing that gave her the right to be: wifedom, motherhood. And now she wanted out.

When the first thing no longer works, you have to get away from it somehow. You need something to set you free. And everyone knows that in order to leave a marriage, in order to change a family, you need a disaster.

Not the kind of disaster that just falls from nowhere onto your head, like a cartoon Acme anvil. Not a huge disaster, maybe more of a mini-disaster. The kind of disaster you have to build with your own hands. (Like you have to do everything else in this goddamn family.) You have to blow up the palace where you're the queen.

Lisa set about methodically creating her own disaster.

A few days after the party, Lisa called to tell me that she had made out with Charlie. It had come out of nowhere, she said. No one was more surprised than she was.

Bruce began to pack to go to Belize. I went out to the grocery store and bought supplies. Junior Mints for when I was feeling sad. A steak for every night he would be gone. A few bottles of wine with those lovely screw tops. I didn't have the energy to fuck around with a corkscrew.

Bruce left, as always, on a 5:30 a.m. flight. He kissed me and was gone, shutting the door quietly. But it was too late. I was awake. I lay there fretting about the stubborn mildew that liked to grow on the south wall of our bedroom.

While Bruce was gone, my mom came over one afternoon to hang out with the kids. "Go on, honey," she said. "Get some work done. Or take a break."

Feeling like I was on the lam, I walked up to the corner market, a sort of glorified convenience store, to buy more Junior Mints and steak and screw-top wine. There I ran into one of the co-op moms who lived in the neighborhood. She was standing in front of the meager cheese aisle looking unhappy.

"What's up?" I asked her.

"I have to take a cheese platter to a potluck and I'm trying to find some local cheese and they just don't have any and I don't have time to stop anywhere else!" She looked near tears.

"That cheddar is organic, at least," I gently pointed out.

"I know, but I'm trying to buy everything locally."

This was right at the beginning of the local-food movement, and her statement still had some power to astonish. I looked at her and thought: This is it. This is exactly what our life has become. We are all trying to buy local food in a convenience store, and failing, and berating ourselves for it. I felt a moment of compassion, and then the guilt set in. Why was I not buying local food? What was wrong with me? Should I petition Ken's Market to carry local cheese?

I was depressed when I got home, but then Lucy climbed on the couch next to me and said, "Come on, Mommy, let me show you the page of the Wooden Soldier catalogue that really makes my spirit soar."

Lisa appeared to be collecting men. I don't know where she was finding them. On the Internet? At yoga class? Underneath an apple tree, like fallen fruit?

She was over at my house all the time, with various kids in tow, talking, talking, talking. But I could never get any information about these men. She wouldn't tell me where they came from, or what she did with them. She got a wicked look in her eye when I asked about them, and then she delicately changed the subject.

What she wanted to talk about was this: What was going to happen next. Where she would live. How Steve was driving her crazy with his apathy.

She was doing something big and important and un-fun: beginning the process of making a new life. She needed the fun, the men, to get her there. The men were the unforgivable act she needed to commit in order to get herself out of that house.

In this way, whatever she was doing with the men (kissing? having sex? dating?) was the most innocent part of the whole situation. It was the part I felt comfortable thinking about and wanted to talk about. I could manage boy talk. I didn't want to think about the other stuff. I didn't want to think about a mother leaving her husband and breaking up her family.

Were the kids somehow clocking what was going on with me and Bruce? We woke up one December morning to the kind of rain that makes giant drops. Everyone overslept. Lucy couldn't find her library book, and bitter tears stood in her eyes as she stormed around the house. It was one of Willie's days to go to preschool, and he sat in an armchair, repeating, "I won't go to school, I won't go to school." He would go to school, of course, and what's more, he would have a fabulous day, but all the same it was demoralizing to listen to.

Bruce yelled at both kids. I yelled at him for yelling at the kids. And then for good measure I yelled at the kids, too. Willie disappeared and I found him on the back porch.

He looked at me. "No time for laughter," he said. (Though he pronounced it "wafter.")

I picked him up and he put his arms around my neck. I swear, every time that kid touched me, he turned me into a happy ape, fervently mammalian. I marched around the house with him in my arms, and Lucy sang the overture to *Seussical: The Musical* while we marched. The three of us were a team, and Bruce went off to work by himself in the rain. I was not sorry to see him go.

Lisa seemed to have narrowed it down to one guy: a person called Carl. But I still got the impression that the identity of the chosen guy didn't really matter. Poor Carl. He didn't know that he was actually a bomb, chosen for his ability to blow things up.

A friend who lived in New York—like me, nearly forty—called to tell me that he was finally getting married.

After I grilled him about the woman in question, we fell to discussing marriage. The day before my wedding, almost ten years before, I had told this same friend that I was getting married for "the sex and the conversation. D'you think that's OK?" And he had burst out laughing. "Yes," he had said, "I think that's the point."

"It's just a matter of values," I said now, on the phone to my friend. "A good marriage has to have shared values."

"Shared values?" he asked.

"Yes," I said. "Similar ideas about how to take care of children, where to live, how to spend money, what's right and what's wrong."

"What's right and what's wrong?" he asked.

"Exactly."

Jesus Christ, he didn't say. That is the most pathetic idea of marriage I've ever heard. What the hell happened to you? But I could hear him thinking it.

Here's what he did say: "What about fun?"

Bruce was home for a bit, and we took our computers downtown to a pretentious doughnut shop that had opened recently. We walked in the door, and there was Lisa. She was wearing high boots and a skirt and a sweater. She was groomed and neat and softly upholstered in her pretty knits. I had not seen her out of sweatpants for half a decade and here she was looking like a French movie star.

She was sitting at a little table, her rangy, slender body slung over a tiny chair. Across from her sat a man of profound ordinariness. His proportions seemed to match those of the table and chair, rather than those of Lisa. He looked like a man who has just discovered that life is going to hold a lot more doughnuts and sex than he had previously anticipated.

"Hey, guys," said Lisa, unruffled.

"Hey," we said.

She waved a large hand across the table. "This is Carl," she said.

I know, I thought. "Nice to see you," I said. "I'm Claire, and this is Bruce."

Carl looked like he wanted us to go away. Bruce looked ready to bolt. I felt glum and had a smile on my face that I was sure looked utterly demented. Lisa alone appeared serene.

"What doughnut did you have?" I asked. Which was a disingenuous question, as I well knew that Lisa no longer ate.

"We shared one of those fluffy ones, with the coconut on top."

"Delicious," said Carl.

"Oh, well, I think I'll go for chocolate," I said. "We better get to work. Deadlines," I ended lamely.

Bruce and I bought our doughnuts and espresso (it was that kind of doughnut place) and found a table in the upstairs mezzanine.

"That's him," I hissed.

"Gee, you think?" said Bruce. "Awkward!"

"Lisa didn't seem to find it awkward," I said. "What am I supposed to do? Not tell Steve? It's just incredibly inconsiderate."

"Well, to be fair, she didn't know we were going to be here."

"She knows I come here to work! She knows it!"

For some reason, I was taking this sighting of Lisa and Carl very personally.

"At least they're not at the, like, Adultery Motel," said Bruce.

"That is a comfort," I said unhappily, and got to work.

My job had in fact taken a turn for the weird. In my role as critic, I found myself returning time and again to the year 1973. In a review of Erica Jong's new book, I wrote extensively about *Fear of Flying*. I wrote about what I perceived as misogyny in the 1960s and '70s work of Shel Silverstein. I wrote about poets from 1973, and I dreamed up and sold stories about the music of 1973. All not quite consciously. Mysteriously, editors began to pursue me to write about this era. Who even publishes writing about 1973? What a strange thing to assign a writer to write about! And yet it was as though they could smell it on me, those brilliant editors; they kept assigning these odd little 1973 stories. Or maybe, more likely, I kept finding odd little 1973 stories buried in my assignments. Maybe I turned every story into an odd little 1973 story.

It was entirely lost on me that 1973 was the year my folks split up.

I never realized what I was doing. I thought I had a new beat. I thought the 1970s interested me because the clothes were better.

This, I am told, is why people go to analysts and therapists. Because without psychoanalysis, without its exposure of the wound, we just circle back to it over and over, without even knowing that we are acting obsessively. We can't leave it alone. I didn't go to an analyst. Instead, I wrote little essays about the wound. I opined on the wound. I discussed the wound's aesthetic merits.

It was a sunny September afternoon. I was out mulching the garden when Steve appeared in my yard. "My wife has been making out with some guy named Carl."

I sat back on my heels and brushed dark brown dirt from my gloved hands. "Feh. I know. I guess I should've told you."

"That's OK," he said magnanimously, as if we were at a restaurant and he was picking up the bill. "I guess I know everything now, but I'm not sure."

"Me, neither. I really don't know any more than that." Lisa called me almost every day and talked to me nonstop, but the sum of human knowledge gained from these conversations amounted to what Steve had just said: Lisa had been making out with some guy named Carl.

I spaded up a couple of buttercups, their roots grabbing at the soil. "Are you OK?" I asked.

Steve smiled his usual half smile, which always looked grudging and right now looked sort of diabolical. "I'd like to kill him. I mean it. I would really like to kick that guy's ass." He spoke lingeringly, as if savoring the idea.

"What about her?" I asked.

"What do you mean?" he asked.

"Do you want to kick her ass? Or what? Do you want to break up with her?"

"What am I gonna do? She's the mother of my children." This sounded like a line to me, but I did him the courtesy of not saying so.

Lisa stopped calling. The plot was moving too fast; no time for updates. Her yoga teacher had a basement apartment in his house that happened to be empty. Lisa took a suitcase and moved there. She would commute home during the day to take care of the children. It was just for a while.

I sat in my office, typing away at my millions of stories concerning 1973. The year it all went pear-shaped. Lisa had gone. She was off to find her fortunes or her heart or her self, just as my mother, all the mothers, had done in that fateful year.

What was she doing right now? Did she have a mattress on the floor? Somehow that seemed like the right way to sleep when you had run away from home. Was she sitting up drinking tea or wine with her yoga teacher, and laughing and talking? Was she making out with some guy named Carl? Was she doing whatever she pleased, whatever she wanted?

Was yoga part of what had made her go? Was it simply that yoga had given her a new body? More confidence? Merely a new set of people? Was it that yoga was a new place to go, and she desperately needed a destination? You could only go out for so long before you had to end up somewhere in particular.

As I revised my latest 1973 story, I drank whiskey and cried a little. As one does. What I felt, in my heart of hearts, was this: jealousy.

Not just toward Lisa but toward my mother, toward all the mothers who shrugged off the mantle of the expected. It wasn't that I wanted to leave my kids; that was something that would never happen. But I was sick of all the virtue. My wicked days seemed far away, almost mythical. Those days seemed like they might've belonged to someone else altogether.

18. CHILD'S POSE 5

1983

Adolescence was a deep well I fell into. Sometimes falling was fun, dizzying, glamorous, exciting, fast. Sometimes it was plain scary. Life was fraught. I bristled against the strictures of my school, my house, my age. Even so, once my brother left for college, weeknights had a cozy, triumvirate closeness. I was somehow bumped into a more major, adult role in the household. My mom, Larry, and I ate dinner in front of the TV and chatted lazily about nothing in particular. And I do mean nothing; our conversation was blacked out with taboo areas, like a censored wartime letter. Here are some of the things we didn't talk about: My father. My grades. My drugs. My sex life.

I don't know why we didn't talk about these things. Maybe pretending everything was OK had become a habit.

We were addicted to *Remington Steele*. We pretended to watch ironically, but we got caught up in the plots and developed a strange attachment to Pierce Brosnan. On this particular spring evening, we half watched the show as we chatted idly about John, the latest in my string of boyfriends (known collectively by Larry as "The Weasels"). We were snickering about the way John ground the gears in his little Honda. The three of us drove aging Volvos and expertly gentled their ornery transmissions. We sneered a little at John—I was always ready to sell out my boyfriends if it meant getting a laugh out of Mom and Larry—and I felt a current of belonging.

All of a sudden, with atypical curiosity, my mother asked, "How many boys have you kissed?" The emphasis was on the "have," and I think it was the inflection that really got to me. I felt a rush of heat and a sudden need to move. I got up from my chair, cheeks brilliant, and walked over to the coat closet, thinking obscurely, "This is the place for me." Our conversation was normally corralled by a groovy politesse, a kind of too-mellow-to-argue languor. It was an impenetrable wall of cool, and it didn't admit emotions like the one I was experiencing now: pure rage.

I stood inside the closet doorway, turned around, and said to the back of my mother's burnished golden head, "That's none of your business." Now the words came out, irretrievable and hurtling, like young soldiers rushing to certain glorious death: "That's like, that's like, that's like me asking you how many men you've fucked."

The room went hot and bright. The lamplight spangled. There was a pounding in my ears like a bloody ocean. There was silence. A strange feeling passed through me. It was as alien and as real as the fury that preceded it. The feeling was happiness. I was happy.

The back of a person's head can be surprisingly expressive, but my mother's was as mute as a piece of granite. There was something about its immobility that seemed hilarious to me. Slowly she turned to look at me, her blue eyes watering with tears. Somehow that struck me as funny, too. I suppressed a giggle. Larry—who had never disciplined me in my entire life—barked out perhaps the only parenting cliché of his career as a kind of stepdad. "Apologize to your mother," he said, and looked silly saying it. The role of repressive father figure didn't suit his bearded, long-haired, judiciously laid-back demeanor. It didn't help that he was lying on the couch.

So I apologized to my mother, barely able to stifle a smile. If her inflection of a single word had sent me around the bend, my smirk enraged her. We were closely tuned to one another's signals in that house; we might as well have been communicating by antennae. "You can go to your room right now. I don't want to see you," said my mom. I opened my mouth, raised my eyebrows, and couldn't think of a thing to say. With a shrug, I left.

It was a night of anomalies. Larry's anger was new. My obnoxious smirking was new, too. Usually I was compliant and bland at home, saving my rebellions for elsewhere. My friends and I liked the magic mushrooms that grew in the shady park near our school, and that's how my sadness and rebellion grew, too: away from the light, hard to find, but tenacious. Out of the house, I ate drugs and drank a lot and let boys touch me. I rode in strangers' vans and bought acid in flop-houses on First Avenue. I courted trouble and called it something else: fun. At home, though, I was no trouble at all. I skated around my mother in graceful loops, managing her, charming her, soothing her. The important thing was to prevent her from getting mad at me. And if I did inadvertently piss her off, my reaction was a dismayed nausea; I had never before found her anger funny.

Upstairs, I sank into the old green brocade armchair in my room. I kept it right next to my casement window, where I could look into the huge pines. Usually I couldn't bear silence or idleness. Alone in my room, I would read, or listen to records, or write in my notebook. Tonight I wanted just to sit there and feel this ill-gotten happiness. The tips of the tree branches brushed my window in a companionable kind of way. I looked at the place near the top of the tree where the boughs crisscrossed to form a perfect face. The face was always there, unchanging. Shouldn't it grow into another shape? The tree was alive, after all, and growing. Shouldn't the face become something else?

I thought about the strangeness of my mother's impertinent question. She tended not to ask questions about my boyfriends since, when I was fifteen, I informed her that I had begun having sex. I had mistakenly taken her at her own valuation: She was a freethinker, open and supportive, a woman of the world, unbound by society's conventions.

Not so much, it turned out. When I told her my news, a pained look had crossed her face, as though I'd stepped on her foot. "Are you using birth control?" she asked, practically choking out every word. "Yes," I said, eager to please. She rushed from the room, looking like she was going to vomit. I never broached the topic again.

The sky dimmed and the neighboring housetops softened into gorgeous anonymity. In the half dark, they could've been housetops anywhere. I had a sudden fantasy of flying over them, like a rainbow-faced woman in a Chagall painting. It was more than a fantasy; it was a pervasive feeling of possibility.

A wash of brilliant springtime lavender infused the sky, and then it was dark. With the dying light my weird ecstasy seemed to fade. I felt a tug from below, as if my mother had hold of a string that ran up through the floor and fastened to my navel. Tug, tug, she pulled. I rose from my chair, resignedly went downstairs, and crept up behind my mother's head. I had stood in this exact spot ten years before when she and my father had just split. We were watching Helen Reddy on TV. Helen was singing "You and Me Against the World" and I wrapped my kid arms around my mom's neck and said, "This song is about you and me, Mom." Even then, I was flattering her. I was canny. My fate was tied to hers, and I had a sense that I'd better not queer the deal. I missed my father with a not-quite pain that was blunt and unnamable. I knew I mustn't mention him. My job, I knew without ever thinking about it, was to be happy. With her. With her decision to live in this house with this man. So I was determinedly happy.

Now, again, I wrapped my arms around her neck, and whispered, "I'm sorry." She turned accusing eyes to me. "Are you really?" I was sorry. I was sorry I had to apologize to her. "Yes," I said, soothing her. She had once told me how, at a hotel where she had stayed on the Riviera, every morning a team of men raked the beach until it was smooth. She loved that. "I'm so sorry," I said. "I don't know. It just popped out." I was wily enough to turn the thing back on her: "I really did feel that you violated my privacy. But I know that wasn't the way to handle it."

"Well," she said, looking down at her lap like Mary in the Pietà we'd been studying in art history. Except that instead of the dying Jesus, there were only her clasped hands. "Just don't ever, ever speak to me that way again." She didn't look at me. Obviously we weren't going to discuss the matter any further. I realized with a start that I really did want to know how many men she had fucked. Oh, well. While her gaze was turned, I took my seat in the chair by the TV.

We subsided into our evening. *Remington Steele* wasn't over yet. Everything was back to normal: Mom, incurious. Larry, benign. And me, with a glimmer of white-hot rage seared somewhere on me, like when you stare at the sun and afterward a white crescent marks your vision.

19. FOOT BEHIND THE HEAD POSE

I dropped through chaturanga. The studio was cast with a cool gray light from high windows. Dark was coming on quickly. I was going to yoga three and four and five times a week, hiding out from my family. Bruce had tried Fran's class briefly but got bored with it. That was fine with me. Yoga was something I wanted to have all to myself. I didn't even like going to class with a friend.

Darkness came and the floor of the studio was pooled with discrete circles of yellow from the overhead lights. We all had that trancelike look of concentration. We were trying to obliterate our minds, obliterate our pasts, obliterate our futures. At least I was. I didn't understand that there might be another way—that letting go might be a good thing. That the desire to obliterate the past and the future was not the same thing as simply letting the present moment occur. Even in my wish to forget, to obliterate, to block out, I was still struggling to control things I couldn't control.

My mind was seeking things to rest upon. Forward and back it moved. Earlier in the day I'd forgotten to pick up a friend's kid from

school and the teacher had called me, irate. Meanwhile, I was thinking ahead: Would I make it through chaturanga this time? Should I
hop back to plank or step gently? What if she wanted us to segue into
scorpion?

I wanted all these thoughts to disappear. I moved with more determination.

"Loosen jaw," said Mindy.

Another beat and then: "Smooth brow."

Another beat and: "Release shoulders."

At the end of the next vinyasa, she asked us to come to a sitting
position.

"This class could use some hip release," she said. "I'm seeing a lot
of congestion."

We went through a bunch of hippy stuff: pigeon, marichi's twist,
squatting, frog. Then we moved into foot behind the head pose, the
most hilariously stereotypical of all yoga poses. As such, it's a fun pose.
Who doesn't love the idea of putting their foot behind their head?

First we cradled our right leg in our arms, rocking it back and
forth and enjoying the pleasantly unfamiliar bicep-y feeling—biceps
don't see a lot of action in yoga. Then we began to navigate our right
heels upward until we could lean our heads forward and, as one, slip
our right feet behind our heads.

It was not where we had thought we would end up when we went
to vinyasa class on this night. We peeked around gigglingly. We
looked very funny.

Our teacher smiled at us but she did not break character, if indeed
a character it was. "Breathe into sensation," she said, and we inhaled
and exhaled. We had forgotten. It was true: When we breathed, we
felt more. When you are literally tying yourself in a knot, this is all
you can do: Breathe into sensation. Stop and take in air and find out
what you're really feeling.

After a while, it stopped being so funny and seemed like it might
be time to stop. Our teacher spoke in a hypnotic voice.

"You might be feeling discomfort now. If it is time to stop, it is
time to stop. But if you can, stay with it. What is discomfort? What

does it feel like? Is it really pain, or are you just in an unfamiliar situation? That's an OK place to be. Soften shoulders."

The seat of little ease. This is what my practice had been missing. Stillness. I was in it now, and it was scary. I was incredibly uncomfortable, and there was nothing I could do about it. I could not move more quickly or focus on the next transition. There was no task to complete, no clock to watch, no child to cradle, no dinner to make, no mother to call, no sad husband to cheer up, no friend to comfort, no father to lend an ear to, no school to clean, no car to fill with gas, no deadline to meet, no editor to appease. There was nothing I could do to solve this. All I could do was be with it. There was just this discomfort.

For years, yoga had been the one place where I paid attention to how I was feeling. I did the poses and actually, right there in that moment, felt them. When I did pigeon, I could feel my right hip, feel it telling me something: to start carrying my kids on my left hip once in a while. The poses gave me real information. My mind tried to slip away into oughts and shoulds, but the poses pulled it back, made it stay right there in the moment. Not always, but often enough.

Then I started vinyasa. Because the cool girls were doing it. Because there was chanting. Because I felt like I always needed to be advancing in my yoga, moving forward, improving. And in devoting myself to vinyasa, I gave up the very thing that made yoga work for me: the staying still, the attunement to what I might actually be feeling. Fran had tried to teach me these things, but in my quest to be "better" at yoga, I had left Fran behind.

I tried to breathe. I felt a radiating sensation in my right hip. I felt something else, and I recognized it, as if it were a ship on the horizon: relief. I was finally feeling my own discomfort, my own lack of ease in the world. Discomfort, anxiety, dread—they had been lurking there all along, and I had been avoiding them, rushing away from them, moving quickly so they couldn't make themselves known.

I sat there with my foot behind my head, like a moron. Who puts their foot behind their head?

I sat there and, sitting, realized: I was very, very unhappy. We were unhappy, Bruce and I. In fact, Bruce was severely depressed and our household, while creative, charming, and often funny, was underlined by his black mood. This was something I had not allowed myself to face, had not wanted to face. If I faced it: What? What next? I knew how to be cheerful, and make the best of things, and turn resolutely from reality. (Bruce had colluded with me in this.) Here's what I didn't know how to do: I didn't know how to deal with having the tallest, saddest husband in the world. I was utterly ill-equipped to deal with that. I didn't want anyone to know it was occurring. I didn't want to know it was occurring.

"Release foot."

I released foot. I shook out my leg and massaged it a bit. Time to do the other side. What ghastly news would it have for me?

I had just finished reading to the children. I sat in the living room with my book; Bruce sat watching a movie in the TV room, which we had begun to call the TV room. Was this some kind of white flag of surrender? Or a refreshing dose of realism? The porch light was on, and it was illuminating the front yard. Through the yellow light, fat flakes of snow began to fall. Snow in Seattle was as rare as emeralds. Seattle was a city wrapped in a tight, choking net of rain. The rain snarled the traffic and dampened moods. Snow was a benediction, a floating, covering cloak that was indiscriminate, unconditional in its attentions. Snow was generous.

Here is my secret: I did not tell the children. I went upstairs and turned out their lights and snuggled them, one after the other, into near-sleep. I did all this without telling them it was snowing.

If I had told them about the snow Willie would have come running down the stairs, his knees pumping in his striped long-john pajamas. Lucy would have followed, with her own devastatingly unique little way of running, where her rump drifted off to one side. They would have run outside in their pajamas and looked up into the night with its new filter of whiteness. Willie's eyes would have squinted with happiness, and Lucy's would have shone. And Bruce would be talking in a large voice and locating mittens. Contentment would have a shelf life. And then Bruce would be telling the kids to go in before they were ready, and then I would be anxious that he was ruining their magical moment, and we would all be getting cold anyway.

And the children would have snuggled under the blankets, their hair damp and their cheeks hard and shiny with cold.

But they didn't do any of those things because I didn't tell them about the snow. I didn't want to deal with their joy.

I continued to sit there in my armchair, with the facts all over the floor. The facts were these: I was powerfully unhappy. I was married to a depressive. I was harboring an underground, blossoming hatred of my parents; I resented their incursions into my family life, and I resented my own constant need to please them. I was distant, almost estranged, from my brother. I felt competitive with my friends and watched them carefully for clues about what I might be doing wrong. I spent my days writing criticism.

I would get up the next day and do the things I was supposed to do, with some approximation of a smile on my face. Cheerful. Meals, the clock of life, would come and go, and I would cook them and serve them, like a wife in an old story, slapping the plates on the table.

Not just any wife; not just any story. I had somehow contrived to re-create my mother's life before she left my father. In response to my 1970s mom, I had become a 1950s housewife. I was obsessed with what my family ate. I was fraught about bedtimes. I did everything I could to make sure nothing, nothing disrupted my husband's work schedule. I had a nice little job that didn't take me away from home. A book reviewer! I might as well have been taking in piecework from the gentry.

I was trapped in a misery of expectations, as if in a blizzard. I was afraid that if I stopped, if I said "Something is wrong here," my family would fall apart. After all, that is what families do. And I couldn't even kick over the traces like my mother had, and Lisa. I didn't want to. I wanted to stay married and stay home and stay a mother, no matter what. I wasn't, wasn't, wasn't going to do to my children what my parents had done to me.

My parents had made mistakes. They had disrupted our family and pretended that disruption had not occurred. This is exactly the kind of behavior that makes kids mad. Kids hate having their order upset, and they hate being lied to. My response, as a child, was to be adaptable and cheerful. As I grew older I had surges of anger about what had happened. I had a kind of flailing unpredictable rage that bubbled up occasionally and then disappeared.

But now . . . my parents were no longer doing anything to me at all. I was doing something to myself. My parents had, long ago in the past, made decisions that had created an unconventional but in many ways contented childhood. Now, with my rigidity and desperation for control, I was swinging the other way, creating an environment that was entirely conventional. Was I creating discontent as well?

I had just one idea—the idea of how things ought to be. A four-person family. An uninterrupted story. A couple of intact children. Happiness and, yes, cheerfulness all day long. No one leaves. No one cries. No bearded men show up. Fathers don't move to houseboats. Everyone sticks together and follows the rules. Even yoga had been reduced to a series of rules. These rules, this idea that things should be a certain way, were sucking the day-to-day joy out of life. My idea of how things ought to be was eating up our family. I was so worried about the children missing their sleep that I couldn't wake them to see the snow.

20. CROW, AGAIN

Bruce was invited to an environmental-journalism conference being held in Austin; he was nominated for an award and they told him it would be a good idea if he showed up, which was a sweetly cagey way of saying he had won.

I came along. I was all for free vacation, and for Austin.

We made our way from air-conditioned airport to air-conditioned shuttle to air-conditioned hotel, but the minute we stepped outside, the heat pressed down on us, a sweaty hand. We stumbled a few blocks, our bodies in an overwhelm of sensation. All thought was pressed from our heads. It felt great.

Every shop we passed seemed to be selling KEEP AUSTIN WEIRD T-shirts, which cracked me up, since Lucy's best friend was named Austin and was, in fact, delightfully weird.

Finally we cried uncle and went to Stubb's, which was air-conditioned, and ate barbecue and drank sweet tea. The heat had reduced us, like a sauce, to our barest components: hunger and thirst and sweat.

It was a perfect day: barbecue; a keynote speech by Molly Ivins, who just couldn't say enough mean things about George W. Bush; and finally, an awards ceremony where Bruce won for a thankless piece he had slaved over about Bush's clean air act.

The room was a typically corporate conference room; a big hotel meeting room with a generic, un-festive chandelier hanging overhead. It was the kind of environment where we rarely ventured, the province of people who used whiteboards and ran meetings. Or did people even use whiteboards anymore? Was it all PowerPoint? That just showed how little we knew of such environs.

Bruce stood at the lectern, hunched over the microphone in his rumpled blazer. He gave an acceptance speech as generically elegant as the chandelier.

Then, as he was winding up, he gazed out from under his eyebrows and said, "I have worked with three great editors over the last years." He named two of his editors—famous, brilliant men. "And my wife, who is the greatest editor I could ask for. My stories are better because of her."

It was a tiny moment, under the glittering light. But I found myself crying. It wasn't that I was so thrilled about being called a great editor. I could definitely think of prettier compliments. This was not the romantic moment I had sometimes asked him for. Nor was it the assurance of eternal security that I craved. It was, instead, an acknowledgment of the real thing that we had built together, in the middle of all my worry and all Bruce's depression. Invisibly, silently, we had been making a marriage where we helped each other. Our marriage didn't look the way I wanted it to look, but that didn't mean it had no value. We had been growing something without realizing it.

You can't see bread rise, but it rises. If you could watch a lump of dough in the time-lapse photography so prevalent in the schoolroom filmstrips of my youth, you would see it rise. If you took time-lapse photos of a marriage, what would you see? Mutual diminishment? One partner slowly devouring the other? A mere string of fights and fucks, signifying nothing? Or would you see something strong, growing slowly?

After the ceremony, we lingered in the hall, chatting with fellow environmental journalists—lots of beards, lots of denim—when a man with bright blue eyes appeared at Bruce's side.

"You won my award," he said. Somehow his beard and denim looked more handsome and cheerful than everyone else's beard and denim. "I'm the runner-up. How about you buy me a beer?"

Bruce laughed and the man, whose name turned out to be Dan, took us off to a bar with a lot of other bearded, denim-clad people. (And that was just the women!) For the next couple of days, wherever we went, there was Dan. It wasn't that he was a pest; it was that he knew how to make friends. He made things simple. He literally said, "I'd like to be friends with you guys." And it was so. To a couple of grouchy eggheads like me and Bruce, it seemed revolutionary.

Dan was at the conference with his buddy Wendy, who helped run an environmental-journalism fellowship in Boulder. The place was lousy with these Boulder people, who really liked to drink beer. Even when they weren't drinking beer, they kept saying the same thing over and over. Come, they said to Bruce. We'll give you a fellowship. You'll get a faculty salary and all you have to do is take classes. Whatever classes you want. Whatever classes will make you a better environmental journalist. How Bruce would end up interpreting this to mean that he ought to take Beginning Hockey is a story for another time.

At the airport, we were quiet. It was lunchtime and we were desperately hung over. My eyes moved drily around in their sockets. The Texas light was high and hard and bright through the big airport windows. We ate barbecue sandwiches and drank our last Shiner Bocks. I bought a stack of magazines and we loaded silently onto the plane. I read *People*, which is what decent people read on airplanes, and Bruce wrote his book, and after a while I leaned my head back against the seat and looked at him with his fucking tap-tap-tapping.

"I was thinking . . ." I said, and trailed off. If this was a different kind of story, this sentence would've ended "that we should have another baby." But that is not how the sentence ended.

Bruce in fact finished the sentence for me: "That I should apply for that Boulder fellowship?"

Bruce applied for the fellowship, and we waited.

Bruce and I felt that people should live where they were from. Our friends felt the same way. We were fiercely proud natives. As the city filled up with more and more newcomers, there was a moral force to our position. We surveyed the scene from the ramparts, considering how best to protect our redoubt: We were here first! Those technology guys with their Ducatis at Caffe Ladro; those wealthy newcomer families filling up all the spots in the summer day camps—they were the enemy and must be kept at bay.

But things weren't working where we were. Our hand had become a losing hand. Seattle was so expensive, and we had no real need to be there. We were spending a lot of money to live in a city that did not employ us. Why were we here, again?

This idea of Boulder set us free a bit. We could leave. We had never thought of it.

Leaving. I thought about the mothers I knew who had left, and whom I had judged.

I thought about Lisa driving across town, her van heaped with clothes and toiletries and yoga mat.

I thought of my mother, driving onto the Bainbridge Island ferry, over the bumping metal ramp from dock to boat, leaving behind her solid house in Laurelhurst and her matron's existence and her handsome husband for a beach shack and a twentysomething boyfriend. Her car was loaded with children, too: me and my brother. Were we like an anchor, or were we part of the thrill?

I had never thought of being a mother who drove away. I had thought I would stay here and make eternal birthday cakes.

I remembered a story my hair colorist, Miriam, had told me one day when I was getting my roots done, about her sister who had three little kids. The sister's house had a garage, but she always parked the minivan on the street, right in front of the kitchen window.

"That way she can see it there," said Miriam. "She knows she could just get into the minivan and run away from home at any minute."

"Has she ever done it?" I asked.

"No, that's the point. As long as she can see it there, she feels OK. It's the idea of it that's comforting to her."

When I thought of driving away, of trying to go somewhere new, of escaping my responsibilities, this is what I saw for myself: a van with me at the helm, filled with children and books and bits of popcorn wedged into the seat. Oh, hell, Bruce would probably come along for the ride, too. If true freedom meant pulling onto I-5 and heading south with no destination in mind and the Minutemen on the stereo and no one but myself for company, then I knew for a fact I would never achieve true freedom.

But leaving with everyone else—leaving with Bruce—this was interesting. I had turned down my chance once before, when he was writing his book about Belize. I had never considered that there might be some value in leaving. I had thought leaving was for sinners and losers and teenagers. And moms on the lam. But all of sudden, it seemed like it might be a good idea. For us, for virtuous grown-ups. Maybe everyone needs to retreat every once in a while, or you don't know who you are or what you've become.

Yoga had been an escape for a while; it had been the word at the end of the prepositional phrase: I was going to yoga. I was at yoga. It was my own small leaving, my world away from the world. But I had become so consumed by it, so grim about it that it had become part of the problem, another spoke on the wheel of obligation.

We realized with something like horror that it was not certain that Bruce would get one of the Boulder fellowships. And over coffee one morning we surprised ourselves with the following conversation:

"I might not get in."

"Oh, you'll get in. You're the golden boy."

"But I might not get in."

"Yikes!"

"I know. I can't stand the thought of not going."

"Well, we could just go anyway. They don't own Boulder."

"We don't even have to go to Boulder. We could go anywhere. After all, we can work from anywhere."

While Willie was at preschool the next day and Lucy was at the co-op, Bruce and I took a break from work and went out to Wide World Books on Wallingford. We pulled a pile of travel books and atlases onto the carpeted floor and began to read. And talk. Our conversation ping-ponged place-names back and forth:

"Ketchum, Idaho," I began, as if opening a round of bidding.

"Madison."

"Iowa City."

"Flagstaff."

"Portsmouth is underrated. It's actually a really cool town. I was there once in 1987."

"Where's that?"

"It's the bit of New Hampshire that's on the water."

"Eh. New England. Who needs it? What about Bozeman?"

"Why not New York?"

"Why not London? Why not Paris? Why not go entirely broke?"

"Paso Robles, California."

"Asheville, North Carolina."

"Asheville!"

It was like going on a trip just reading those names. We wanted a place that wasn't a city. And real mountains. And bakeries. And affordability. And lots of stuff to do outside. We could have what we wanted, we realized. As simple as that. It struck us as funny.

We went home with an A-list: Ketchum. Asheville. Flagstaff.

There was some preservation instinct at work in us. We needed to leave. We needed to flee our families and to flee what we had been. It was time to try to unlearn some of what we had learned. I had learned to be anxious, and to cover it with cheerfulness and effort and virtue; Bruce had learned, simply, that to be a provider is to be alone and sad.

In Sanskrit, the second sutra reads: citta vrtti nirodhah.

Citta means mind; vrtta means fluctuations or disruptions; niro-dhah means restraint.

These three words have been translated in lots of beautiful ways, but my favorite was this: "Yoga is to still the patterning of consciousness."

This translation echoed a poem by William Stafford that I had loved in high school: "A pattern that others made may prevail in the world / and following the wrong god home we may miss our star."

We had followed a pattern that others had made for us. It was hard to see how we could unlearn that pattern unless we left. It didn't mean leaving each other. It meant leaving our parents. And our home. We, too, would flee. But we could all go together.

The grandparents weren't happy. None of them. My mom wept and immediately began to research hotels in Boulder. My dad said, "Sounds like a great opportunity," and draped an arm across my back. "It's only for a year, right?"

Asheville was surging to the front of the pack when the letter came: Bruce had gotten the Colorado fellowship.

I went across town to a new studio, where they taught only vinyasa. It was very glamorous, with swirling red paint on the walls and thumping Bollywood soundtracks on the stereo. I unrolled my mat and looked around. There were many of the same pretty, taut-armed girls I'd seen at my own studio—apparently they chased vinyasa around town like surfers chasing waves.

The teacher, new to me, appeared in front of the class, adjusted some knobs on the stereo, and began calling the shots.

This vinyasa class included crow. I could do crow by now, but it was a tentative affair. Today I planted my hands, placed my knees upon my elbows, and lifted into the pose. The work that I had been doing all these years, the strengthening of my arms in chaturanga and my core in bandhas, had been building all along. I could fly, a bit.

21. MOUNTAIN

We packed and rented our house and surrendered our place at the co-op for the next year and got the kids signed up for school in Colorado.

It was finally time to go. Just as I had foreseen in my vision of my escape, we loaded our VW van with toys and books and CDs and pillows and a DVD player for the children that was clearly not going to work; such convenience items never worked for us. We had somehow unwittingly been installed with anti-normalcy devices that prevented us from being able to partake in the mainstream solutions that appeared so effortlessly functional for our friends and relations. This had started early: teething rings and pacifiers; baby-proof nail clippers; and now DVD players—it wasn't that we didn't want them to work. It was just that they didn't.

So we got in the van. Since we had rented out our house, we spent our last few nights with my mother and Larry. Early on an August morning, we hugged my parents and were hugged, and we drove away. Bruce looked like a shot arrow. It was, in fact, a very dramatic and possibly violent moment. The VW van hurtled forward with sureness if not a great deal of velocity, and our parents sent skeins of webs at us, as if they were a team of Spider-Men. Don't go, don't go, don't go.

We went. We pulled down the dark street with its massive canopy of deodar cedars. Memory has us careening around the corner as if we were in a getaway car.

Lake Washington was glittering in the morning sun as we crossed it, the 520 bridge looking as narrow as an unspooled tourniquet in all that glittering water. We made our way to I-90 and drove east, emerging after a couple of hours from the density of the coast, its forest-green shroud giving way into high open mountains. You could see between the trees! We drove over the Blue Mountains, into sunshine, and sunshine, and sunshine. It had been there all the time—imagine!

As we drove across the rooftop of southeast Washington, I thought of a conversation I had had many years ago with my grandfather, my father's father, a true Western outdoorsman. He had made his fortune in the fur industry. When he was dying, my cousins and brother and I would gather at his apartment in his retirement home high above downtown Seattle and listen to him talk. One cool spring evening, my cousins and I sat with him in his aerie, and we all fell into a silence. For some reason, we had been talking about Colorado, and now we were lost in our various thoughts. Suddenly my grandfather, not a poetic man, interrupted the silence with these words: "Ah, the strange mountains of the West!" That was what I was driving into: the strange mountains of the West.

When we stopped in Boise for dinner, the temperature was in the nineties. We played in a fountain and watched the punters head into a concert. They were going inside, which seemed foolish. We would continue hurtling forward. It seemed like the rightest activity imaginable.

In Ketchum we lay on my cousin's lawn and felt the mountains looming above us. They were brown and sere and without trees. Sagebrush was everywhere. The landscape was paramount.

In Park City we took a tram to a mountaintop. We walked the trail like it was a shelf and we were a row of books, arranged just so: mom in front, kids in between, dad in back. This way the children would not be eaten by mountain lions. Our new life was so simple! We hadn't yet learned that aspen groves are single living organisms; we hadn't yet learned to sniff the ponderosa pines for the vanilla scent, as sweetly sexy as a straight-A student at the prom. We would learn these things later. For now, we hiked and stopped at a stream and ate cookies and felt that if there was more to life than this, then we did not want more.

On the border between Utah and Wyoming we stopped at a rest area where we could stand in both states at the same time. Our bodies hurt. So far no one, not even the children, had been able to get the DVD player to work. I had busted the budget that morning at a Park City bookstore, loading up on books for the kids. We were eating poorly. We stood with one foot in Utah and one in Wyoming. The kids shrieked, "We'll be split in half!" The wind scoured the bare brown earth. Sagebrush was still everywhere. Our van had a strange squeak on the passenger side, which we had now been listening to for days on end. Our bodies had that squeak inside them; we were as gnarled and cramped as a hand that had grasped an oar for hours on end. We touched our toes, not that it would help any.

An elderly, heavyset white man approached us with a smile. "Say, didn't I just see you folks at the IHOP back in Ogden?"

"Nope, it wasn't us," I said with a returning smile.

"Well, I could've sworn it was you."

"No, we just came from Park City, which is the opposite direction."

"Are you sure?" He looked darkly at me.

I laughed. "I'm sure I'm sure."

He walked away shaking his head.

We were strangely pleased by this conversation. Things had shaken loose for us a little. We were on the road. We were too hot during the day and cooled by the desert air at night. These were new kinds of air for us; it dawned on us that we would be living in new air. We were bodies hurtling down the highway, deeper and deeper into the strange mountains of the West. Somehow it seemed possible that we might have been in Ogden that morning, eating pancakes. We might be any-where, doing anything.

September in Boulder was blue-sky beautiful and hot enough to make you cry. The heat shimmered across the prairie in almost visible waves, the way you can see the rising temperature move through olive oil in a sauté pan.

The heat began early in the morning, a good worker. I woke with my limbs on top of the counterpane, where they had not started out the night before. I rolled over and sniffed the air. The smell of death, with its famous sweetness, tendriled around the house. No corner seemed immune.

We had found a house in Chautauqua, a cluster of buildings built in the meadows at the foot of the Flatirons, the bit of the Rockies that edges Boulder. Chautauqua was created at the turn of the last century by a group of Texas schoolmarms who couldn't bear the summer heat in the Lone Star State and built this community of frame cottages clinging to the base of the mountains.

The cottage we lived in was owned by a group of grown-up sib-lings who'd been left the house by their mother. Don't ever rent a house owned by a group of grown-up siblings, unless you know for certain that they suffer from a collective disorder involving being very organized and keeping everything clean. It was an old frame house, the kind of house where wooden hallways lead to dead ends and doors lead to brick walls. Every corner, every drawer, every closet of that house was crammed with the crap belonging those sibling owners. If I thought I had messy drawers back at home, I was in for a shock. Here, for example, is an inventory of what was in the right-hand drawer of the hutch in the dining room, just one of perhaps fifty similarly crammed drawers in that house:

a chicken-shaped ceramic candleholder
KFC hand wipes
a pack of Camel Wide cigarettes

a deck of forty-three playing cards with a picture of the Eiffel
    Tower
a newspaper clipping about a 1987 wrestling match in Beaumont,
    Texas
mustard packets
lint
candle ends
gum wrappers
rubber bands
a tube of deodorant
a box of tampons
an old-looking and beautiful Meissen china platter

The house had a smell. It was rats, or mice, or death, or decay. Something bad. It was inside my nostrils all day long, the greasy, sweet smell of death. And no one else could smell it.

Every year the University of Colorado brought together five fellows, journalists from different media who covered the environment and boggled at their luck in finding this cushy setup.

Aside from Bruce, all the fellows this year were women. Jerri, an expert on water politics (big stuff in Colorado) at a Denver daily, was a tough reporter who looked like a lady who lunched, slender and delicate and gray-blond. Amy was an Alaskan photographer and editor with hair to her waist and a face like an open book. Kailani was a fierce, beautiful Hawaiian native-rights activist. And petite red-haired Leigh was a broadcast journalist who used to do something called the "Nasdaq stand-up" on some station that was just an assemblage of consonants to me: CNN or MSNBC or CNBC. The collectible dolls of environmental journalism, I called them. But not to their faces.

We were sitting on the grass outside the Chautauqua Auditorium. We were too cheap to buy tickets and go indoors. Anyway, Jerri, a local, said you could hear the music perfectly well outside; it was a Boulder thing to do, sitting on the lawn and stealing a concert while drinking wine. The temperature was finally dropping. Cool air was sluicing down the mountainside. It felt delicious against my skin. Kailani shrugged an ankle-length down coat over her thick hooded sweatshirt.

"Kailani, it's like sixty-five degrees out. What are you gonna do when it's below zero?" Jerri laughed.

"Layers," answered Kailani, through blue lips.

The fellows had interesting careers, and well-formed opinions, and an ability to hold their liquor. Here's what they didn't have: young children. Three were childless; one had older kids. They didn't want to talk about kids, they didn't want to hear about kids. Eventually they would come to love and cherish my kids (and vice versa). But they still didn't want to talk about them.

I found it strangely restful to have my motherhood stripped away as a conversational topic. We were there, lying on the grass outside the open-air auditorium, to listen to (if not see) Rosanne Cash, a singer who did not interest me very much, except maybe in her provenance. But I had a feeling that she wasn't going to spend a lot of time spinning yarns about her old man.

But the music wasn't the point. The point was to sit on the mountainside, in the cooling grass, and drink a bunch of wine. The mountain air felt alien. Jerri poured more wine. Rosanne Cash's voice emanated, disembodied, from the auditorium. I was among strangers, happily.

The next day pixieish Leigh came over to check out the smell.

She walked around the house. "I have a really good nose," she said. She had a neat little figure and eyes that missed nothing. She scared me a bit.

She sniffed the walls, the floors. "I'm not getting anything," she said as she sniffed under the sink.

"You're standing in, like, the epicenter of the smell," I said.

"Let's go out for a glass of wine tonight," she said.

That night we went to an expensive bistro, of which there were many in Boulder. On the upside, the help was friendly and, like every-one in Boulder, strappingly good-looking. The kitchen hands climbed the brick walls in the back of the dining room, as though they were bouldering their way up a climbing route.

Leigh ordered me a glass of Viognier and said gently, "You've had a big life change. When I moved to London, I broke out in a rash all over my torso. You're under a lot of stress, moving your family across the country. Your body is a mysterious thing."

My body was not a mysterious thing! "There is a smell!" I said. I resented the idea that my body was expressing something my mind didn't know. "It's not stress." But I had at least found a friend, even if she did think I was insane.

Bruce bought me a very expensive German air purifier. It was proba-bly the most expensive gift he ever gave me. I knew what it was: hush money. Here's your German air purifier. Now for god's sake shut up!

What with the mysterious smell and the strange dead-end hallways and the drawers filled with the detritus of other people's lives, my house, the house I lived in, ceased being a place of self-expression. I didn't buy it little treats or plan ways to fix it up. I barely cleaned it. I was freed from the vanity that makes a little shell around a house. I huddled amid the mouse droppings in my tiny office, my bathrobe wrapped tight, and did my work, and shivered.

I was thirty-nine when we moved to Boulder—nearly forty. I have this theory: Women in their forties stop being vain about their looks and start being vain about their houses. I was a renter; I had no house to be vain about. I was a renter in a beautiful dump. The idea of impressing guests with my lovely home was nothing short of ridicu-lous.

Not only that, but most people I met in Boulder had themselves lived in Chautauqua at one time or another—in college, or when they first came to town, or when they were remodeling their house. Like all the houses in Chautauqua, my house wasn't so much a house as a Boulder institution. Former tenants wandered in when they found the door unlocked. Students stoned out of their minds banged on the windows at 3 a.m. and demanded the use of our phone. Hikers bushwhacked through our yard. My house did not in any sense belong to me.

The sharpness had barely come into the night air when it was time for school to start. My Lucy, my darling, educated for years in cooperatives where I could keep an eye on her, was off to public school. The first day, I brushed her hair, a doomy feeling in my stomach. Hard to send her off to an unknown school, with unknown people.

Then she and Bruce headed out the door to walk down the hillside. On the doorstep Lucy lifted her face up to be kissed. Her gaze was blue and level, fearful and resolute.

"Have a good day, sweetie." I hugged her.

"I will have a good day," she said. She looked like a baby to me then, undefended.

Willie and I climbed into the VW van and headed down the hill. I had found him a cooperative preschool at the big Presbyterian church downtown. It seemed a little Jesus-y, but at least it was a co-op. We parked around the corner and walked through the sunshine. Willie held my hand. He had a wonderful, cool, paw-like grip. His shaggy yellow hair fell in his eyes. His orange backpack was on his back. He wore his favorite purple T-shirt and a pair of long blue stripey shorts. He was like a walking box of crayons; he was like happiness itself, roaming around at large.

The other moms were unloading their little boys and girls out of SUVs. The boys had haircuts and the girls had tight pigtails. The moms had twinsets and crosses on chains at their necks. When a small army of these moms and kids were gathered around us, heading toward the entrance of the school, Willie looked up at the chapel and said, in his very loudest voice, "Church! I've always wanted to go there!" Every head swiveled, or so it seemed to me.

I got my godless hippie child settled into his classroom. The teacher was a martinet-looking person, with steely gray hair, gimlet eyes, and a strong nose.

She squatted down next to Willie. "Hello, there," she said in a voice that was as soft as moss. Taking him by the hand, she showed him where to hang his backpack. She introduced him to a shelf full of wooden blocks and smoothed his hair as she walked away. She reminded me of Rosey Grier singing "It's All Right to Cry" on the *Free to Be . . . You and Me* album—a gentle warrior. She made me less nervous about the picture of Mr. Jesus H. Christ on the wall. I was beginning to see something: Boulder might be a bubble of liberalism at the edge of the prairie, but the prairie was, after all, right there, like a giant grassy driveway leading to the Midwest and then on to the Bible Belt.

I felt reluctant to go to work. (Not exactly a novel sensation.) Normally I would have forced myself to at least go to a café with my laptop, but I was . . . I was lonely. And I was feeling the exhilaration that sometimes goes hand in hand with loneliness. So I shirked.

I made my way down Pearl Street, the bricked-over main drag that had been turned, in the early 1970s, into a pedestrian mall.

I had hung out on Pearl Street before, two decades ago, when the street was lined with dirty kids sitting on the ground in front of incense-smelling shops. Then, there was an edge in the air: Was it transcendence, born of devoted chanting? Or was it drugs? In Boulder, in the 1980s, it was either, or both.

In 1987, my brother lived on University Hill with a bunch of other climbers. University Hill stretches below Chautauqua; my brother lived a couple of blocks from the school where Lucy was now spending her first day.

I was driving across the country, back from college, with a few friends. We had acquired an Airstream trailer and were towing it west, tag-teaming in two separate pickup trucks. We slept in rest areas. We had a CB radio and chatted between our pickups as we rolled through the blond arid expanses of Kansas, making up handles that we thought would sound off-putting to potential predators: "Come in, come in, Lard Ass. This is Ugly Mug lookin' for a big ten-four."

In Boulder, Julia and I detached ourselves from the caravan and stayed on for a couple of weeks, sleeping wherever we could find a spot: on my brother's couch; in the back of her Toyota pickup, which had a canopy; at the house of my brother's friend, where we were evicted in disgrace, having left our dirty underpants on the floor (the young make poor houseguests).

Boulder Valley, empty of its students, was like a bowl that held only the remains of a meal: the hippies, the rock climbers, the locals, the Buddhists, the bike freaks, the poor. You rode your bike through the tree-lined streets and the air was filled with the Grateful Dead and the Violent Femmes.

We hung out with my brother and his friends. Back then, climbing was alternative culture and comfortably combined a diet of millet with a punk aesthetic. The climbers were just one stratum of the multilayered weirdo cake that was Boulder. People roamed the streets barefoot. Hair was either to your waist, or shaved off entirely, or looked like it had been cut with nail scissors (which was, in fact, how my brother and his gnarly friends cut their hair). Work was palpably not being done. Time was to be spent in the mountains, or hanging out on Pearl Street, or playing your guitar, or sitting satsang.

I toured through all this with my friend Julia. She was an ideal companion, a perfect Californian, six feet tall with long straight hair and a face as open as a piece of buttered toast. She would try anything. I once saw her eat a peanut butter, lettuce, pickle, and mayonnaise sandwich. We rode inner tubes in fast-flowing creeks. We ate dinner with the Hare Krishnas. We hiked far into the mountains and took acid and solved society's problems. (See, we're really all like ants and . . .)

Every day was sunny; every afternoon thunderstormed, the piled-high clouds scudding into town and unleashing a big can of whup-ass all over everything. When the rain came, you sat in the Trident and drank your espresso and read the newspaper. After an hour or so, the clouds blew out of town like a crack team of cleaning ladies jumping into their van, and everything was scoured and scrubbed and smelled just great.

I borrowed, or took, my brother's bike and Julia borrowed, or took, someone else's, and we rode over to Daddy Bruce's Bar-B-Que, where we met a bunch of Buddhist guys—white boys with no hair or long hair. Come chant with us, they said, at Naropa, the Buddhist university just down the street that had been started by Chogyam Trungpa Rinpoche. They gave us a time and a place. (What were they doing there, at the barbecue place? It wasn't like Daddy Bruce offered seitan.)

I tried to get Julia to go with me. Julia, who would try anything, begged off on chanting with the Buddhists.

"They're scary," she said. "It's like they're looking right through you." She started cracking up. "It's like they're looking into your soooul." Julia thought everything was funny.

It was true; the Buddhists gave off an air of knowing what they were doing and it seemed like they might know what we were doing as well. We were still teenagers, with a teenager's natural shiftiness. We didn't want people knowing what we were doing.

Even so: chanting. What was it? Curiosity won out. One sunny afternoon, just before the clouds came, I slipped into the dusty front hall of the brick building that housed Naropa. I was about fifteen minutes late—standard for me at the time. I heard some deep repetitive vocal noises coming from behind a door. It was as if the room beyond was filled with a bunch of whales with really terrific rhythm.

I sat down outside the door and listened for a while. I would have stayed longer, and maybe gone inside, but somehow the sounds repelled me. They said, Go away, this is not for you. This is for serious people with the voices of whales. I couldn't even pick my dirty underpants up off the floor. How could I chant?

Julia and I parted ways, and I said goodbye to Boulder as well. Time to go back to Seattle and earn a little cash.

I picked up Willie and took him home. A couple of hours later, I went to get Lucy at school. I stood on a bench in the throng of slender moms so she could see me. She came out and said hello to me demurely. I couldn't tell how her day had been. We went home, and when we got there she immediately climbed into my lap. Her eyes looked teary. She said, "Thank goodness you're so big. That way I fit into your lap."

I was big and solid for her, and I held her until she had recovered from school.

Next to corpse pose, mountain is the simplest pose in the yoga lexicon. Mountain is confusing because you're just standing there and the teacher wants you to think you're doing yoga. Teachers talk a lot during mountain, maybe because they've finally caught their breath. Or maybe because on some level they don't really believe that mountain is yoga, either, so they surround the pose with a lot of verbiage in order to bolster its status.

The trick to mountain, say the teachers, is to weight all four corners of your feet evenly on the ground. The trick to mountain is to drop your tailbone toward the ground. The trick to mountain is to lift your breastbone without pooching out your rib cage. The trick to mountain is to keep the back of your neck long. The trick to mountain is to soften your belly. The trick to mountain is that there is no trick.

The teachers talk and talk and talk during mountain, and the students grow more and more suspicious. All of a sudden they're not in a class. They're in a negotiation. The teachers are trying to convince them of something—the importance of simply standing there—and the students are not sure they're buying it. After all, the greatest law of negotiation is this: He who's talking is losing.

On the other hand, maybe the teachers really mean it.

As with all yoga poses, my relationship has changed with mountain over time. First it seemed simple, easy.

Then, as I was flooded with information, it seemed overwhelmingly complex. My mind traveled all over my body while I did the pose, checking my feet, my butt, my gut.

Then I sort of started to enjoy it. Often when you do mountain, the teacher asks you do it with your eyes shut. In this way, mountain is again the twin of corpse; it takes you, if you'll go, directly to pratya-hara, the elusive inward-turning that Fran talked about. When you get there, what do you really feel? For me, mountain was a feeling of heaviness.

Teachers tend to use the idea of rootedness to describe mountain: Root your feet into the ground, they say. But I like to think of it as heaviness. Be like a mountain. Be heavy. Don't make your feet or your body go anywhere. It's sort of a radical idea: to be unready, to be immovable. Inertia, you realize as you stand there, is a kind of power.

The very word "mountain" sounds heavy. It's just a great word. It's rock-sounding. It sounds kind of massive. There was the proto-heavy-metal band called Mountain. There was Jerry Garcia's girlfriend, Mountain Girl. The Crucifucks—Steve Shelley's band before he joined Sonic Youth—did "The Mountain Song."

Heavy, inert, solid, intractable. These are not things women are supposed to be. I was, Lucy said, big enough for her. And I was glad to be.

22. SEATED FORWARD BEND

I wandered lonely as a cloud.

I walked from the back door of my cottage in Chautauqua right into the Front Range. This sounds like the kind of fact that you might find in a brochure about the amenities at a resort; I assure you it was more salient than that. It was more salient than any fact I had encountered since my husband took my hand and I knew he would be my husband; since my children were born.

I cranked up the German air purifier, drank a lot of coffee, and headed for the hills. By myself.

I was, at first, scared to go hiking in Boulder. A famous book had been written a couple of years before about the mountain lions who were coming into town and eating everyone. At least I guessed that was the gist. I was too scared to read it. At the first party we went to when we arrived in town, I met the fellow who had written the book. He was a small man with a wry demeanor who briefly detailed for me a few of the more grisly eviscerations from the book.

My mother read it. My mother reads everything. She called me up on the phone.

"How far is it from your car to your door?"

"Mom, it's fine! Nothing's going to eat me."

"Well, I certainly hope you're not letting the children play outside."

As it happened, our house was across the street from a fenced basketball court where the neighborhood children congregated and yelled and flung balls at each other. I told my mother this.

"Did you know that mountain lions can jump fourteen feet? How high is the fence? Have you measured it?"

Even so, the trails literally started at my back door, and their lure was irresistible. When I wasn't working, I was hiking. I dragged my kids with me, I went by myself, I made Bruce come along. The strength of the trails' allure surprised me. I come from a family of mountaineers; I considered myself an urbanite, an anti-mountaineer. Now I tumbled out the back door of my house right onto a sunny trail; it was wide and well traveled; it lead back in the mountains to other, smaller, lonelier trails; and on and on it went, far back into the Rockies.

For the first time in a long time, since I drifted for months on end through those meadows on Stuart Island, life became more real outside than in. Reality is an easy commodity in the Front Range. There's weather, and there are animals that are thinking about eating you, and there's all that beauty. It sort of whomps you on the head. It's strange that we use the word "unreal" to describe beauty—it's my experience that beauty drags us by the hair into the real.

Bruce spent his days studying, going on field trips, surrounded by colleagues. He was a social creature, down in town. He was blossoming with the attention, the light, the work, the lack of worry. And meanwhile I hiked alone. Each day I made notes in my diary on where I had hiked and at night I went to sleep recounting to myself the contours of that day's trail. As I had once lulled myself with yoga sequences, now I fell asleep thinking of how many feet I had ascended and what animals and birds I had seen.

I fell in love with the physicality of the trails. They ranged in width from a road to the narrowest footpath. They were made of beautiful

stuff, the red sandstone that was an important ingredient of the
Flatirons. They were hard and well-worn and intentional. These were
not the foot-smoothed brown ribbons of Stuart Island; they were not
stories told by feet. They were made lovingly by hand—Boulder's
trails were planned and provided for and protected, like beloved children. The trails had history and meaning as public spaces; they were as
much a part of the built environment of Boulder as its town hall or its
pedestrian mall. It was strangely moving to me that my experience in
the woods had been thought of and planned for by those people long
ago. I was also interested in how I lived when I was out on these trails.
I experienced a new range of emotions. Fear ruled; there were the
bears and the mountain lions and you never, ever forgot about them,
especially when you were hiking alone, especially somewhere far back
against the mountain, especially when you continued past a WARN-
ING: MOUNTAIN LION sign because you were so deeply curious about
what might lie ahead. There was nothing you could do to protect
yourself against mountain lions, except to carry a big stick. They were
not like bears, whom you could warn away with a loud voice or
singing. The main danger of bears was that you might surprise them.
Mountain lions, on the other hand, would track you, moving invisibly
through the trees until the perfect moment to pounce on you.

Euphoria came hand in hand with fear, like twins born of the same
mom. Walking alone on a high mountain trail, I felt like the top of
my head might come unattached and lift cleanly off. Nature seemed
even better at delivering this sensation than yoga.

These feelings were hemmed in by a new set of mores and social
codes, as feelings are. You think you're in nature, where emotions can
run as untrammeled as the wilderness itself. But you're wrong. The
trail is a vessel for human interaction. And human interaction seeks
form and organization.

I could hike way, way back into the mountains, leaving as early as
I could bear and hiking for hours. Huffing through the thin air, I
would round the corner and come upon, to give just one example, a
plucked-eyebrow college girl walking her dog, a plaster cast on her
hand. On her feet: flip-flops. In her good hand: a Frappuccino. It

reminded me of the travel experience we've all had. You head to the very ends of the earth, to the far shores of Banda Aceh or the deserts of Patagonia, and there you will find . . . a German. No matter where you go in the world, a German will have beaten you there, clad in a sweaty black T-shirt and a smug expression. Boulder people were just like that: They infested every corner of the mountains. There was no escaping their ubiquity. Human interaction was as much a part of these mountains as the trees or the giant rocks.

In fact, human interaction on the trails often raised the hairs on the back of my neck. A typical hike would elicit a series of responses, each at least as coded and subtly emotional as any cocktail-party exchange. For instance, this is a rundown of a hike I took up Gregory Canyon one Tuesday morning.

Here comes someone behind me. They're approaching quickly. I was assaulted on the street on a sunny Sunday afternoon in San Francisco when I was about twenty-two; some character ran up behind me and got his hands right up my skirt. Ever since then, I can hardly bear the sound of a human approaching me from behind. The feet behind me are moving quickly, pounding softly on the earth; probably a trail runner. Do I turn around and look? Do I acknowledge him or her? I glance over my shoulder; we lock eyes; I give one of those "I'm harmless" smiles and he returns the exact same look.

I walk on. Someone is approaching from ahead. It's an older gentleman; this means we will greet each other. Old people almost always acknowledge you and, with a certain dignity, expect acknowledgment in return.

"Good morning," I say to the approaching figure. I like to get them before they get me.

"Good morning," he says. He has Coke-bottle glasses and a pair of sturdy hiking boots that are so old and worn and richly brown that they look almost like living parts of his body. He has a kind eye and I suspect he might be experiencing a bit of that head-removing euphoria. All this I can see as he approaches under the ponderosa. Ah, yes, he has more to say.

"A beautiful morning!" he announces with a grin, like an MC at a wrestling match introducing a fighter.

"It sure is!" I say, being sure to include an exclamation point to match his. He nods and we pass, leaving a lot of space between us at the crucial moment. Our shorthand, predictable language is code for this: "I'm edging toward the transcendent; I think my head might lift off; I can't believe my luck."

These gestures, all of them—the backward glance, the chat, the pretending not to see each other, the grimace of blamelessness, the moment of passing, the stepping aside of the descender so that an ascender might climb past more easily—they were, I was sure, ancient gestures. What was older than a path? When I approached a woman on a trail from behind, I was aware that my footsteps might be menacing. This approach, and all those other movements and grimaces and courtesies, were old gestures. It was easy to grow romantic about the ancient lineage of these moments, these feelings. Anyone who ever trod a track must have had these moments: an African tribesman of long ago; a poet on a pilgrimage; a woman following her husband toward the West in the grip of manifest destiny.

In this way, walking the trails was like yoga. The kinesics were absolutely old; the idea of the sheer number of other people who had done them before me was overwhelming and at the same time thrilling and liberating.

The first snowflakes fell, fat and white. By morning they were drifted onto the hood of the car. Leigh called. "Go outside and blow on the snow!"

I went outside and blew. The snow lifted into a sparkling cloud, airborne and utterly weightless.

That night we lay in bed. The mouse smell had momentarily abated. Lucy had been asked on a playdate. Willie had used the bathroom, on his own, at preschool. I had completed an assignment in my icy little office. Bruce was gleeful, like an escapee. He spent the days going to classes, tooling around town on his bike, drinking beers with the lady fellows.

So we were happy as we lay in bed. Slowly the house began to shake. The wind began to beat harder, and the house began to move all over, like a loosely jointed dancer. I thought of the Robert Frost poem "The Silken Tent" and the line "it gently sways at ease." The wind outside was fierce and toothy, but the house moved suavely, a house that had lived at the edge of a mountain meadow for a hundred years and knew how to take it.

The wind grew. You could almost feel it expanding in size, like a balloon. And then—were we imagining it?—things began to heat up. The room grew hotter and hotter. I stripped off my pajama top and then my bottoms. Bruce began to toss and turn. It seemed impossible, but the wind grew more harsh, and the temperature rose even more. I felt like I was inside a test tube, rattling and hot.

The wind blew in my room and took over my body. I had heard rain loud on the roof and felt nights hot on my skin, but I had never had a wind invade my house and my head quite like that.

The next morning, I dropped off Willie at preschool, and his teacher told me that the wind was called the chinook. The chinook wind comes down fast from the mountains, the quick compression causing the air to heat up, sometimes up to fifty degrees within an hour. (A year later, I measured the temperature rise during a chinook and found a thirty-degree rise within an hour and a half.) The chinook is a foehn, which meteorologists use as a general term for these hot winds coming down the leeward side of a mountain range.

Willie's preschool teacher had lived in Germany. She told me that when the foehn came, people got headaches and generally felt crummy, and the German pharmacies sold special sugary foehn drops to ward off its effects. After I left the preschool, I took my computer over to the coffee shop, where I ran into Fritz, a dad from Lucy's school, who seemed elated by the foehn, as people are by weather that is unusual yet nonfatal. Fritz told me that he had left his office window ajar and found his papers wildly strewn across the floor, as if the room had been tossed by a cadre of movie baddies.

I shared Fritz's feeling of occasion, and when I stopped by the library to do some research for an article, I took a moment to look up the foehn.

The foehn, I learned, was first recorded in the Alps but is found all over the world. The Santa Anas contain the occasional foehn, nicknamed "murder winds" and immortalized in Joan Didion's 1965 essay "Los Angeles Notebook." The mistral of southern France is a foehn. The sirocco is partly made of foehn winds. Any number of ill winds around the world are foehns, from Appalachia to South America to Croatia.

The foehn is famous for making people sick, for bringing headaches, even for causing crimes. Auden: "Sirocco brings the minor devils."

The mountains in Seattle were faraway things. They produced a pleasant aesthetic response, not much more powerful than the feeling you got looking at a beautiful photograph. The Flatirons came after you in your bed, throwing hot wind at you and freaking you out. I had moved to a place where emotions could be produced by mountains.

I didn't have time for yoga. When I was off the trails, I had work to get done and then kids to care for. My body tightened. It hurt to sit down. Stairs seemed endless. Hiking was my vocation, and it was changing my body.

I began to do some home practice. My practice was simple: sun salutations, twists, a sequence leading through the warriors to triangle to half moon to standing splits. And a lot of seated forward bend to get at my hamstrings.

After my aforementioned hike up Gregory Canyon, I forced myself to unroll my mat in the death-smelling living room. I moved into a vinyasa somewhat creakily.

Home practice sucked. The gestures and movements that were so thrilling in class seemed flat and dull when done at home alone. In class, tension hummed in the room as bodies moved in and out of shapes, failed, succeeded, breathed. There was a feeling that you were participating in a very slow but very real transformation. At home, the same movements became mere stretching exercises—the boring part of PE.

There was a focus that happened in class, a sharpening of intention and attention. What was it that happened in yoga class that gave these movements greater value? Was it simply the exchange of money? People who do Weight Watchers say that paying money for the program is a big motivator—it places a value on their effort.

Or maybe it was having a teacher who was leading you. Maybe there is something in us that wants to relinquish agency, wants to be led, wants to become apprenticed to a teacher, and this very deep part of us is satisfied by a class setting.

Or maybe it was just being in a room with other people. Maybe the feeling—the thrill—was created through these other bodies in the room; the focus jumped around the room from person to person, intensifying as it went.

I leaned out over my legs. To lay your torso down on top of your legs, your stomach curled like a fat little dog onto your lap. To feel your chest reaching toward your toes, like a lover who knows her love will always be unrequited. To let your nose get to know your shins.

This was a pose that felt right to do alone. To turn inward. This was the most alone of the poses, the kind of alone that you were as a kid. Contented in your own world. Living inside your own geography. Recognizing that your body was its own territory, bounded and united and sufficient.

My life was shrinking. There were no calls, no people dropping in. The fellows turned up and then went away. They didn't take over. I didn't try to please them; it would've seemed ridiculous, they were such non-pleasers themselves, to a woman. My family life had been, to some degree, a performance that might please all around me. A performance to prove to everyone else, and to myself, that everything was fine. No, not fine. Perfect. Now my family life was my family life, private, almost secret, a pile of bears in a den, writhing and furry and intimate. I had no public.

And now that there was no public, something mysterious was happening: The object of my worry and shame—that is to say, Bruce's depression—had gone away. Probably there were a lot of reasons for this. The lady fellows, for one thing. The sunshine. The journalism faculty, who treated him as a respected colleague.

It begged a question. Had my misgivings caused his depression in the first place? With me watching over him like a hawk, making sure he was sticking with the program, maybe he had felt crowded and overwhelmed.

Bruce walked Lucy to school every day, and they bumped off cheerily. No yelling. No complaints. Just simple happiness: a father and a daughter walking to school together. I was not part of the picture. I didn't try to organize their walk or make it work. I just said goodbye. I would get Willie off to school, write a few hundred words, and hit the trails. Alone.

My kids got the words "geography" and "geology" mixed up, but in Boulder geography and geology were in fact often the same thing, and they came to rule me. The mountains defined the way the city lived. Seattle was, for me, governed by its social history—when I was there, I lived by Muriel Rukeyser's line "The universe is made of stories, not atoms." Every street corner had a story, and I mean that quite literally. In Boulder, the atoms were back in charge. Weather came into my house and shook me up. The ivy climbed through the window frame. When I walked in a rain I didn't just come home wet; I came home with mud making my hiking boots into platform shoes. Nature wasn't the romantic, sentimental thing it is to people who never go there. It was immediate and forceful. It might eat you. It had started to eat me.

23. CORPSE

The hoary old chestnut says that when the pupil is ready the teacher will come. When I lived in Boulder, teachers seemed to fall out of the sky on top of me. It rained teachers.

After I'd been in Boulder for a while, an editor at *The New York Times* asked me to do an article on contemplative education at Naropa, the hybrid Buddhist/beatnik university. My editor was an efficient-sounding person, and I didn't tell her about sitting on the floor in the hallway of Naropa in 1987, too freaked out by the Buddhists and their whale vocalizations to walk through the door.

Naropa was a beloved Boulder institution. I did some preliminary research and discovered that it began life as the Naropa Institute in 1974. That summer, Chogyam Trungpa Rinpoche—a Tibetan Buddhist teacher who made his way to the United States by way of Oxford—founded the institute to integrate Eastern and Western studies. He invited artists from all over the country, the artists invited their buddies, and the gathering ended up with a head count of 2,500. Many of the participants decided to stay in Boulder, including the poet Allen Ginsberg. He stayed on to help start the elegiacally named Jack Kerouac School of Disembodied Poetics. I drove past Naropa almost every day. The main building was an old schoolhouse on Arapahoe Avenue. The campus was cheerful and prosperous-looking, with new, modern buildings and green lawns surrounding the old brick flagship.

Students wandered its sunny sidewalks looking as though their goal in life was to fulfill every stereotype you might hold about what a Naropa student should look like. They wore dreadlocks and moth-eaten cardigans and hand-painted leather jackets and floor-length patchwork skirts. As for shoes, it was motorcycle boots or nothing at all. I found the Naropa students, from the vantage of my car with my children's demands in my ears and my deadlines looming, very dear and a little bit ridiculous; surely not the effect they were going for.

The *Times* wanted a piece on the way the school integrated contemplative practice into its coursework. The PR office at the school connected me to a few professors who fit the bill. I was to spend a week visiting classes and talking with Naropans. My first class was to be "The Contemplative Artist," taught by someone named Robert Spellman. I would be expected to participate in all the classes I attended, the PR lady told me. The first rule of the freelancer is that a job is a job, even if it might potentially involve chanting.

On a scorching September morning I put on a short skirt and a tank top, slung around a few jokes with my husband about how I was going to come back a woo-woo Buddhist cult member, and headed to Naropa's Arapahoe Campus, a repurposed modern office block. Boulder turns pretty quickly to prairie once you head east from the slabs of the Flatirons, and it was strange to see this shiny cement-and-glass office building, here on the flat prairie, adorned with Tibetan prayer flags. It was stranger still to see students sitting cross-legged, with their hands in the forefinger-to-thumb gyana mudra, meditating on the grassy strip that separated the parking lot from the building.

The building had that warm institutional smell that campus build-ings have; it's unique and universal to colleges, and has something to do with body odor and something to do with cleaning supplies. Students smiled and bustled about; a girl with a mohawk directed me to the studio where my class was going to meet. I pushed through the door tentatively. The cement studio floor was lumped with zafu cushions, those round, hard, cotton-covered pillows that look like something the hookah-smoking caterpillar in *Alice in Wonderland* might sit on. First lesson: Never wear a short skirt to a class with the word "contemplative" in its name. With much adjusting, I navigated my way down onto a cushion. The room filled with students who gracefully dropped onto their lumps.

The door opened, and a gray-haired man walked in, looking utterly out of place in the studio. He wore chinos, a pale-blue button-down shirt, horn-rimmed glasses, and an alert, stern expression. He was the tweediest patrician you ever saw. He greeted me, nodded to the students, sat down on a zafu, slipped off his polished brown oxfords, folded up his legs, placed his hands upon his knees, and meditated silently for twenty minutes.

When he finally opened his eyes, they looked deeply refreshed, as if they were lawns he'd just watered. Then he smiled and looked around at his students and said, "If we set an intention of being a good, holy meditator, and we're not aware of that intention, we're going to become a certain kind of jerk."

He proceeded to talk for the next half hour, trying to explain to his students what they had just been doing. He spoke in metaphors. His talk looped from Dolores Umbridge, a villainess from the Harry Potter books, to Saint Brigid of Kildare. He talked about the sanctity of the housefly and he talked about the frontal lobe. His talk seemed to spread in all directions, trying to find a way to bring each of his listeners home. He wanted somehow to scoop them up, offer each of them the most compelling metaphor, the one that would make them want to sit, make them want to devote themselves to the process of meditation.

Finally he swung one of his metaphors out like a giant net, and it caught me. He talked about Tom Brown, a tracker based in New Jersey. Brown said that if you want to see wild animals, you have to go into the forest and hold perfectly still. If you are still enough, the wild animals will come to you. He had my attention immediately; Bruce had gone tracking with this very man for a story. Spellman said that sitting in meditation worked just the way the tracker described. If you're still enough, the wild mind, the mind that isn't preoccupied with oughts and shoulds and the minutiae of life, will approach you and make itself known.

Holy crap, I thought.

Then it was time to draw.

"It's important to stay loose if you want to make art," said Spellman as we fanned out over the studio.

The sun was streaming in the high windows. The room smelled a little dry, like chalk dust, and a little eggy, like tempera.

"Stay loose," continued Spellman. "It especially helps to release the body a bit when you're moving from one activity to another. OK, so let your jaws go limp. Totally limp. And stare into space. Maybe stare up a little. Just let go. I'll be right back, I'm going into the other room to get some supplies. Remember: Loose! Limp!"

He came back ten or twenty seconds later and looked at us all standing there, jaws slack, arms hanging at our sides.

He started cracking up. "Man, you guys look really, really funny."

We sat at long tables and did blind contour drawings of pots and urns. I made a phenomenally ugly little sketch of a creamer. I was happy. We were all there together, silently making marks on the page. These marks I made in Spellman's class were a mess. I was ridiculously proud of them.

I met Bruce for coffee afterward. I was bubbling over with news of my art class.

"Spellman is it," I said. "If a person was going to have a guru, he'd be the one."

Bruce, who had seen me leave the house four hours earlier suspicious of the very idea of Naropa, let alone contemplation, said, "God, you're like Woody Allen in *Radio Days*. You know, the scene where he goes next door to complain to his Communist neighbors about the noise and he comes back spouting the party line."

———

My skepticism softened a bit by Spellman's intelligence and also his horn-rimmed glasses, I continued my week at Naropa. I went to a seminar on contemplative practice with Judith Simmer-Brown, who was a big deal in Buddhist circles.

After we had talked about the assigned reading, she told us it was time for a meditation exercise. That sounded a little scary. At least I was wearing pants.

She set up a makeshift stage to one side of the tall, dusty classroom. She asked each student to stand on one side of the stage, bow, and walk silently to the middle of the stage. Each person stood there, without moving, laughing, smiling, or speaking. The goal was to stand silently and look in the eye of every person in the room. Embarrassment flickered across some faces; some stood comfortably, rooted in the ground, staring intently into every eye.

When the students were done, Simmer-Brown looked at me. Really, these people had some kind of mesmerizing power. She didn't look at me expectantly or with any kind of suggestion in her eyes. She just looked at me. I found myself rising and walking to the front of the room.

I paused at the edge of the stage and bowed. My hands were shaking and I tried to think of it as my humanity, as the prana body. I was really wigged out, but there was no turning back.

I walked onto the stage, which suddenly seemed very real, not makeshift all. I stood there, my hands shaking at my sides, and looked at all those student faces: the girl with the purple hair; the boy with the dreadlocks; the girl with straight brown hair and rimless glasses who looked like she might have been valedictorian of her high school in Lincoln, Nebraska. Then there was Simmer-Brown herself. I had imagined she might nod at me approvingly, but her face was entirely impassive.

In fact, all their faces were impassive. I hadn't seen it before, when I was sitting among them on the floor, my reporter's notebook on my lap, a fool's prop. Their faces showed neither approval or mockery. No one smiled at me. No one frowned, either. Simmer-Brown had some-how taught them nonjudgment. They were looking at me without any judgment in their eyes at all. This meditation exercise was working in two directions; it was as much a challenge for the audience as it was for the stage walker.

I went home shaken. There had been a heightened sense of reality in the room. It was like the exact opposite of being on drugs: too much clarity. It was interesting to think that when judgment fell away, what you ended up with was clarity. I had always leaned on judg-ment—in my work and in my life—to make sense of the world for me. But maybe it wasn't helping. Maybe it was muddying the waters rather than clearing them. I was old enough to know myself, to know that I would never be able to see the world without reflexive judg-ment. But maybe I could at least try. Those students had tried, and the charge they gave off could've lit up a small city.

The next day I went to yoga in the Naropa gym. The teacher, who had red hair and was clearly in no way Indian, spoke in a thick Indian accent and told a story about a monkey. I didn't feel quite as wildly critical when he did this as I might've in the past. After all, many of the things I had encountered at Naropa should have annoyed me or irritated me, but ended up enchanting me instead.

I had thought the feeling of the place would be sanctimonious—after all, isn't that how many of us think of Western Buddhists? They seem like they know something you don't, and they know they know it, and they're smug. But instead the nonjudgment I had encountered in Simmer-Brown's classroom seemed to be a form of permission. It was OK to experiment, to try new stuff. The students, even the teach-ers of Naropa seemed to fling themselves into enterprises.

Long ago, I had noticed that when Fran was really cooking in class, she would rely heavily on the phrase "Why not?" She would suggest a pose—for instance, side crow—and then she would answer her own suggestion: Why not? She verbally warded off the judging mind, the mind that had many, many reasons why not. This was the feeling I got from Naropa; it was a place where judgment was not so much killed as outwitted. I had thought the vibe would be anti-intellectual, but that was not the case. It was a place where the teachers were using their smarts to step around judgment. This upset my notions of what smart looked like.

The red-haired yoga teacher with the Indian accent did catch my attention with one thing he said: "Those of you who are really bad at yoga, you're in the right place. I hope everyone will allow themselves to be really crappy today, to walk away from being perfect. The real yoga isn't in the perfect pose; it's in the crappy pose that you are really feeling. You want to feel it from the inside out, rather than make it perfect from the outside in."

We did an extra-long savasana, which seemed very Naropa. Of course savasana was important here. We lay on our backs on the gym floor.

The gym was a huge airy rectangular box, filled with light. The floor was crowded with mats. Not just students but faculty and office workers who had come in for a lunchtime class. This was my favorite kind of yoga: filled with all different kinds of people of all different shapes and ages.

My mat was dusty. Had I ever washed it? I didn't think so. I rubbed my fingers softly on it and found a little pine needle embedded there. The knob on the back of my head pressed into the ground; I rolled my head a bit back and forth, feeling the shape of the knob.

The person next to me was making snuffling, pre-sleep sounds, which seemed friendly. The teacher walked around the room. I could hear his footsteps. My sweat was beginning to dry a little, and I was cooling down. As silently as possible, I pulled my sweatshirt from where it was heaped next to my mat and spread it over my chest.

I lay there, with the dust in my nose and the pleasant weight of my sweatshirt on my chest. And I realized: I was meditating. There was nothing scary lurking beneath the surface. There was just . . . this. This reality.

I had a sudden thought: What if the opposite of good wasn't bad? What if the opposite of good was real?

After my yoga class, I dizzily wandered down the street to meet my friend Dan for a beer. We sat in the front window of an Irish pub in downtown Boulder. Giant pink clouds rolled thickly down the mountainside. We looked out the window and laughed. It was so beautiful, that was all we could do.

Dan asked the waitress for our pints in his gentle, flirting way. We sipped our stouts and he asked, "How's the Naropa story going?"

I reddened. I was embarrassed by how much Naropa had come to mean to me. I was embarrassed by how important the work that went on there felt to me. I was embarrassed even to apply the word "work" to what was going on over there. These were not really things you could write about in *The New York Times*.

"It might be kind of hard to write," I said.

He gave me a knowing look. "I once had to follow the Dalai Lama for two weeks for *Newsweek*. At the beginning I was totally skeptical of the whole Dalai Lama thing. It seemed like a kind of industry to me, like a spiritual sideshow. But then I started listening to him talk, and I saw the way he moved through the world, and he made me rethink everything. *Newsweek* wouldn't use any of my copy. I didn't cover the Dalai Lama. I believed him."

I handed in my story; they edited out all the wonder and left in the facts, and that's newspapers for you. Probably for the best. Who wants wonder in their morning newspaper?

24. THE JUMP-THROUGH

The handyman, who was a woman, stopped by to check on the smell. I was sitting outside in a tank top, reading a book for review. The sun was so hot that my upper lip was filmed with sweat. It had snowed three inches the day before. Boulder weather was schizophrenic.

"I'm not smelling anything," she said with a sniff. "Call me if it keeps up. I gotta go, I have yoga in twenty minutes."

"Oh!" My attention was wrested away from the smell. "Where do you go?"

"I go to Richard Freeman. I don't know why anyone goes anywhere else."

"Where does he teach?"

"He has the Yoga Workshop. Haven't you ever heard of him?"

I had, in fact, heard of him. He was some kind of famous ashtanga master, one of the early adopters who moved to India in the 1960s and '70s. I had seen him somewhere—a magazine or an ad or a video cover. I could picture gray hair, intelligent eyebrows, and bike shorts.

"You should definitely go to him," she said. "He's a genius."

And with a swish of her long gray ponytail she was gone.

My hurried morning sun salutation wasn't cutting it. I decided to try the Yoga Workshop. There was a beginning class on Sunday. I would try that—ashtanga sounded intimidating. Or looked intimidating, if you went by Madonna's arms.

I asked around about Freeman. He was, it seemed, part of the Boulder old guard: the freaks, the chronically broke, the hippies. He was world-famous but kept his studio in the same little cinder-block structure where it had always been. He was, everyone said it, the real deal.

As soon as he started to move, you could tell he really was a genius. He floated through the most basic movements of sun salutation A, hovering over the ground like he was inhaling helium rather than oxygen. His body was perfect intelligence; every inch seemed to know where it was in the air and how it related to every other part of his body. I thought of acrobats. I thought of flight. I thought that my understanding of the possibilities of the human body had until that point been tragically limited.

Mostly I sat there with my mouth open in amazement like a cartoon dog: "Aaawrooh?"

After he demonstrated the sequence, we joined him in the movements. It was so exciting being in the same room with him that my usual tremor turned into a thrumming vibration. When I lifted my hands to meet over my head, they shook so much that they could barely find each other; they finally bumped into one another like two old friends who couldn't quite recognize each other anymore.

His instructions were precise and phenomenally helpful in helping you relax in the postures. "Release the tongue to the palate of the mouth," he said, and I did, and my jaw unclenched and could not clench again with my tongue in that position.

His talk was thoughtful and funny, a perfectly judged combination of wisdom and comic patter. As we held revolved triangle, he said in his somnambulant voice, "Just think of it as a very complicated breathing exercise."

Best of all, this! He said "exheel" and "inheel." Somehow when he said it, you knew that Mindy and her ilk were copying him, rather than the other way around. I had come to the source.

This was my first real run-in with lineage. The genius had studied for years in Mysore with K. Pattabhi Jois, who in turn studied with Tirumalai Krishnamacharya, the father of modern yoga. Krishnamacharya had three students who famously shaped contemporary yoga: his brother-in-law, B.K.S. Iyengar, who founded the eponymous school of yoga that was deeply concerned with alignment and precision; Krishnamacharya's son, T. K. V. Desikachar, who continued his father's teachings and promulgated viniyoga, a kind of very gentle therapeutic yoga; and Jois, who made a lifetime work of studying, developing, and promulgating ashtanga yoga, the dynamic form of yoga that, in its popularized, simplified form, had come to be known as vinyasa.

True ashtanga, as taught in the Jois lineage, was much more rigorous than the vinyasa classes I'd been attending. The vinyasa movements I had learned were used as a kind of glue in ashtanga yoga, holding together a set series of poses. In fact, there were several of these series, a series of series, if you will. They were known as the primary series, the secondary series, up through the sixth series. The series were followed in a set order, and were bookended by introductory and closing chants and movements. The primary series alone was enough to keep you busy for a lifetime. The poses ranged from the simple to the difficult, and were linked by a complex, elegant vinyasa dance that involved jumping, rolling, hopping, balancing, and, in the genius's case, floating.

In beginning classes, we simply explored the vinyasa sequence and sometimes broke down some of the poses from the primary series. We worked on the interstitial tendons that held the sequences together; for instance, we might spend some time on the jump-through, which is the archetypal ashtanga movement. You start in downward dog and leap (or float) the feet between the hands to end up in a seated position. Go try it right now and when you're done laughing (or crying), come back.

Cognitive dissonance: You watched the genius do the jump-through and it was the purest, simplest thing you ever saw. It was so visceral watching him do the jump-through that it made a believer out of you, the way the sight of someone speaking in tongues can convert a sinner. You watched the genius jump through, and you believed deep in your heart that you could do it, too.

You got ready. In downward dog you zipped your gut tight in anticipation. You would be strong; this time, you would make it. Exhaling, gathering strength, you leaped . . . and skidded your feet into the mat, or landed them with a thud next to your hands.

On the rare occasions when I actually accomplished the jump-through, I was so excited I could barely contain myself. I glowed with pride. I lost track of what I was supposed to do next. Which was just the opposite of what the jump-through was designed to accomplish. It was meant to keep you in flow, to keep the poses from getting stuck.

The genius just flowed right out of the pose, onto the next thing, and the next, and the next.

The primary-series classes were so difficult that I sometimes wondered if I was actually doing the poses. I would ease my way into a pose—for instance, arm pressure pose, where the legs were hooked over the tops of the upper arms and the feet crossed in front. I would be in the pose, and at the same time, I would feel that I had a mere toe in the water compared to the genius and his disciples. (Of course I was not supposed to compare.) They seemed immersed. Which isn't to say that classes there were a drag. There was a sweet seriousness in the air in this little cinder-block building in downtown Boulder. Some people had been coming to the same classes there for two decades, trying to get the juice that had traveled from Krishnamacharya to Jois to Freeman. The lineage had a power that could not be denied.

Yoga is the closest thing many of us will ever encounter to a pure oral tradition. No substitutions, so far, have even come close to approximating the experience of learning from a live person. As I discovered early in my practice, learning from a video doesn't quite work, nor does a book, even if it's a book as close to the source as Iyengar's *Light on Yoga*.

Many writers have talked about the mystery of transmission. For some reason, it's important to learn yoga from a live person. Maybe it's simply seeing the poses done in three dimensions. But it feels like something more than that. When your teacher shows you how something is done, there's a feeling of possibility, a transmittal of something like faith. Yes, this can be done. I'm seeing it right before my eyes.

When you took a class with Freeman, there was a strange sense of fate: Had everything led to this moment? Had you been climbing the rope of lineage, without even realizing it? His teaching and his understanding of his own role in the lineage gave off a kind of heat. It was crucial, what he was transmitting. He had to get it off his chest. At least that was the way I read it.

Each time I went to class I grew more deeply appreciative of the serious community he had built; of the humility of the surroundings; of the fearsome articulation of his body; of the clarity of his direction.

I always went to the beginning class on Sunday mornings. I walked. Afterward, Bruce and the kids would pick me up in the VW van.

"Well, he's a genius," I said each time, and so we headed off for our day.

"What do you mean he's a genius?"

"He just flies through the air," I said, propping my feet up on the dashboard.

"Do geniuses fly?" asked Willie from the backseat.

At the same moment, Bruce said, "That doesn't mean he's a genius. It just means he's super fit."

"No, it's more than that. It's like, everything he does is just simple. He's found a way to not think about everything so hard. He just does it. It sounds horrible to say it, but he's totally in the moment."

"If he's not thinking, doesn't that make him the opposite of a genius?"

"No! Why do you have to question every sentence I utter? Why don't you just trust me?"

"I'm hungry and I want to go to the library," said Lucy.

Normally this would have started a big fight between Bruce and me, one that could easily have lasted hours, even unto bedtime. This time we both stopped and sort of looked at the situation for a minute, like it was a strange bug we'd found on the kitchen counter. It was just an argument, not a harbinger of doom. And then we talked about what was for lunch.

It seemed like a natural decision to stay another year; we were having a great time. But not in the mouse-smelling house. We moved to a house that looked like a massive ski lodge, high up in the mountains. The owners were going to Ecuador for a year to work on their Spanish. Our kids would have to take the bus five winding miles down the steep mountainside into town. We would get a lot of snow, the owners told us. We would see elk and bears and mountain lions and bobcats and wild turkeys. We would be real mountain people. Talk about reality: The house came with its own snowplow. Set on a knoll, it looked over the parkland called Walker Ranch in one direction, the Continental Divide in another. We giggled with delight all day long. Leigh came up for dinner the first night. As we slurped our soup, she looked around at the grandiose Aspen-y interior and said, "You know this is not how people really live, don't you? You realize you will have to go back to real life."

"We're pretending we're in the foreign service, like diplomats," said Bruce.

"Whatever. Just as long as I can move in, too."

Right away I started having strange animal encounters. I, not a morning person, wandered coffee in hand into a herd of elk on my front stoop. The glass-paned door to the garage had giant muddy paw prints on it, from some bear who had been gazing through the window longingly at the garbage cans therein. And I found a chipmunk in my kitchen. It looked like it was about to break into song like one of those friendly creatures in a Disney movie.

A few weeks after we moved in, I had a call from my mom. I mean, I had a call from my mom every week, if not every day. She was determined not to let little things like a major mountain range and a thousand miles come between us. Anyhow, I had this particular call from my mom:

"Hi, honey. Are Lucy and Willie there?"

"They're in town. Lucy's playing at Juliana's house and Willie is at Amar's. I was just heading down the mountain to get them."

"Oh, too bad. Well, have them call me when they get home. I want to hear what they're up to."

"OK, it'll be a couple of hours."

"Well, talk to me a minute. I'm glad I caught you. Your dad and I are thinking about going through with a divorce."

"What?"

"We're just talking about it."

"That is so great! Way to go, you!"

"It seemed like it might be time."

"You realize this is a deeply weird conversation, don't you?"

"I suppose, honey. Have the children call me."

"Alrighty!"

I checked my e-mail before I headed out. There was a note from my dad.

Dave and Claire:
Just wanted to let you know. Your mother and I are exploring options for divorce. I'll keep you posted.
xo Dad

This seemed to come out of nowhere. Had they simply wearied of my brother's nagging? Had I subtly altered the emotional landscape by moving away? Just as their real story had lain under the surface unspoken all those years, now its resolution was equally unclear to me. Did all parents do this, or just my own? Their decisions and their movements were made behind a scrim. You could ask them what was behind the scrim—was there something back there?—but you would not be answered. "We tried our best," they told my brother and me over and over. They said it with perfect earnestness. And that was all we ever got out of them. Deep in my heart, I suspect this was because they had no idea what was actually going on between the two of them in their very eccentric marriage, and would rather not think about it themselves.

When I was twenty-two, the age my mother was when she got married, I was a college dropout living in Australia with my boyfriend, an eternally sunny character who had hair down to his butt and sang in a punk-rock band. We lived in a little cinder-block house on a busy road in an industrial city just south of Sydney. It was a kind of paradise. Huge sticky orange blossoms grew in the yard, blossoms whose names I never learned. Why bother? We lived with the surly, stringy-haired guitarist from my boyfriend's band and a utopian-minded teenage punk rocker who treated us like we were her old mum and dad, but in a nice way. Other utopian teenage punk rockers paraded through the house, eating our food. The beach was a block away. When I was low on money, I spent my days driving a forklift and loading boxes in a Sydney warehouse. I also modeled nude for life drawing classes at the local art college, something I would never, ever do on my home continent. When I had a little money, I spent my days lying on the beach under an umbrella reading Tolstoy. When I wanted a change of scene, I stuck out my thumb and hitchhiked a thousand miles to Queensland.

I wrote all day long in a little journal that I kept in my backpack. I was in touch with my feelings and terrified of my ambitions. Sand drifted into the bed and I lived on Cadbury chocolates. I could make a daylong journey out of going to the shop for sweets, as I learned to say. I lay on gritty sheets and ate chocolate Freddo Frogs and plowed through *Anna Karenina*. At night, sand would somehow sneak into my mouth, finding its way back to my molars.

Drugs would've filled up the days, but who could be bothered? Drugs were a lot of work. We didn't even bother to drink; too expensive and we were having plenty of fun anyhow. If my boyfriend's band was playing, or someone else of interest, the whole household headed up to Sydney and its sweaty rock shows. Or if it wasn't a night to go to Sydney, my boyfriend and I left our cinder-block house as dusk fell and walked barefoot along the busy road to the little vegetarian restaurant in town, where we ate gado-gado. We held hands while we ate. The restaurant was charmingly named the Plant Room, though of course my Australian boyfriend pronounced it "thi Plahnt Room." The Southern Cross shone overhead!

I continued in this vein for many years.

I made my way around the Pacific Ocean, from Australia to San Francisco back to Seattle to Southeast Asia and back to Seattle. Boyfriends came and went, but I was entirely in charge of my own life, right up through my twenties. If it had been my mother's era, or my grandmother's, and on and on, back into the mists of time, I, a twentysomething woman from a good family, would have been married and a mother already. Probably for years.

It's astonishing, even vertiginous, to think about the precipitous speed with which that change came. Hundreds of years of history asked that women be married by twenty or twenty-five. My mother was married in 1962; some reports claim the median age of first marriage for women at that time to be twenty-two, others claim twenty.

And yet by the time I was in my twenties, among my friends it was considered the norm to remain unmarried until your late twenties or early thirties. In twenty years, the span between my mother's youth and my own, the norm of early marriage was subverted and puffed away, like a dandelion clock, as if it had never existed. I never gave a thought to getting married. When a boyfriend or two asked, seemingly sincerely, it was all I could do not to laugh at the very thought. Are you kidding? I wanted to ask. Are you crazy? (But of course I did not say this out loud.)

My mom and her sisters and her friends, on the other hand, were married by twenty-five, and thrilled with their lot. They had been taught for their entire lives that marriage and adulthood and even motherhood would bring freedom and happiness and all good things.

My mother describes growing up in the 1940s and '50s and yearning for adulthood. Childhood was to be endured, a long tunnel leading to the light of adulthood. Pleasure was for grown-ups. You might have fun along the way, but you were, in essence, waiting. Nowhere is this more perfectly captured than in Nancy Mitford's 1945 novel *The Pursuit of Love*. Sisters Jassy and Linda, weary of their seemingly endless youth, discuss the passage of time as they loll about the drawing room:

"What's the time, darling?"

"Guess."

"A quarter to six?"

"Better than that."

"Six!"

"Not quite so good."

"Five to?"

"Yes."

Back then, time was a bad penny for young girls; it could not be spent fast enough.

My mother had my brother when she was twenty-four. Pick any counterculture landmark, and when it occurred she was already shackled to husband and kids: She was pregnant with me and had a two-year-old when *Sgt. Pepper* was released. At the time of Woodstock, she had a two-year-old and a four-year-old. When *The Female Eunuch* came out in 1970, my brother was starting kindergarten and I was hanging around the house demanding more blueberry yogurt. Like countless other women, she had followed all the rules for making a good life. The narratives she had read all her life said this: Freedom came with marriage. Get married, have children, run your own house, and be free of your parents forever.

This notion might sound retrograde, but without it, we would have no Jane Austen. Her women, forthright and independent and smart, belong in marriage because marriage was the institution that gave women agency, power, success, adulthood, pleasure, and money.

Now all of a sudden, the narrative of liberation wasn't the old narrative. Within the period of my mother's young adulthood, the narrative of liberation reversed: Get un-married and be free of your husband forever. Then you will find freedom, and riches, and love. It's time to go. Just go.

(What would the narrative be for their daughters, for me? The most truthful one told so far was the one where we were expected to do everything: family and job, children and self-realization. Our emblem, if not our narrative, was one of a many-armed woman, a Hindu goddess, trying to do everything at once. Those who chose not to work, or chose not to have a child, were in the minority. The significant majority of women did both.)

This grand departure of my mother's generation was told in the fiction of the times. Most famously, of course, there is Erica Jong's *Fear of Flying*, the story of a woman who leaves her crazy husband to drive around Europe in a two-seater convertible (of course) with a sexy academic. Isadora Wing uttered these words, which make a fine summing-up for the general mood: "A good woman would have given over her life to the care and feeding of her husband's madness. I was not a good woman. I had too many other things to do."

Isadora's flight was both descriptive and prescriptive. For some, her journey was an escapist fantasy, a substitute for the real thing. Novelist Lois Gould blurbed the hardcover: "She'll take you farther from home than you ever dreamed you'd go." For other women, Jong was a siren, calling them to the other side. A 1975 *Newsweek* profile of Jong gives an idea of the book's impact: "Runaway wives appear periodically on her doorstep, announcing their intention to move in with her."

Jong's voice was joined in chorus by a whole string of books, some of which were passed around like samizdat, some of which became best sellers: Alix Kates Shulman's *Memoirs of an Ex–Prom Queen*, Sue Kaufman's *Diary of a Mad Housewife*, Marge Piercy's *Small Changes*, Lisa Alther's *Kinflicks*, Dorothy Bryant's *Ella Price's Journal*, and Marilyn French's *The Women's Room*.

In these books, being a protagonist meant ending a marriage. Where the fate of every woman in a romance story is to be married, the fate of every woman in this literature is to be un-married. These books were interested in what it meant to be a woman, not a wife. Memoirist Mary Cantwell later described the moment thus: "I discovered that I did not know much about women. That nobody knew much about women. I began to think of myself as a woman."

These new novels of women lined the shelves in the house where I grew up. (Except *Rubyfruit Jungle*, which was passed between sixth-grade lockers and massively dog-eared. The sex horrified and called to us, but we most loved the passage where the heroine tricks a dupe into eating rabbit turds disguised as raisins. The book—for we only had the one copy—fell open to that passage, not to the later, stickier sex passages.) By the time I was twelve, I had read them all. I didn't read them as examples of radical thought: I read them as bonbons. I read them alongside *Gone With the Wind* and *Rebecca* and *Pride and Prejudice* and all the other books through which girls typically wade on their way into the deeper end of adult fiction. To me, they all told the only story I was interested in reading: the flight to freedom.

These books came out mostly between 1973 and 1978, a bit late in the freedom game for everyone else. At this point, the culture had spent almost a decade selling the idea of freedom to just about everyone. Which was all to the good for the unencumbered, but how did you drop out if you were a mom? I try to imagine what it would have been like to hear this constant message—youth is good, freedom is good—when you had bent your considerable energies to one thing: marriage.

The question arises: What happened? How come we got to sail like fabulous free birds through our twenties, working or studying or partying? How come we were not expected to marry? The answer, I think, lies in our mothers' difficulties, their sticky pulling away from the marriage contract. It's impossible not to acknowledge: Their difficulty is our boon. They wondered, and wandered, and questioned marriage so we wouldn't have to.

My assumption that I would delay marriage, and consequently delay having children, was complete and unquestioned. I never thought about the privileges of growing up with this kind of freedom; the idea of marriage-as-yoke was as distant to me as the idea of wearing a bustle. It wasn't a freedom I cherished; it was a freedom I assumed, and maybe abused. (Then again, maybe a freedom isn't real until it can be abused.)

I certainly never connected the dots between my freedom and my mother's story. If I thought about my own life in terms of feminism at all, I thought about it in heroic, nineteenth-century terms. I thought of the women of Seneca Falls, and I thought about my favorite heroine, Jo March. I thought about suffrage and the ERA and women occupying the offices of *Good Housekeeping*.

I didn't think to put my mother in this lineage. I didn't see how her leaving my lovely father for her young boyfriend had anything to do with feminism.

Like Freeman transmitting the lineage of ashtanga, my mom had transmitted the lineage of feminism. Of course, it did not look so grandiose as all that—it looked like a shabby gray house on Manitou Beach, like a bearded young man with a ready laugh—but that is what it was: a lineage of female self-determination.

These women, the moms who left home in the early 1970s, were a vanguard movement—whether or not their intentions were political. They were the ones who broke the back of expectation. Like union members on strike, they were the ones who would no longer tolerate the working conditions of early marriage and early childbirth, and so they staged a walkout.

Maybe being their kid was tough. Maybe divorce is not what most of us would have chosen for our parents. Maybe we are angry at them, or compensating for them, or sad about what we lost as children. But maybe, just maybe, this is also true: If they had not done what they did, we might have lived utterly different lives. If they had not made new lives, when it was our turn to become young women, we might have found ourselves living ghosts, stuck in the old life they left behind, the life of marriage at twenty-one and a kid at twenty-two; we might be living that life one more time in some kind of eternal return.

And know this: We ourselves might be the ones to flee, to break up marriages, to grab our confused children by the hand and get in the car and drive. Some of us still need to do that. Lisa felt a powerful need to marry and have children early in life; and then she had to leave, to find her way alone.

I wonder if my mother saved me from this fate. Maybe she did this thing for me, like she did so many other things for me, without calling much attention to it.

Without our mothers and their mass 1970s exodus to who knows where, we might not have gotten those crucial years of learning who we were. I am not sure any of the mothers meant to give us this gift, this terrible gift of freedom. In fact, I know for sure that my mom was unnerved by much of what I did with that freedom: the dropping out of school, the flight to the other side of the planet, a flight that made me look suspiciously like someone who literally could not get far enough away from her family. (All I can say is: I invited them to visit!) But they gave it to us. They bought our freedom with their courage.

I recently interviewed a historian for an article I was writing about women's suffrage in Washington State. A cool, elegant woman, she was composed and unemotional throughout our discussion. I got a lot of good facts out of her. As I clicked off my tape recorder and gathered my things to leave, she held up a finger: Just a minute! She pulled a page from a sheaf of photocopied papers and told me she wanted to read me a quote from Susan B. Anthony. Here is what she read: "We shall someday be heeded, and . . . everybody will think it was always so, just exactly as many young people think that all the privileges, all the freedom, all the enjoyments which woman now possesses always were hers."

As the historian read, her voice caught and her eyes teared up. I thought about offering her a Kleenex. Unembarrassed, she continued with Anthony's words: "They have no idea of how every single inch of ground that she stands upon today has been gained by the hard work of some little handful of women of the past." She wiped her eyes.

Blinking behind her glasses, she said, "We all ought to remember those words."

Of course, it is not so simple.

On the one hand, maybe my mother's rift with expectation gave me the freedom to slowly become the writer and mother and wife that I became.

On the other hand, there I was hitchhiking through Australia, climbing into cars with strangers. I would, in time's fullness, become a wife and mother who was so worn out by the chaos of her childhood that she turned her own marriage into a trap. But when I was young, I was as free as I pleased. And that freedom was messy and sometimes scary.

Is that brand of freedom what I would want for my own daughter or son? A thousand times no. It's possible that my parents' split caused me to be a less stable young adult. In her book documenting her study of children from divorced families, *For Better or for Worse*, E. Mavis Hetherington writes that at the twenty-year mark in her study, she found that 20 percent of her subjects were "troubled." These troubled youths "were having difficulty at work, in romantic relationships, and in gaining a toehold in adult life." Let's take a look at my twenty-two-year-old self down in Oz: I was driving a forklift in a warehouse; I was living with a man I met on a street corner; and I was subsisting on a diet of chocolate and sand. A trifecta!

Maybe both perspectives are true. Maybe I was both liberated and a disaster. I know I felt a great deal of terror at the basic sketchy facts of my life during those weird years. I know that other people didn't seem to have such a complicated relationship with the demands of school, or work, or day-to-day life. And yet, let's not forget: I loved the wild adventure of my life.

We can't really know. Maybe I would've been an even flakier kid if my parents had stayed together. In a way, social observation is a kind of speculative fiction: If factor a or factor b had been different, then result x or result y would have occurred. Maybe I was simply afflicted with a serious case of youth. As the Ryan Adams song says, "To Be Young (Is to Be Sad, Is to Be High)."

If the notion of what might've been is inherently unuseful, all we can do is rely on corollaries, like a one-legged skier who relies on two smaller skis that he guides with his hands. And here is what we know: More women and men got divorced in the 1970s. More women put off marriage now. And first marriages that start when the woman is twenty-six or older are 70 percent more likely to be successful than marriages that start at twenty-one. Overall, this new freedom is a boon.

I wasn't my mom. I was hidebound by my need for security. But somehow I had made this leap, just this little leap, with my family, across the country. Now here we were, all together, dazed and happy. We'd done it!

Events are not what make up family life. Family life exists in the nonevents: the meals, the arguments, the reading together, the back-yard soccer, the getting ready for school. We hid alone together on our mountain and reveled in the nonevents. Bruce and I had a bedroom at the top of the house, three stories up, where you felt like your fore-head was grazing eight thousand feet. (Coloradans are obsessed with the metrics of altitude.) The room was huge and airy and mostly made of glass; it shook in the thirty-mile-an-hour winds that scoured the mountaintop. In that high room, there was a high bed. Bruce is six four; the mattress was at his chest height. We needed stairs to get in.

A Saturday afternoon: No one wants to drive up or down the mountain for a playdate. The family is aboard, about, above, across the bed, with comic books and radios, with arguments and elbows to the nose. Willie creates an obstacle course, leaping off the bed onto various cushions. Lucy reads *Harry Potter* and listens to *Wait Wait . . . Don't Tell Me!* at the same time, while riding the exercise bike next to the bed. I fold laundry. Bruce spends some time debating with himself about what he should eat next.

Simple.

We were entirely content. I folded the last towel and said to Bruce, "So, do you think we should stay? In Boulder?"

Bruce gave me a look. "I think we should think about it."

25. WHEEL

The genius would never have claimed perfection or excessive goodness. But that is how it read to me: perfect and good. And I had this idea that perfect and good were just what I didn't need. It was a fledgling idea, and I had an instinct that it needed to be protected and nurtured. Even I could see that. The genius was truly incredible, but it seemed like it might be nice to take incredible off the menu for a while and just enjoy ordinary.

I started trawling around town for yoga classes. I was on the prowl. I was like Diane Keaton in *Looking for Mr. Goodbar*, except without the drugs. And the men. And the death wish. And the good hair. But besides that, I was exactly like her.

I found a few studios that were perfectly pleasant and clean and all, but were rife with Boulder syndrome—too fit, too young, too much facile spirituality. I had become more accepting since my early yoga days, but I still found it tough to have a buff twenty-year-old explain the nature of human existence to me.

There was a joint in the strip mall on the eastern edge of town. It looked like a better place to do a meth deal than to do yoga. It was extremely parking-lot-y. I had been resisting the joint in the strip mall on general principles. Leigh had taken a class from the owner and described her as "compassionate." Coming from a die-hard New Yorker like Leigh, it was hard to know if that was a compliment or an insult. Still, I decided to try a morning class. I unrolled my mat. There were people of all ages and sizes and genders. This was good.

A freckle-faced woman in her fifties came in. She was wearing a sloppy T-shirt and didn't have the best figure. I mentally kicked myself for assessing her figure. What was this, the judgment of Paris? Why do I do this? She sat down in the teacher's spot, in the middle against the east wall, and looked around at us. It was the look of a teacher who was about to begin class: Are you with me? Are we ready? Except here's what happened next:

The teacher, whose name was Katharine Seidel, began to massage her feet. This wasn't that unusual; classes occasionally opened with what is termed self-massage, which always cracked me up in a juvenile way.

Only this time, instead of leading us into foot massage, she said, "So I was just thinking, I saw Laurie Anderson play live once. With Lou Reed. You know they're an item, right? They were inCREDible. Laurie especially. She was just, like, incandescent."

Her face lit up a bit at the thought. It was strange to be talking about Laurie Anderson at yoga, but maybe the teacher was headed for some kind pithy yogic wisdom. Sometimes teachers trotted out these little stories at the beginning of class. However, as I've said before, they were usually more Indian-sounding than this. This sounded like . . . chat.

"It was so amazing to think that no matter what happens, she just keeps making her art. She has such perseverance . . ." She trailed off. "Do you guys like Laurie Anderson's music? It's kind of weird, don't you think?"

A couple of people volunteered that they used to listen to Laurie Anderson back in the 1980s.

The teacher smiled at them and then said, "OK! Anyhow! Let's do some poses."

We started doing postures. She had an incredibly calm presence. It wasn't phony calm or ostentatiously calm. It was calm like a bird on a wire; it was calm like "What's going to happen next?"

She watched us as we worked. It was like being looked at by a benevolent kindergarten teacher with a fabulous sense of humor. She occasionally punctuated class with statements such as "You guys are really gonna hate the next one!" These lines were delivered in an unforgettable voice: low in register, slow, humorous, deliberate, deadpan.

Just when I was starting to think she was some kind of crazy proponent of laughter yoga, she asked us to sit in marichi's twist, the seated pose where you twist your body against an upright bent knee and gaze out over your shoulder.

"This is an interesting pose," she said in her throaty voice, which sounded like a meandering trail. Her sentences got where they were going, eventually.

"This is one of the relatively few poses in yoga where your gaze ought to extend beyond your mat. You look into the distance. There are fewer poses like this than you think. Most of the time, you should keep your gaze close to you. Keep your gaze within the area of your mat. That will keep your concentration where it needs to be: inside."

This was possibly the single most useful piece of yoga advice I had ever heard. Keep your gaze within the area of your mat. It was so simple. It was the physical description of that lecture Fran had given all those years ago about pratyahara, the practice of turning attention inward. It was a very specific instruction in how to keep from being distracted. It was much easier to keep my gaze within the area of my mat than it was to "practice pratyahara."

Also, I was enchanted by the phrase "keep your gaze close to you." I loved the idea of the gaze as something that might be husbanded or herded, like a sheep. The gaze, in this phrase, became a resource. It would always be there to help you, if you took good care of it.

At the end of class, we meditated. From the way she sat, it was obvious she was someone who meditated a lot. I watched her. When she shut her eyes, there was true unself-consciousness on her face. This is a rare thing to see in another human being, especially with their eyes closed. She wasn't protecting herself; she wasn't showing off; she didn't give a shit if anyone was looking at her. How could I tell all this? I don't know. Maybe by her freckles.

When she opened her eyes, they looked wet and glowing.

I started going to Seidel's class regularly. I always thought of her as Seidel. She fit right in with Spellman and Freeman. As a teacher, she seemed to have two settings: entirely exterior and connected, through laughter, jokes, and smiles; and entirely interior. There didn't seem to be that third place, where most of us live all the time.

Though most of the strip-mall teachers had been trained by the genius, their classes were as far from ashtanga as you could imagine. They were anti-vinyasa. Their yoga seemed to be about not trying, about finding the most efficient, least effortful way possible to do a pose. They did not link poses very often. It was like they were scientists, and the studio was their lab, and the poses were their experiments: What happens to the outer hip of the standing leg in bird of paradise? What about the vertebrae C3 and C4 in bridge?

They had weird ways of isolating and relaxing secret muscles, muscles heretofore undiscovered by people who dwelt beyond the strip mall. You would lie supine at the wall, gently twist your legs overhead in some surprising configuration, and grow slowly bored, wondering when the action was going to start. Then you would try to move, and discover that you had somehow Rolfed yourself. Surprise!

They were big on the thoracic spine. This is the fancy term for the middle of your back, which they felt didn't get enough attention. They seemed almost to have taken a political stance on this. They felt the thoracic spine had unfairly been exiled, and needed to be repatriated into the rest of the body.

They were, in fact, obsessed with skeletons. They wanted us to forget our muscles and remember and trust our bones. "Do this pose with your skeleton!" was their refrain. "Let the muscles go and trust the structure." The idea was to stop gripping yourself into place with your muscles; instead, find a skeletal alignment that was sustainable, that didn't need muscular support to be held for some time.

One sunny morning Seidel led us in bridge, trying to teach us to trust our bones and to stop "efforting" with our muscles. My habit of muscling my way into a pose, my trick of engaging the bandhas in order to endure a pose—these were not acceptable strategies at the strip mall. No efforting allowed. We lay on our backs, knees bent, feet standing, and lifted our hips in the air. I pushed my hips up hard, trying to get a good arch in my back.

"No, no, no!" said Seidel, sounding like one of those old-biddy ballet martinets. "Too high, all of you! Lift again, not so high. Just push up, only using your legs. Don't use your butt muscles at all."

We tried again. I concentrated on my legs.

"Still too high! Listen, just lift your hips a couple of inches from the ground."

We tried this. It felt like cheating, to just lift a little off the floor. Weren't we supposed to lift as high as possible?

"Now, just hammock your weight between your shoulders and your knees. Make no effort. Stop holding on with your muscles. Release your buttock muscles! Just let the arrangement of the bones hold you up."

I couldn't really feel anything.

We came down.

"What are we supposed to be feeling?" I asked.

"Exactly!" she said. "What are we supposed to be feeling? Who knows? We're working with the subtle body. It's gonna surprise us. We just have to get out the way."

"Do it again," she said. "Don't use your butt. Just let it all happen at a deep, structural level."

We did bridge in this manner a few more times. She walked around the room, checking our bottoms to see if our glutes were tensed.

Then she wanted us to try wheel, also known as full backbend. If there is a pose that's all muscle for me, it's backbend. I sort of shove my way into it, like it's the doorway to the Bendel's Christmas sale and I'm one of those shopping-crazed matrons in an old *New Yorker* cartoon.

Backbends have always been hard for me. I'm a huncher. I hunch when I stand and I hunch when I write. Sometimes I suspect that years of breast-feeding left me curled forward like a fist or a flower.

As I prepared for wheel, I thought back to Fran, all those years ago, offhandedly describing the feeling in my chest as fear. It was no joke. It was scary to unfold my chest, to open something that remained so habitually closed.

I thought of Fran, and fear, as I got ready to do wheel. Preparation for wheel was always a psychodrama for me. I was too weak. I wasn't flexible enough. I was sure that I would collapse on my head with a clonk and end up with a broken neck.

As I ran down my litany of pre-wheel worries, like a fighter pilot going down a checklist, Seidel said, "I don't know about you, but I'm kind of a hunchy person. I don't mean I have great hunches about things. I mean, I hunch a lot. When I'm at yoga, I do the opposite of hunching. I open. I draw my shoulders back. I used to think that if I did enough yoga I would learn to stop hunching in regular life. I would teach myself at yoga to become a non-hunchy person, and I would go around all the time with wide, open shoulders."

I positioned my feet a few inches from my hips. I slid my hands behind my shoulders, palms facing down, fingers pointing down my back. I felt that strange pulling in the backside of the arms that comes in backbend preparation. This opening of the wrists and the triceps is a sensation that is unique to backbend and its variants; nothing I did in day-to-day life replicated this feeling.

With the profound feeling of doubt—and its Kierkegaardian twin, faith—that always accompanied rising up, I pushed into wheel. I panicked. I stopped breathing.

"OK, so now you're up. You're freaking out, right? You're panicking. That's cool. Just ignore it."

We all made strange "meh, meh" sounds that were our substitute for laughter.

"Now, you know your legs are strong. Use them. Stop using your arm muscles and your back muscles. Think about legs and core. And let your back muscles drape over the arc of your spine. Think of your skeleton in this pose as architecture, and just drape over it."

And there, for a split second, I had it. My muscles released. In fact, they did not release themselves. I released them. I let go. It was scary.

But for a second I trusted that everything was fine. The structure was sound. It would be OK. And it was heavenly, like my muscles were syrup poring over rock.

"Great!" she said. "Come on down, for god's sake."

We let ourselves down.

"Anyway. I think of yoga as a kind of counterweight to the way I behave in the rest of my life. No matter how hunched I am the rest of the time, I know that for at least an hour or so every day, I'll have beautiful, open shoulders. I've given up on having them in the rest of life. I just enjoy them while I have them."

A counterweight. This seemed to me the pithiest description of transformation I had ever heard. You didn't lead up to it or analyze it or try to apply it in different situations. You just created optimal situations for being different, and then you were different. You didn't have to worry about changing everything about yourself, or fixing the fear, or being someone new. You just acted like the person you wanted to be, when and if you could.

It was easy to think of yoga as a cure, a program, a teleology. You were going to end up somewhere really great if you just stuck with it. I often thought about what yoga would give me: yoga butt, open hamstrings, equilibrium, a calm mind, that mysterious yoga glow. And it was true, a person would be more likely to have those things if she went to yoga than if she, say, played Tetris for hours on end. (Always an option.)

The idea was, you got better, looser, stronger while you were at yoga, and then you exported that excellence to the rest to life. You learned how to act right at yoga, and then you acted right, or righter, when you were in your car, or at the grocery store, or putting your children to bed.

What if, as Seidel said, we just enjoyed the way our bodies and minds were when we were at yoga, and stopped freighting it with expectations? What if the whole point of yoga wasn't getting ready for the future, but was instead finding whatever pleasure we could in the present?

26. HANDSTAND

The next morning, I woke up as usual. The sun shone on the mountaintop as usual. The week before, I had told a man I met in a bar that I didn't know why I felt better here in the mountains than I did in Seattle. He had said, "Gee, maybe it's that big fiery ball that comes up in the sky every day."

My bed faced west. I could feel the sun, that big fiery ball, behind me. I rolled from my bed and went to face the tasks of morning that unspooled before me like the ribbony dirt road that led to the bus stop: wake kids, make breakfast, lunch, clothes, hair, teeth, walk to bus, kiss goodbye.

The kitchen, like my bed, also faced west. The sun hadn't made its way over here yet. There was Bruce, with a coffee for me in his hand. Every day he greeted me with coffee. Muzzily I poured Raisin Bran into a bowl. As often happened in the morning, the minutes stole by, like mice running along the baseboards. You didn't even see them go past.

I looked up. The others were talking to one another, an activity that was not available to me in the morning. I glanced at the clock and: It was late! It was time for . . . hair.

I snatched up the hairbrush. Lucy, seeing me, ran. Finally I caught her in the living room. She resignedly sat down on the arm of the sofa, broken. I dragged the brush through her hair.

"Ouch," she cried. Lucy, who could make beautiful sentences of unexpected shape and vocabulary, always uttered this ordinary cry when her hair was brushed. I would've thought, before I had children, that in this narrative I would have related to the child. That was just the kind of person I was. Yet now I ignored her cry, maybe even pulled the brush a bit harder. I gathered handfuls of thick hair for a ponytail. The ponytails I made were slightly inept, not quite neat. Maybe this messiness made me pull the brush even harder, determined to exert control over this unruly mass.

Sometimes, during hairbrushing, I realized I was creating a memory in my child. Lucy would maybe always hate having her hair brushed, hate this naked moment of control.

Lucy looked at me. "You are churlish," she said. "You are full of churl."

She kept looking. My own hair needed a trim and a dye job and stood in a wild corona around my head.

Lucy pointed this out. "Mommy. Your hair is messy." Pause. "Your hair is a disaster."

She snatched the brush, seeming to catch the violence of my movements, and plied the brush on my messy, sweaty crown. This was intolerable to me, to have my hair brushed by my child. I gave a shout and snatched the brush back. Our eyes met. Lucy had my number. She looked at the brush in my hand. "That," she said, "is an instrument of torture. Now you know."

I looked at her. I wasn't exactly giving up or giving in. I just thought, Why not? Why not let her go to school with messy hair? Does it really matter? I took the brush gently from her and threw it on the couch.

It was bus time. I slipped a down coat over my pajamas. Outside, we saw the sun breaching the shoulder of Green Mountain. From a

few paces behind everyone else, I watched my daughter walking down
the road to the school bus. Bruce and Willie walked ahead, one very
tall, the other very short, a visual joke. My daughter's body was
straight and tall. Her ponytail swung, curly and confident and tangled. My daughter was everything I had not felt I was as a child:
straight and beautiful and true. And still I tried to make her more perfect, more acceptable, more tidy. Less real, more good.

What if I applied Seidel's idea of a counterbalance here and now?
What if I didn't have some goal for how I might act but simply acted
differently? Simply stopped being so preoccupied with doing things
perfectly. Caught myself at it before I fell.

I kissed my children goodbye at the bus, giving an extra squeeze to
Lucy. Later that week I went to class at a yoga studio that I didn't normally frequent. It was a kind of yoga mill, a chain that had outlets in
half a dozen states. It was a strange dynamic: You literally felt like a
cog in a yoga machine when you went to class there. University of
Colorado sorority girls jammed the place, with its big, ultraclean,
characterless yoga rooms, masses of corporate branding, and annoy-
ingly expensive towel policy. I suppose in some weird sense there
was a purity to it. If yoga is about moving past the importance of the
self, this place made you feel as depersonalized as possible. Well,
except for the mirrors everywhere. Those kept reminding you who
you were.

But this was the only yoga class I could make it to. The yoga mill
offered about twenty classes a day. It was like the Honey Nut Cheerios
of the yoga world; always there for you, in lieu of a real meal.

Its class offerings were hilariously off-brand. Hot Yoga, which I
pictured written in the same black-on-white lettering they used to use
on generic beer, was simply an unlicensed Bikram. Same locked knees,
same demented huffing straight-legged sit-up. Same heat. Power Yoga
was ashtanga done very carelessly. Sometimes I saw the genius's students laboring in these mines as teachers. They had to follow the yoga
mill's prescribed series, so they couldn't include any of the genius's
daffier instructions. Somehow "billow your knees like sails in the
wind" just wouldn't sound right here.

I was at Power Yoga, which was essentially the same sequence I did at home alone, a couple of sun salutations, a simple linking of standing poses, some twisty chair, some seated stretches. Toward the end of class, the instructor said, "Let's try handstand today. Please pull your mat to the wall."

Inversions would seem to go well with the mill's relentlessly youthful and physical approach to yoga. And yet we rarely were asked to perform them there. Too many lawsuits, probably.

But maybe this particular teenage supermodel teacher hadn't gotten the memo. I stared at her. Now that she had said that word—handstand—I realized with a sudden feeling of guilt that this was one of the reasons I went to the yoga mill in the first place. I took secret not-quite-conscious solace in the knowledge that I wouldn't be asked to do handstand. This was the one pose I would not do. I had overcome my hatred of chaturanga; I moved through it as best I could. But handstand—all your weight on your palms—it was too much. I couldn't trust myself that far. Long ago, I had mastered headstand, but the balance required for handstand seemed beyond me.

I pulled my mat over and thought about flipping up into headstand, which was no problem for me. My forearms, my shoulders, I knew they were strong. But in a trice, I made a decision: Fuck that. I was a Boulder lady now! I could hike up and ski down! At ten thousand feet! Certainly I could pull off a handstand. I would trust my skeleton, like Seidel said, and not overthink it.

I situated my hands a little away from the wall. I spread my fingers. I lifted into downward dog and began to walk my feet toward my hands. My bottom (or my "botto," as Lucy called it) rose higher and higher in the air. The crucial moment came. I kicked with my right leg, kicked with all my might, zipping my stomach tight as I did so. For one moment, my legs were up the air, I was inverted. And then I fell, mostly on my mat, with what seemed like the loudest sound that has been made by any human body ever.

I sat up with red cheeks. The small person who was teaching the class rushed over. "Are you OK?"

I sat up, rubbing my head like Harold Lloyd after a pratfall. "I'm good."

"You sure?" She looked nervous. Maybe she had just remembered that she wasn't supposed to teach inversions when there were slightly chubby middle-aged women in the class.

"Yeah, I think I'm fine." I moved around a little to show her that my various parts were still functional.

"You know, next time you should think about your core." She patted her stomach.

"I know, I know," I said. The excuse was about to tumble out of my mouth: Two C-sections had given me a weak core. But the fact remained: I fell.

We finished class and I sheepishly got the hell out of there. I wasn't suing them. This time.

On the way back up the mountain, I started to recover from my humiliation, and I got to thinking about inversions. What is it about them that is so scary? Certainly it's a matter of strength; our arms are not as strong as our legs, and we'd look pretty funny if they were. But it's more than that. Inversions are upsetting. They ask us to remove our familiar perspective. The world doesn't make the same sense it did in the moments before you kicked up. That change of perspective could be difficult, even intolerable.

I looked up "inversion" in our compact *Oxford English Dictionary* when I got home. Its initial definition was simple: a turning upside down. I went down the list: a turning out of the contents. This was a good description of what happened at yoga sometimes. The reversal of a ratio. This was interesting, given my small epiphany on the mat the other day in savasana. Yoga had helped to reverse the goodness-to-reality ratio in my life.

I had started going to yoga because I wanted other people to admire my goodness. I came to yoga with my plate held out, asking yoga to give me the same old stuff I'd been receiving all my life, repackaged and in a groovier new form. Going to yoga was part of my goodness project. And yet what yoga seemed to be teaching me was this: Who cares? Who cares about goodness? Who even cares how it looks? There's only this: a woman in a heap on the floor. No one ever said reality was going to be dignified.

If I wanted to look at how things really were, I was going to find imperfection. What would real look like? Without good there, gussying it up, brushing its hair?

I wanted to learn how to exist inside this anastrophe, this reversal of the old ratio, this inversion.

27. LION

We were doing a series of painful calf and foot releases. We did downward dog with the tops of our toes rolled under, bringing more and more weight back onto the feet. We kneeled with a rolled mat resting on top of our calves, then set the full weight of our butts on the rolled mat, so its lower bulge dug deeply into our calves.

"Gee!" said Seidel. "This really hurts! You hate this, right?"

We all nodded and laughed, hoping she would tell us to stop.

"You want me to tell you to stop. So. Stop if you want. Or you can hang on a bit longer."

Someone groaned. Seidel laughed.

"Right! Ugh, right? OK, so here's what we do. We do lion."

Lion: the pose where you took a deep breath. You exhaled it with a giant, loud "Hah!" As you hah!-ed, you opened your mouth wide, stuck your tongue way out, bugged your eyes, and gazed upward.

We did it. A deep breath. A giant exhale, tongues out, eyes bugging. And again, and again.

"O lion of realization," said Seidel. "That's the beginning of a poem that Yogananda wrote. You know, the guy who wrote *Autobiography of a Yogi*. O lion of realization . . ." She trailed off. "You'll be shocked to hear that I can't remember the rest."

We rolled off our mats and laid down to recover for a moment.

Lion had always bugged me. It seemed self-consciously unselfconscious. It was such an extravagantly free gesture that it called attention to its own freedom. Look at me! I don't care if anyone is looking at me! There was something in lion that reminded me of the laughter of hippies. You know the hippie laugh. It says: I'm light of heart! Yet aware of my foibles! And also free! Very, very free! This laugh is often heard at, say, lectures given by non-Westerners. If the non-Westerner makes even the feeblest joke—the kind of lame crack that back home would earn him maybe a wry smile and a raised eyebrow—his American audience will erupt in hippie laughter. It's the kind of chuckle that you hear from students when a yoga teacher tells an extra-funny story about monkeys, or a dharma teacher talks about losing her temper in traffic.

There are other behaviors that go with the knowing hippie laugh: Public singing and dancing come to mind. For instance, in the aisle at Whole Foods. I'm so free! I'm just gonna let loose with a little jig right here next to the tahini!

Lion felt part and parcel of all that to me. It felt like phony freedom. It felt like an exclamation point where a simple period would do. But I wondered: In my attitude wasn't there something of the little old lady peeking censoriously from behind her lace curtain? I thought of my old friend from college who, reading my book criticism, e-mailed me to say, "Your métier appears to be disappointment." Why was I so annoyed by lion? It's not like it was hurting anyone.

Van Morrison has a song called "Listen to the Lion." It's the most Van Morrison-y of all Van Morrison songs. Morrison growls and roars and hardly utters any intelligible words at all, other than "Listen to the lion inside of me." (Though there are also some demented ramblings that appear to be about sailing to Caledonia.) It's a completely spastic, unrestrained gesture of a song.

Back in college, we used to have a silly rubric: Never have sex with anyone who doesn't like Van Morrison. They will be bad in bed. This notion was based on the fact that Van Morrison is embarrassing, and sex is embarrassing.

And. Lion was embarrassing. It made you feel like Van Morrison, all uncontrollable noises and strange eruptions. Lion was, in its way, unforgiving. You couldn't do it partway. The smart brain, the one that paid my bills and remembered to buy anti-frizz stuff for my hair, got totally upstaged. In fact, the smart brain could really screw up lion. If you actually thought while you did lion, you ended up with a lame minor distortion of your face. Lion was like the tango; it had to be done with absolute commitment. Otherwise, why do it at all?

Seidel, wily enough to know she was onto a good thing, had us do lion throughout class that day. By the end, I was roaring alongside everyone else. I felt a lot embarrassed, a little free, and a tiny bit bad-ass. These three teachers—Freeman, Seidel, Spellman—were like cartoon wives hitting me over the head with a frying pan. Get over yourself! You're gonna fuck up! And it'll be OK.

With their voices in my ears, I could just about face thinking about going home again.

I walked into Bruce's office to check in about the kids' schedule. Outside, the northern flicker—it was always the same one—was hammering his beak against the side of the house. His tattoo punctuated our workday. Often I would find Bruce and the flicker staring at each other, half comically, half confrontationally, through the glass. But today Bruce was sitting silently with his head in his hands.

Uh-oh.

"I can't figure out how we're going to pay for everything," he said.

I had seen this before: the drooping flower of his head, the bent back.

"We always seem to figure it out."

"I can't figure out how I'm going to do enough freelancing to support us."

I was making my usual genteel pittance.

"Well, let's see," I said. "Let's make a list of all the money we have coming in over the next couple of months." I somewhat officiously got out paper and pen, and together we made a list that did appear frighteningly paltry. So I did the next thing I usually did; I made a list of stories I could pitch. If I sold every story on my list, we could conceivably pay all our bills. For one month.

It was true that our financial life was a house of cards. It was also true that Bruce was congenitally ill-suited to such a life. On the other hand, here we were, writing together, in the middle of a weekday, in the middle of the mountains. You could not expect to have all that and financial stability, too.

I said as much, but it was no help. This time Bruce's depression came quickly and entirely. By that night he was sleepless; and he stayed that way for two weeks. I tossed and turned anxiously next to him.

Two weeks turned into a month.

I was worried. I didn't tell anyone what was going on.

I fell into my old habits. At first I was sympathetic, but then I grew anxious, short-tempered, and even bitchy.

"Go to sleep!" I said at night. "Drink some Nyquil."

And in the day: "Go for a walk! It's beautiful out."

But after a while, a new feeling emerged. I felt something new. Part of me felt like: So what?

I lay down on the couch in his office and I said it.

"So you're depressed. So what? It'll go away eventually. It's not the end of the world. You were happy until two weeks ago. You seem happy most of the time. This is a blip."

"I hope so," he said. His hair stood up all over his head. I could tell what he was thinking. He wanted to go back to work.

That very day Leigh called to see if we wanted to go to a party. I told her, "Bruce is depressed. I'll come by myself." There. I had said it. The world hadn't ended. Nor had my marriage. Maybe each trial didn't make another chink in the armor of marriage, bringing it to its inevitable end point: divorce. Maybe each trial made a marriage.

Right in the middle of all this came our tenth wedding anniversary.

My mom came out to take care of the kids so we could go away for the weekend. We could not think of any place on earth we preferred to where we were, so we stayed put and planned a series of long hikes and dinners out.

The evening she got in, the two of us sat over a glass of wine at the kitchen table. We talked about the usual things: gossip about the cousins.

There was a lull in the conversation.

"So, I got a lawyer."

This made me feel unaccountably anxious. I don't know why this should've surprised me. If they were getting a divorce, they'd need lawyers, right? I mean, if they were going to get a real divorce.

"Oh. Um, how is that?"

"She's great! She's younger than you, and so smart. She's been explaining a lot to me about how the process works."

Clearly my mom had decided that a young, smart lawyer was the chicest and most ideal lawyer to have.

"Has she met with Dad's lawyer?"

"We're preparing for that meeting."

Preparing for that meeting! What the hell! What was to prepare? Were they going to get in some kind of divorce battle?

"Well, good luck to all!" I gave her a little hug. She was all bones, Seidel's perfect student. It was funny, she snuggled away with the kids, but with me, there was a reserve. Was she protecting herself from me? Or did she dislike hugging adults?

"You'll watch out for lions tomorrow, won't you?"

"Mom! It'll be fine."

I went to bed worried that night. If lawyers were involved, things could turn toward conflict. This separation that had been a stable arrangement for thirty-five years; what would happen with the introduction of a volatile element? Would the balloon of goodwill pop?

It was odd to think: The lawyering up made me appreciate the serenity and friendliness that had been there all along. It reminded me that my parents' weird setup had come from good intentions. Conflict avoidance, and good intentions.

Whatever happened next, I would just have to live with it. The thing was in motion now, becoming reality. Lawyers are as real as it gets. And somehow, despite my nervousness about the whole thing, I trusted my parents to act with truly good intentions.

The next day, our actual anniversary, we decided to hike up to the Continental Divide, the ridge of ridges that we could see from our bedroom. It was a clear fall day. The sun was shining and we had big plans to make the Divide quickly and then go into Nederland (the scrappy mountain town above Boulder, affectionately known as Ned) and eat a lot of ribs.

We were hiking through a forest, thick for the Front Range, toward a draw. Thick forests meant animals. I began to get that scrambled feeling in my chest. Mountain lions had been killing dogs in this area all year.

The feeling by now was familiar: suppressed terror based on an idea. It was hard to know how much terror was the right amount of terror for the given situation. As Bruce and I walked, I played with different amounts of terror. I imagined I could feel the lion stalking us, leaping from tree to tree as it waited for its perfect opportunity to pounce and devour us. Then I downshifted a little. I imagined the lion appearing in front of us on the trail, holding us in its gaze. I imagined myself snatching up a stick (in this particular version, there was always a stick right to hand) and making myself large and yelling at the lion. Then I really went for it and tried to imagine what it would feel like in that first moment when the lion flung its weight upon you. What would that snarling, moving weight feel like?

In Boulder, mountain lions were cocktail-party chat. I had listened, over a glass of Malbec, to a story about an old woman and an old man, husband and wife, who were hiking in California. A mountain lion attacked the old man and held his head in the grip of its mouth. The old woman got a giant stick and bashed the lion on the head, repeatedly. She pulled her husband's head from the lion's jaws.

To have your head in the lion's jaws. I contemplated this idea with something approaching jealousy. We fear an idea, and we hike along, and the fear grows bigger and bigger, until finally we find ourselves craving its realization, if only to escape the idea.

We emerged from the woods into a high, wide, treeless draw with a narrow creek running through it. No more animals. We hiked on and on; the open, gray meadow seemed to go on forever. The hike was making Bruce cheerful—it was very difficult for him to be glum while hiking—and it was making me less crabby, less anxious. We gossiped about the children as we walked.

"Do you think Lucy will be invited to Olivia's birthday party?" I asked.

"Oh, my god. What I think is that you need some co-workers to gossip about. Rather than third-grade social life."

"Don't you have to go into an office every day if you want to have co-workers? That's what I heard. Anyway, do you think Olivia has sent out her invites yet?"

"You're mentally ill, you know that?"

As we chatted, a flake fell from the sky.

"Snow alert," I said happily, anticipating a dusting.

By the time we reached the Divide, which was at twelve thousand feet plus change, we were in thick snow. The ridge seemed knife-edged and narrow. We decided to walk along it a bit, to look for a tarn that was supposed to be a little ways ahead. The landscape was bare, with not even a shrub. Great boulders littered the ground, which was the color that decorators call "greige."

As we walked, the snow fell more thickly, and then more thickly still, until it occurred to us that we were in something like a blizzard. As we turned to head back down, we heard thunder. Then, through the clouded white, a flash of lightning came up from the west side of the ridge. We stood exposed on the ridge and watched the fatal yellow flash through the scrim of thick white, the realest thing we ever saw.

I had spent two years worrying about mountain lions and now here I was on a mountaintop in some kind of unholy lightning/blizzard combo storm. I had been worrying about the wrong goddamn thing. All my precautions were for nothing. Reality found me, and instead of being slobbery and muscular, it was cold and light and flashing.

"OK," said Bruce. He patted me on the back and smiled at me, a dazzling smile that was both entirely inappropriate to the moment and exactly what I needed to see. He was, after all, my husband. Not just the father of my kids, not just the fourth wheel. He was someone who could floor me with a smile. "Get behind me, and put your hand on my backpack."

I tightened the distance between us. I rested my hand on his yellow pack. Together, we made our way down the ridge, in what we hoped was the right direction.

28. MONKEY

 Isabel came for a visit, in her little car. She was driving across the country to hang a show in Kansas City and then Austin—the work was being shipped.

I stood in front of my house waiting for her, looking across the meadow to where, in the distance, I could just see the mountain road at the end of my driveway. There was her car, zipping along.

She unfolded from the driver's seat, tall and tomboy-ish and beautiful and the teeniest bit formidable. We went straight up on the roof and had a beer.

"We're thinking about staying," I said.

She was distracted by the Continental Divide.

"Good. I was kind of sick of listening to you complain about Seattle."

"I know. I was sick of myself. But I'm happy here. I have space."

"Space from what? I mean, obviously you have space." She gestured with her hand and we kind of laughed at the excess of space around us—twenty miles of mountain air. "But what do you need space from?"

"Um, Seattle. My family, I guess." I told her how happy we felt with more time for just us.

"Oh, you don't really want space from your family. I ran into your mom at the grocery store."

"Which one?"

"The QFC in the University Village." This was the fancy-ass mall near my mom's house.

"What were you doing there?"

"Fatal error," she said in a robotic voice.

"I'll say."

"Anyway, you'd miss your mom. She's so cute!"

"Hmm."

We went into Boulder. We walked through its streets, filled with beautiful children and cute shops. We walked along the creek, which was urban and full of fish at the same time, which you might have thought was oxymoronic. We walked by the expensive New Age pharmacy and the handmade-paper shop and the four places to buy antiqued garden furniture. We climbed the old wooden stairs to Upstairs at the Kitchen, the bar I favored.

Isabel settled herself on a chic woolly pouf. She ordered a whiskey sour. She stirred it with its darling little stick.

She said sternly to me, "You can't live here."

"Why not?"

"It's not real. It's too pretty, too adorable. It's like Carmel, only more New Age and in the mountains. It's, like, all cute shops. That's it. Cute shops and Tibetan prayer flags. You can move away from Seattle, but you can't move here."

We ordered the cheese platter (which came with figs!) and talked about Lisa. Still out of the house; no longer with Carl; madly doing yoga. Oh, dear. I was missing plot points out here in the mountains.

Isabel stayed for another day of drinking and hiking. Where did she get her energy?

Early on the following day, she headed off in her little car. It was a sparkling, chilly early-winter day. Before she left, she took a picture of Bruce and me in front of our house, our arms wrapped around each other, the sun shining. In the photo, we look old and happy. We walked the quarter mile to the end of the drive to pick up the newspaper. We didn't wear coats, just T-shirts. We were becoming Coloradans; we didn't feel the cold so much anymore.

"She is so great," said Bruce as we let ourselves into the house. He set about making one of his incredibly smelly fried-egg sandwiches. He was one of those skinny people who requires massive infusions of calories all day long. I poured myself some cereal.

"She says we can't stay here," I said. "She says Boulder is like Carmel, but with Tibetan prayer flags."

He laughed. "Well, it is. But isn't the whole point that we don't really care what anyone thinks?"

"True. But she does have a point. And I miss her so much."

"I think," he said, "that we would really miss all our friends if we stayed. And our families. I mean, it's good here. But it's not perfect."

"It's not perfect. And I miss my family. I mean, my other family."

"Well, at least you know which is which." He smiled at me.

"How do we know we won't just go home and be miserable? Maybe we're simpler than we think. Maybe we're just happy here 'cause it's sunny."

"We don't know. We might be in total misery."

"Yeah! We might!"

"I think it'll be OK. I think we know how much we like our family time now, and we'll make sure we get it."

"Maybe. But it's gonna rain. A lot."

I thought about the fact that I had grown up with the Northwest landscape, that I had lived with it all my life. Bruce had even written a book about Mount Rainier. I thought about salt water a lot. Could I get along without it? When I drove down the mountain, I was confronted with the empty plains stretching out toward Kansas. Even after living there for a year, every time I drove down the mountain I expected that emptiness to be filled with salt water. I had a daily moment of cognitive dissonance: Where am I?

I decided to check in with Spellman. He had given me his phone number and for months we had meant to meet for coffee. Maybe I could consult with him, as though he were Yoda? Maybe this would help.

We met at the Boulder Dushanbe Teahouse, a building that was given to the city by its sister city, Dushanbe, in Tajikistan. An elegant, airy structure, it was painted blue and filled with tiles, murals, and a huge fountain.

We sat next to the fountain and ordered iced teas.

I meant to ask him about what I should do, but found myself blurting out something else: "Are you a Buddhist?" Spellman's mind was so nimble and refined that he made such a direct question seem a bit coarse.

"I sit," he said.

That set me on my heels for a moment. Eventually I resorted to that old warhorse: "Why?"

He paused. "Because I want to experience this." He waved a hand.

I found this strangely flattering, that he wanted to experience this. I understood that he meant what is usually called the present moment, but "this" was a much more interesting way of putting it.

Spellman seemed uninterested in defining himself as a particular kind of Buddhist, or as a Buddhist at all.

We talked about Naropa for a while. The fountain tinkled away and the sun shone in. It was very pleasant.

I asked him what it meant to be a good Buddhist.

"I'm not sure 'good' is a very helpful word," he said. "If you're busy being good, you're probably going to miss this. You're going to miss the real stuff that's going on all around you. No, 'good' doesn't really come into it."

He leaned forward, his gaze direct behind his horn-rims, looking as always like he was going to tell the best joke ever, maybe one about a horse who goes into a bar. He said, "I think you might want to expunge that word from your vocabulary."

I never did ask him about whether or not I should go home. Like

Yoda, he would just give me some "know thyself" answer. And I already did.

I went home and told Bruce what Spellman had said, about the uselessness of being good. "Huh," said Bruce.

I thought about my mom bringing the news of her new lawyer to me, gingerly, carefully. What I thought mattered to her, to them. It didn't matter in the same way here.

I missed them—my parents and their cagey ways. I even missed being annoyed by them. Boulder was a tonic, a place where your path (in all its meanings) could be the most important thing in your life, and you could be surrounded by other people on their very special paths. You could learn things here, about yoga and the nature of reality and yourself. But what was the point of knowing them in a bubble? I had a mom and a dad and Larry and a brother and more cousins than I could count on all my fingers.

Some people can go away and make new lives and be fully realized and transformed. They can live on a mountainside in the sunshine and be uncomplicatedly grateful for the reality they've chosen and/or created. Not me. The problem of understanding my family and my history, in a real way, would, I suspected, take me the rest of my life. I could practice reality, and imperfection, and messiness in Boulder, but really, it felt like avoiding the whole point. Reality was at home, with my family. My other family.

The next week Bruce and I were hiking and I brought up the topic again.

"We could make a list," I said. "Pros and cons."

We walked a narrow trail along the south fork of Boulder Creek. Up here in the mountains it was more river than creek, boiling and surging between giant rocks. We made a list: one for Boulder and one for home. Boulder had many more pros than home did.

"Um, it seems like a clue that we keep calling it 'home,'" said Bruce.

We had been children, really, until we moved to Boulder, unable and unwilling to direct our own destinies. It was embarrassing to admit, but we had finally grown up. And as grown-ups, we felt confident about going back.

We went home to call my mom and e-mail my dad to say we were coming back.

"Oh, honey, that's great. Is Lucy there? Or Willie? Can I talk to them?"

I got the kids for her.

"My mom seems so serene about the whole thing," I said when I had handed the phone over to Lucy. "Like she was expecting us to come back all along. Couldn't we get a little excitement? Do they always have to take us for granted?"

I was already getting fed up and we hadn't even gone home yet.

"God, they're so aggravating!"

"Well, we don't have to live right on top of them," said Bruce. "All we know is we want to live in the Northwest, and somewhere where there's nature. I mean, I'm willing to accept the absence of sun, but there definitely seems to be a corollary between our happiness and the presence of trees."

"So let's make a list," I said.

"Like before we came here."

"Exactly."

"OK, Portland."

"Too urban."

"Olympia."

"I think it gets like thirty inches more rain a year than Seattle does. Can that be right? How about Eugene?"

"Too far. Bellingham."

"Too cold. Orcas Island." This was a remote hippie enclave near Stuart Island.

"Too far from an airport. What about Bainbridge Island?"

"Huh."

It was perfect. We would have nature. We would have a moat, protecting our little family from too many familial incursions. If we went back, we would need that moat. If we went back, we would basically have to be assholes and say no a lot. But sometimes we could say yes.

We would be unto ourselves, but the ferries would be there, plying their routes east and west across the sound, connecting us to everyone else.

The rest of the school year was spent throwing parties for our friends and bawling. Sometimes, as I drove up the mountain to my house, I had to pull over on the side of the road and cry, it was so beautiful there. Sometimes Bruce cried, but only when he thought about all the skiing he would be leaving behind. And Lucy cried like crazy. This had become her home. I had nothing to say to her. I just sat there and let her cry it out. I didn't want to rush her through her feelings or make her pretend everything was okay.

And at the end of the year, we said goodbye. We packed boxes. Leigh wept. I, to my shame, couldn't cry as I hugged her. I wanted to cry, to be friendly. But I was too excited to finally get on the road.

We left in a whirl, flying down the mountain in our VW van only a few days after school let out. We shoved a few last bags of trash in a campus Dumpster and stopped on our way out of town to eat an early dinner at our favorite hamburger joint, the West End Tavern. Our hair just slightly touched with the smell of meaty grease, we took off for Seattle, for home, as the hard afternoon light turned soft. We drove west on I-70, through the Eisenhower Tunnel, over Vail Pass. Trees infested with pine beetles made the only change in color as we drove through stand after stand of conifers; every so often we'd see a dead tree, standing alone, rust red, entirely distinguishable among the thousands of trees around it. Weird to think that a thing could be so singled out in its dying. We bickered pleasantly; I had begun to think of bickering not as the beginning of the end of the world but as just another way families communicate. We carried Bruce's depression and my anxiety with us, on the roof rack, as it were. They weren't going to leave us alone. They were just part of the deal.

Lucy sat silently, reading hard as we drove away from Boulder, the home she had grown to love, that we asked her to love. And I let her read. I didn't ask her to be present for something she wants to miss; I didn't ask her to be part of my story when she really didn't feel like it.

We rolled into our campsite near Vail just after the sunset, and in the gloaming Lucy and I walked down to the fee station to pay. We could hear the river nearby, and smell the smells of other campers. Lucy, who had recently sat in my lap and wept about our departure, jumped and giggled with joy and insisted on stuffing the envelope into the little slot. The temperature was in the thirties and dropping, but we were mountain people now and didn't give a shit. Also, Lucy and I were sleeping in the back of the van under about five quilts. By the time we got back to camp, the men had built their tent—Willie talking at the top of his lungs all the while—and we rolled into bed, our earlobes fresh with cold.

Morning found Bruce and me doing shots of bottled espresso and breaking up camp. Everything seemed inexpressibly funny; the tent; the van; the two hats Bruce wore; Willie dancing around, elbows out. We headed into Vail to find something to eat.

Maybe you have never been to Vail. Maybe you have some kind of idea about Vail. It sounds great. You are thinking: It is high in the Colorado Rockies and maybe full of . . . elk? And clear mountain streams? And kindhearted, twinkly-eyed people? All wrong. Vail is a wide spot on the interstate, overlaid with a demoralizing veneer of faux-Austrian classiness. (The skiing is truly great, I am told. I have never been able to tolerate the place long enough to strap on a pair of planks and check it out properly.)

From Vail, we drove into superlatives. We sailed down the Western Slope, one of the best place-names of all time. We made camp near Maroon Bells, the most beautiful mountains in Colorado, and flirted with little Basalt, a town that might have been home in another life. We gunned through Utah and then through Idaho. We saw all that sagebrush that we had seen on our way out to Colorado, from the opposite direction.

We sang along to an old Meat Puppets song:

Coming down from the mountain
I have seen the high and mighty
I will go again someday
But for now I'm coming down.

We were going home because we wanted to. We had located our faculties of desire. We were not going home in order to be good or to do the right thing. We were going home because we felt like it. And amazingly this feeling, the feeling of doing exactly what we wanted, imbued the trip with a profound sense of adventure. In the years we had lived in Boulder, we had driven back and forth a few times. This was familiar territory now. But the feeling of doing what we wanted, of being driven not by need but by desire, made it feel new. At least for me and Bruce. The kids were hungry and thirsty and pissed about the long hours of driving and sad about leaving their friends in Boulder and carsick and couldn't get their CD players to work.

There was much intramural bickering.

"I want book five!" said Willie, grabbing *Harry Potter and the Order of the Phoenix*.

"You're not even through book four! You can't have book five. That will ruin everything!" Tears.

In yoga, the splits are called monkey, or hanumanasana, after the monkey god Hanuman. Hanuman was a pal of Rama, who was an incarnation of Vishnu, sometimes thought of as Hinduism's supreme god. When Rama's wife, Sita, was kidnapped and taken across the sea to Sri Lanka, Hanuman leaped across the sea and found Rama's wife. The splits symbolize Hanuman's great leap. Fran used to say that hanumanasana was the pose of friendship, of connection.

Lord knows splits aren't easy. Grown-ups, at yoga class, easing into hanumanasana look like an entirely different species of animal from the cheerleaders who, like little springs, pop into the splits nonchalantly. A cheerleader doing splits is the physical embodiment of the phrase "no biggie."

When I went to yoga and attempted splits, I was surrounded by bodies that had lived for a while. Bodies that had accrued troubles the way my own had. Everyone had their list. Mine was: two cesarians, bursitis in my right shoulder, a hernia, chronic vertigo, thyroid disorder, an old ACL tear in my right knee from skiing, plantar fasciitis. The list got longer and longer without my realizing it; aging occurs while we're (determinedly) looking the other way.

When we prepared for splits, the room erupted in commotion as these bodies rushed around fetching the props that we proudly eschewed in every other pose. You needed at least one block, if not a few. Maybe a blanket. A strap; why not? You only wished there were more props, props that had not yet been invented. Maybe harness-y things currently only used by S-and-M enthusiasts.

When we settled into the pose, we started in a wide lunge, and then, bracing our hands on the floor on either side of our waists (or on towers of blocks) we began easing into the pose. Though easing was the wrong word. Maybe difficulting? I always had an excited, special-occasion feeling when I started splits; it was the Christmas Day of yoga poses. But not the joyous Christmas of childhood; this was the Christmas of adults, bringing with its joy a full sack of dread and effort.

Looking around the room, it looked, in fact, like the Christmas of the damned. My neighbors' faces were contorted in, at best, grim determination. At worst, wild-eyed anxiety. Oh, there was my ACL.

I kept dropping my weight toward the floor. Finally I was fully in the pose. (This didn't happen until I had been practicing the splits regularly for about, oh, three years. No kidding.) I was in it. Yoga teachers talk about energy a lot, and I could feel it thrumming through me now. I had no friends, really, in the class, but there was something gregarious about the pose nonetheless. We talked, which was rare in class, egging each other on.

Goodness knows I wasn't doing splits as we drove across the country, not literally anyhow. But there was a similar feeling of energy, and connection, and difficulty and joy as I leaped over mountains toward my old life, the life where they knew me and I knew them and we would never, ever recover from each other.

EPILOGUE: DOWNWARD DOG

Dear Dave: Rain five days and I love it. A relief from sandy arroyos,
buzzards and buttes, and a growing season consisting strictly of June. Here,
the grass explodes and trees rage black green deep as the distance they rage
in. I suppose all said, this is my soul, the salmon rolling in the strait and
salt air loaded with cream for our breathing.

—Richard Hugo, from "Letter to Wagoner from Port Townsend"

 The seagulls caw. The sky is elaborately colored from
dark to light with every shade of gray in between, like a
sunset that has forgotten to take its meds.

As we drive down to Manitou Beach, my mom says, "There's the
cliff I used to think about driving off."

We get out of the car. The wind blows our hair into tornadoes.

Ahead of us, a row of houses faces the beach. I can't quite tell
which one was ours. They all look shabby: summer beach rentals. A
couple of the houses are more prosperous-looking, newly shingled,
with carefully tended plants in pots on the decks. These are obviously
lived in year-round.

"I think it was that one," I say, pointing at a gray one much like
the others. I think I recognize the front window where we once ate
toasted pumpkin seeds.

"That's it," says my mom.

My mom is tight-lipped. She doesn't like this outing. She doesn't
know why I want to be here. I don't know why I want to be here. I
guess I just want to believe it really happened. I guess I want us both

to acknowledge reality. We've never been here before. She hates it here. It reminds of her of the time in her life when everything that had been solid gave way under her feet, like wet sand.

She and my dad are inching their way through the divorce, carefully, together. But they are progressing.

"This place is creepy," she says.

"I know. It's weird, isn't it?"

We walk farther down the beach until we come to a vacant lot, if shrubbery-grown hillside can be thought of as a vacant lot. In 1997, the hillside gave way and slid down onto the house of a Bainbridge Island high-school biology teacher, killing him, his wife, and his two small children. The cliffs look stable, but clearly are not.

"Why did you want to drive off a cliff?" I ask her.

"I don't know. Everything was changing. I wanted to start a new life, but I also wanted to take good care of you kids. It seemed really confusing."

Of course, my first thought is childish, literally: outrage that she would've considered leaving my brother and me.

"Of course I never would have done it," she says. "I would never have left you and your brother." There it is: Motherhood means always turning back.

Her spare body is swathed in layers of fleece and cotton, but she's still shivering.

"Do you want my coat?" I ask.

"No, I'm fine."

I put my arm around her anyhow. She's not much for this kind of snuggle, but I'm in the mood.

I find it a little embarrassing that I have come to live on the same island where I experienced part of the terrible year of 1973. When Bruce and I decided where to move, we had not had on our checklist this item: site of childhood sadness. I had in fact pretty much forgotten that this was where I had experienced the brunt of my parents' separation.

It's kind of interesting, though, don't you think? I had learned that what I wanted was to live in a place where I could, sometimes, practice being more real and less perfect. And here I was, as if by magic, in the place where the shit hit the fan and then everyone pretended it wasn't really happening. I was getting a second chance.

All the time I was growing up, I wanted to live with Stan and Mimi or Sally and Billy or Eric and Annika, in a house in the woods by the water. I wanted to live on an island with two (two!) parents who were best friends. Now that's where I live, only I'm the parent, living with my husband, who has turned out to be my best friend. God only knows what my own children will grow up wishing for, but I profoundly hope they get it, at least for a while, at least eventually.

Now Bruce and I are connected to our families by water, water I know by heart. I've swum it, or walked alongside it, or ridden across it in tugboat, rowboat, sailboat, ferry. I know its movement like a catechism. Wallace Stevens wrote a poem called "The Westwardness of Everything," and that's how the water moves. The water comes down the Cedar River from the Cascades to Lake Washington. It arrives near the doorstep of my brother, who lives close to the lake in Medina. A mutual friend asked about my brother the other day. It used to be that my brother and his wife, with their insularity and private family rituals, made me feel angry and left out. But I found that I no longer minded; I even understood. After all, my family and I had learned to be happy by hiding on a mountaintop. I surprised myself by answering, "He and his wife have a very private life, a kind of secret garden." She and I agreed that this was a lovely way to live.

From Medina, you follow the water west across Lake Washington, past the house where my family lived for decades, with and without my father. Then you go through the Montlake Cut, originally a log sluice, a narrow, man-made passage bound by concrete, into Portage

Bay, and on to Lake Union, the frankly urban lake where my father bobs around on his houseboat.

To the north, Lisa lives in a little house with three of her kids. Across town, Steve lives with their eldest. Lisa is studying to be a yoga teacher. She's dating a nice guy.

She and Steve are not divorced. They are separated. The kids shuttle between them. They constantly powwow to strategize the children's schedules and well-being. They live as a family, but a family that sprawls across town in two different houses, with Lisa's boyfriend and Steve's girlfriend added to the mix. I don't see her very often. I'm a little unsettled by the diorama-like re-creation she has made of my own childhood. It unnerves me. Even so, it doesn't seem like a bad setup, when you see it from the outside. In a way, it helps me let go of my own history a bit. It seems, from the outside, like a fine way to conduct a family.

Everyone else is much the same. Ruthie continues to pour her considerable energy into her children. Isabel's art just keeps getting minimal-er. We ride the ferries back and forth to take walks together.

From my father's house, continue west. Through the Fremont Cut, still moving in freshwater, to the Ballard Locks, which connect the lakes to the sound. Everything happens here. There are salmon climbing the salmon ladder, sea lions waiting to eat the salmon, tourists with caps pulled over their ears or with sunburned shoulders depending on the time of year, locals with opinions about the sea lions, pleasure boats with thrilled skippers navigating the locks for the very first time, workboats like Larry's for whom the locks are just another part of the job. (Though even the men and the few women on the workboats grow animated as they pass through the locks, calling out jokes and reddening with effort as they move their lines around.)

West into Puget Sound and its wild, cold, possibly dying waters. It took going away and coming back, many times, to realize how northern this place is, and how truly cold. My husband loves to announce: "We live in the North! The North, I tell you! Living here is like living in Alaska, but we don't get any credit for being tough."

Through the cold waters, to the north, you come to a hillside in Everett where Bruce's parents live, looking over mysterious Hat Island, where no one ever goes. To the south, Vashon Island, where Mom and Larry live and forget there ever was such a thing as a hippie. They golf a lot. Larry still runs his tugboat company; it's thriving. South of Vashon lies the city of Tacoma, where Larry now has a boatyard in the Hylebos Waterway, a boatyard of such deep filth and profound funkiness that the whole family bursts into the *Sanford and Son* theme song whenever this boatyard is mentioned.

I like knowing where I am, and where everyone else is. I feel like we're keeping track of one another, but not binding one another, the way we would be if we were connected by roads instead of water.

My island lies west of Seattle, south of Everett, north of Vashon. My island is like a triangulating (or quadrangulating) station for family relations.

After we've lived on the island a few months, my dad and I go to Manitou. It's June, which means rain. We look at the house.

He says genially, "Huh. Are you sure that's it?"

"I'm sure. I remember roasting pumpkin seeds in the kitchen right there."

I start to well up, and he takes my hand in his. He says, "I liked living here." And then he tells me about how he read that until the early part of the twentieth century, Native Americans from the mainland would canoe over to Manitou Beach to set up camps in the summers because the clamming was so good.

When I was younger, this would have totally pissed me off. I am having a moment! An emotional moment! And he's talking about clamming! Now I breathe in slowly and I find I like the feeling of his large bony hand holding mine and I like the sound of his voice in my ear. "If you think about it, the Indians would have found salmon, crabs, bottom fish. Blackberries. Salal."

Here on Bainbridge, I drive across the west side of the island to do yoga in a pretty wood-frame hut crowded all around by Douglas fir.

It's taught by (and located in the backyard of) a woman I went to high school with. Though we don't remember each other very clearly, I find comfort in the fact of this connection. She teaches a vigorous hot-yoga class, a kind of mash-up of power yoga and Bikram and ashtanga. She's very gifted, with a style and a voice all her own, but sometimes I think I'm just in it for the warmth. I love to go into that hot room, with all those other human bodies. On windy days, the tree branches lash around outside. Inside, I can't hear anything but the hum of the heaters and Jen's low voice giving me my marching orders.

We hang out in downward dog a lot. Home, vinyasa teachers sometimes call it. The pose you flow out of and back into, like water.

Downward dog is the pose that I've thought about more than any other pose. I've adjusted it up, down, in, out. I've sucked it in and I've let it go. I've strengthened in it and I've softened.

When I started out, all I cared about was getting my heels on the ground. This was a goal, a measurable way to tell that I was improving. And I wanted desperately to improve. Jonathan insisted that my heels didn't matter. All that mattered was keeping my fingers spread and my back straight. I pretended to think about my fingers but in reality was obsessed with dropping my heels.

After a year or so, I was able to get my heels to the ground and maintain a straight back. Now I focused on my ability to drop my chest in the pose. I hammocked my chest down between my arms, letting a strong arch come into my back. I wanted to be the girl whose chest was almost to the floor; the bendiest.

Then Fran told me I was going to hurt my back doing it that way. Strengthen your core. I wasn't sure I could find my core. Well, just draw your stomach up toward your spine. Oh!

This kept me busy for a couple of years. My hands spread, my heels on the ground, my stomach sucked up to my spine. But now Mindy wanted me to think about rotating my shoulders outward. Now I rotated my elbows so their eyes pointed as far as possible forward. This elbow rotation drew my shoulders wide and kept me from collapsing all my weight into my arms.

This really kept me busy. For years. Fingers spread, heels down, shoulders rotated, stomach in. Then I met Seidel. "What's up with your stomach?" she asked. "You're creating all this weird tension in your back because you're using your core so much." With her freckled hand, she softly brushed my upper back. "Whoa!" It was as hard as a rock. "Soften up," she said. "You're probably too young to remember that Archie Bell and the Drells song, 'Tighten Up.' Well, you gotta soften up!"

One pose. Ten years of thought. Ten years of engagement. Ten years of dialogue. And I am still interested. That's the incredible thing. My downward dog these days is not an unmitigated disaster but not exactly a thing of beauty either. Sometimes I run through all the instructions in my head, my mind moving restlessly across my body. Sometimes I just dump right into my shoulders and slump my back and generally make a mess.

Jen walks past me, rests a hand on my back. She grabs my hips and firmly pulls me backward: Let's straighten this thing out! I find I don't really care. I'm just happy to be someplace warm, close to home.

I thought I would do yoga all my life, and I thought that I would continue to improve at it, that I would penetrate its deepest mysteries and finally be able to perform a transition from scorpion directly into chaturanga. But here's the truth: The longer I do yoga, the worse I get at it. I can't tell you what a relief it is.

In the middle of winter, Bruce and I finally drive to Manitou Beach.

As we head down the hill to the beach, we pass the big art deco marshmallow of a building that used to house the old folks' home.

"That's where the old people used to roam on the lawn in their bathrobes."

"Really?"

"We had to pass them to get to the bus stop."

At the beach we park the car in the lot and walk the bulkhead. I tell Bruce about how my brother and I used to walk it every morning.

Bruce gives my hand a squeeze and I burst into tears. I think it's the squeeze that does it.

A woman with no-nonsense gray curls comes out of one of the more prosperous-looking houses. She has her purse and is clearly headed for her car in the lot.

"Hello," she says.

I wipe tears from my face. "Sorry to be crying in your front yard."

"Oh, don't worry about it. We get people crying down here all the time. They come back to see the rentals where they lived. So many people have lived here at upsetting times in their lives, during a divorce and whatnot. I always say we should put a psychologist's couch right here on the beach."

I stop crying and cheer up a bit. There is something weirdly comforting about the idea that I am one of many people who have come back to this gray beach looking for something.

"I'm freezing," I say to Bruce.

"Me, too. Let's go home and have some hot chocolate."

But we don't leave. Instead we stand there on the bulkhead, looking out across Puget Sound, as if waiting for the arrival of something new.

ACKNOWLEDGMENTS

First thanks to my agent, Anna Stein, a wonder. This book is hers, too. Except the bad parts. And thanks to the generous Peter Terzian for getting me to her.

The brilliant, tenacious, and compassionate Courtney Hodell gave me the edit of my (or any writer's) dreams.

Thanks to all at Farrar, Straus and Giroux for their unfailing intelligence and kindness. Mark Krotov made my life more gracious. Thanks to Charlotte Strick for the beautiful jacket, and to Jeff Seroy for his wit and deep knowledge. Thanks also to Kathy Daneman, Abby Kagan, Zachary Brown, and Karla Eoff.

In the UK, thanks to all at Bloomsbury, especially my editor, Helen Garnons-Williams.

For housing book and author, thanks to Hedgebrook, Gordon and Dawn Janow, Chris Thorsen and Diana Roll, Stephanie Bourgette and Ken Grayson, and Linda Mangel and Steve Fradkin. Above and beyond: Scott Loveless and Teresa Howard.

For help along the way, thanks to Jeanne Garland, Emily White,

Trilby Cohen, Wendy Redal, Leslie Dodson, Daniel Glick, Robert Spellman, Sherri L. Smith, Erika Schickel, and Tracy Ross.

For conversations like vitamins: Victoria Haven.

Thanks to all my yoga teachers, especially Fran Gallo and Jen Breen. I'd also like to acknowledge Stephen Cope, who writes about yoga with rare heart. Cope's books introduced me to Chip Hartranft's elegant translations of the yoga sutras, upon which I have depended.

Being written about in a memoir is officially no fun. A huge thank you to all the people who appear within these pages.

There aren't enough words to thank to my amazing, brave, tolerant family: Donna Dederer, Mike Dederer, Dave Dederer, and Larry Jay. This book was inspired by my mother and her life.

Lucy Barcott and Willie Barcott make every day my lucky day.

Dear Bruce Barcott: God only knows what I'd be without you.

A NOTE ON THE AUTHOR

Claire Dederer is an essayist, critic and reporter. Her writing has appeared in *Vogue*, the *New York Times*, *Slate*, *Yoga Journal*, *Real Simple*, and the *Nation*. She lives on an island near Seattle with her husband and their two children.